JONATHAN SWIFT

AND THE ANATOMY OF SATIRE

JONATHAN SWIFT

AND THE ANATOMY OF SATIRE

A Study of Satiric Technique

JOHN M. BULLITT

HARVARD UNIVERSITY PRESS · CAMBRIDGE

1953

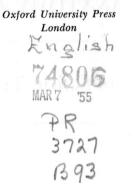

Library of Congress Catalog Card Number 52-12254
Printed in the United States of America 3-1-55

Foreword

THE GREATNESS of Swift's writing lies both in the intellectual content of his satire and in his technical and inventive brilliance. In the range, universality, and power that result from the union of the two, his achievement as a satirist becomes almost unique. The intellectual temper of Swift, the variety of his interests, and the background of his ideas have been more thoroughly discussed than his technical accomplishments. The present volume has concentrated on the latter aspect of Swift's art in the belief that such a study offers a promising means for investigating one of the great literary forms—for investigating, that is, the character, potentialities, and limitations of literary satire. To that extent, this book is concerned with the "anatomy" of satire. It should not be forgotten, however, that satire was Swift's chosen expression for "anatomizing" human nature and life in general. Therefore, his satiric devices are not, in Coleridge's phrase, imposed *ab extra* on his materials, but evolve organically out of his intellectual perception of the disparity between reality and expectation that provokes the comic spirit. In fact, sheer formal analysis, separated from other concerns, could not be more incongruously applied than to Swift: for the mistaking of the means for the end—in literature as in everything else— is one of the principal objects of his own satire. Accordingly, it has not seemed necessary in this study to discuss in detail every device employed by Swift—his use of myth and allegory, for example. The concern has been with those aspects of his satiric craftsmanship which most intimately join with and express his intellectual attitudes and values.

In writing this book, I am indebted for helpful suggestions to the work of Professors Ricardo Quintana, Maynard Mack, Herbert Davis, and Dr. Miriam Starkman. Professor Harry Levin kindly read and criticized the chapter on "The Rhetoric of Satire"; Dr. Irving Singer has assisted me with various points of philosophy touched on in this study; and Professor W. J. Bate has been helpful in discussing the manuscript with me in detail. Above all, in the preparation of this book, as in so many other respects, I am grateful to be enlisted among the many students of the eighteenth century who owe so much to the knowledge, acumen, and friendly patience of Professor George Sherburn.

J. M. B.

Cambridge, Massachusetts
October 1, 1952

Contents

I Exposure by Ridicule   1
  The "Ridiculous Tragedy" of Life
  The Social Sense of Shame
  Affectation: The Source of the "True Ridiculous"
  "Gay Contempt"

II Satiric Detachment: Invective, Diminution,
   and Irony   38
   Invective
   Diminution
   Irony

III The Rhetoric of Satire   68
    Swift's Razor
    Ridicule as "Eloquence": The Neoclassic Background
    The Example
    The Enthymeme

IV The Mechanical Operation of the Spirit   123
   The Subjective Element in Mechanism
   The Comedy of Mechanism
   The "Converting Imagination"
   Misdirection

V The Triumph of Artifice   158
  Art versus Nature
  The Puppet Symbol
  Recurrent Symbols of Height and Depth

   Notes   193

   Index   210

"To this End, I have some Time since, with a World of Pains and Art, dissected the Carcass of *Humane Nature,* and read many useful Lectures upon the several Parts, both *Containing* and *Contained;* till at last it *smelt* so strong, I could preserve it no longer. Upon which, I have been at a great Expence to fit up all the Bones with exact Contexture, and in due Symmetry; so that I am ready to shew a very compleat Anatomy thereof to all curious *Gentlemen and others."*

I

Exposure by Ridicule

The "Ridiculous Tragedy" of Life

In its most serious function, satire is a mediator between two perceptions—the unillusioned perception of man as he actually is, and the ideal perception, or vision, of man as he ought to be. It is often argued, therefore, that satire can become a vital form of literature only when there is a fairly widespread agreement about what man ought to be. The satirist needs the conviction that fixed intellectual ideals or norms can give him, and the assurance that he will receive understanding from his readers. This may help explain why the most successful flowering of satire in the history of literature took place in the later seventeenth and early eighteenth centuries. But if satire is best able to develop from a basis of general agreement on intellectual and moral standards, it is not necessarily chained for that reason to passing conditions and values. The unillusioned perception of man as he actually is can go beyond the mere noting of abuses and customs that have only topical interest, and can expose weaknesses or vices that are a perennial danger. Also, the values and ideals by which man is weighed and found wanting can have enough range and flexibility to be of persisting importance. This superior clarity and range characterizes the most effective satire of this era, as of any other. The writing of its greatest practitioner, Jonathan Swift, especially rises to an enduring universality through the compelling power with which he presents attitudes and reactions which have been common to many minds at many times.

The genius of Swift's satire was not narrowly "original": it was directly opposed to that suggested by the unhappy and bewildered Esther Vanhomrigh, when she said: "Could I know your thoughts, which no human creature is capable of guessing at, because *never anyone living thought like you . . .*"[1] Few people may have *felt* like Swift, but many have *thought* like him. Hence his satire is characterized by a penetrating if at times corrosive realism, and may therefore be described as a genuine exposure of things as they are and too often tend to be. As one of his commentators has justly said, the theme of Swift's writing may be summed up in the injunction: "It is not as you think,—look!"[2] This tendency of mind is the implicit premise shaping not only Swift's technical virtuosity but even more deeply his most fundamental attitudes, and it found its earliest and most explicit expression in *A Tale of a Tub.* In "A Digression Concerning Madness," Swift develops the central theme of all his satire—the idea that man's mind is contented only by the "*Superficies* of Things," and that happiness is "*a perpetual Possession of being well Deceived* . . . The Serene Peaceful State of being a Fool among Knaves." Swift's conception of reason, as opposed to the delusive imagination, was of an instrument "for cutting, and opening, and mangling, and piercing, offering to demonstrate" that only delusion could make man think the externals of life conform with its internal reality. It is not surprising to find Swift, in this connection, continually referring to the "anatomy" of life and to himself as a kind of rational surgeon.[3] In an earlier chapter of the *Tale,* he says:

To this End, I have some Time since, with a World of Pains and Art, dissected the Carcass of *Humane Nature,* and read many useful Lectures upon the several Parts, both *Containing* and *Contained;* till at last it *smelt* so strong, I could preserve it no longer. Upon which, I have been at a great Expence to fit up all the Bones with exact Contexture, and in due Symmetry; so that I am ready to shew a very compleat Anatomy thereof . . .

King Lear's desire to "let them anatomize Regan; see what breeds about her heart," was practiced by Swift upon the world, and his "Experiment" with a dandy was only the first of many operations:

Yesterday I ordered the Carcass of a *Beau* to be stript in my Presence; when we were all amazed to find so many unsuspected Faults under one Suit of Cloaths: Then I laid open his *Brain,* his *Heart,* and his *Spleen;* But, I plainly perceived at every Operation, that the farther we proceeded, we found the Defects encrease upon us in Number and Bulk . . .

But Swift's realism, his vigorous, persistent, and at times almost tortured attempt to see things as they are, to "inspect beyond the Surface and the Rind of Things" even though the resulting wisdom proves to be a nut which "may cost you a Tooth, and pay you with nothing but a *Worm*"—this intense realism stands opposed to another quality with which it cannot be reconciled: his equally intense idealism. For to Swift, the discovery that "in most Corporeal Beings, which have fallen under my Cognizance, the *Outside* hath been infinitely preferable to the *In*," presented an unbridgeable disparity between the *real,* as he saw it rationally, and the *ideal,* as he desired it—and it is the horror of perceiving this continual disparity which informs the frightful understatement of his observation: "Last Week I saw a Woman *flay'd,* and you will hardly believe, how much it altered her Person for the worse." [4] The essence of this idealism was the almost too earnest desire to make the inner reality resemble the more simple surface which the "imagination" presents. And from that very earnestness of desire, reality has appeared even more shrunk and deformed and horrible by contrast. This analytical and dissecting tendency of Swift's realism, combined with the poignant idealistic desire to rid life of the disparity between what actually "is" and what merely seems to be, provided the central impulse behind his satire.

It was impossible for Swift to perceive such a disparity between the real and the ideal without reacting strongly to it. Patrick Delany tells a revealing anecdote about Swift: "A friend of his, found him in this condition one day; and

Swift, putting the question to him, whether the corruptions and villainies of men in power, did not eat his flesh and exhaust his spirits? he answered, that in truth they did not: he then asked in a fury, why,—why,—how can you help it, how can you avoid it? His friend calmly replied, because I am commanded to the contrary: *Fret not thyself because of the ungodly.* This raised a smile . . ."[5] Swift's smile must have been a grim one indeed. For Swift was incapable of a smug or carefree detour around the problem of evil and imperfection in the world—a detour summed up in the classic phrase of a blind optimism: "Whatever is, is right." To shatter this complacency, to make men share with him his own painfully acute awareness that what most often seems "right" in the world is merely the surface colouring of "Artificial *Mediums,* false Lights, refracted Angles, Varnish, and Tinsel"[6]—in short, to force upon mankind his own realization that what truly "is" only *seems* "right" to minds content with being "well deceived," was the guiding intention of Swift's satire. Accordingly, we find in him an urgent need to speak out, an impelling drive to express his own dissatisfaction, because, as he wrote to Pope, "I never will have peace of mind till all honest men are of my opinion."[7] It is, then, very characteristic of Swift that when he was most personally involved in some deep and private disappointment, he should want to vent his anguish in words. "I am angry," he wrote Arbuthnot in the year 1714 when he was first separated from his closest and fondest ties: "I am angry at those who disperse us sooner than there was need. I have a mind to be very angry, and *to let my anger break out in some manner that will not please them* at the end of a pen."[8] In one way or another, the general compulsion and need for expression which this statement reveals might be applied to almost everything Swift ever wrote.

Granting this urgent need for expression, Swift's *reactions* to his highly developed and perceptive moral insight and the embodiment of these reactions in his works differed from time to time and according either to his sense of the importance of the disparity he found between appearance and reality or to the conditions of his own experience bearing down and influencing this perception. For to be angry was by no means his only reaction to life, and the variety and complexity of his satire testifies to his own varied and complicated responses. Indeed, these responses often appeared to be operating almost simultaneously and are responsible in part for the unique tension which distinguishes Swift's satire from that of all other satirists—a tension arising from a state of mind which he once described as "a struggle between contempt and indignation . . ."[9] This struggle does not, of course, even faintly suggest any ambiguity in Swift's perception of the incongruity in life; it merely helps to define the range of possible reactions towards the perception. A concise statement of the diverse possibilities of Swift's response is found in his belief that a reasonable man, when confronted with the disparity between pretended virtue and its concealed folly and viciousness, must be "tempted, according to the present turn of his humour, either to laugh, lament, or be angry; or, if he were sanguine enough, perhaps to dream of a remedy."[10] The "turn" of Swift's humour led him to see life sometimes as a comedy, sometimes as a lamentable tragedy, often as a source of angry frustration—and most frequently and effectively, perhaps, in such satires as *A Modest Proposal* or *Gulliver's Travels,* Swift reacted in all ways at once. We may recall Horace Walpole's familiar statement that "the world is a comedy to those that think, a tragedy to those who feel," and closely relevant to Swift's own fundamental beliefs and attitudes is Emerson's comment: "The presence of the ideal of right and of truth in all action makes the yawning delinquencies of practice remorseful to the conscience, tragic to the interest, but droll to the intellect. The activity of our sympathies may for a time hinder our perceiving the fact intellectually, and so deriving mirth from it; but all falsehoods, all vices seen at sufficient distance, *seen from the point where our moral sympathies do not interfere,* become ludicrous."[11] Certainly, the general and prevailing tendency of Swift's mind and emotions was towards the interference of his "moral sympathies" with his intellectual perceptions, and, as a consequence, his view of life veered constantly towards a tragic conception. But if Swift seldom found life to be wholly a laughing matter, only rarely did he permit himself to view it as wholly tragic: life to Swift became a comic tragedy. "The common saying of life being a farce," he wrote Pope, "is true in every sense but the most important one, for *it is a ridiculous tragedy, which is the worst kind of composition.*" [12]

When Swift's comic sense of the ridiculous dominated his imagination, when he was able to view even a vicious person as "an instance added to millions how ridiculous a creature is man," [13] his satire frequently attained a level of high and even exuberant comedy. For Swift was not by nature a lugubrious man. Although a serious, intellectual intention dominated the writing of *A Tale of a Tub*, there is in this early satire an effervescence, a playfulness of sheer animal spirits, which render whole sections of it broadly laughable. The play of wit, of piling, for example, one image upon another, often pushes his ideas to the region of the absurd and fantastic. His delight in puns and verbal wit of all kinds, which so amused and attracted his many friends, especially Sheridan, frequently find their gratuitous place in even the most serious of his satires. As "Isaac Bickerstaff," he so controlled and disciplined his sense of comic absurdity that he elevated a practical joke almost to the level of a fine art. This sparkling and bubbling vitality is an aspect of Swift's work which one should not overlook. Even more important, of course, to Swift's comic satire was the comedy inherent in the very disparity he perceived between appearance and reality—a disparity which is laughable only when presented without the explicit interposition of strong feelings and moral outrage. It is this comedy which is so closely allied to tragedy and which, even while it evokes laughter, can offer a searching commentary upon life.

In addition to Swift's native exuberance and the comedy intrinsic to all affectation and pretense, two other aspects of his comic satire deserve mention, because they condition and modify his satiric techniques. In the first place, Swift shared with many of his contemporaries the conviction that laughter was generally a more forceful and effective instrument of moral reform than the serious discussion of good and evil. Accordingly, we find Swift defending comic satire for its *objective utility*, its usefulness as a stimulus to reform. Good humour, he said in an article written soon after the publication of his most scathing indictment of mankind, *Gulliver's Travels*, "is certainly the best ingredient toward that kind of satire, which is most useful, and gives the least offence; which *instead of lashing, laughs men out of their follies, and vices,* and is the character which gives Horace the preference to Juvenal." One significant element in Swift's satiric comedy is this belief in the moral utility of laughter. Another important element, which influenced Swift on a deeper and more personal level and which colored and modified the rest, is suggested by his observation in the same essay that comic satire, written without malice, affords the writer an innocent "personal satisfaction"; and Swift demands "whether I have not as good a title to laugh, as men have to be ridiculous, and to expose vice, as another hath to be vicious. If I ridicule the follies and corruptions of a court, a ministry, or a senate; are they not amply paid by pensions, titles, and power, *while I expect and desire no other reward, than that of laughing with a few friends in a corner.*"[14] Now, the "personal satisfaction" Swift found in comic satire goes much deeper than he admits even in this passage. In fact, much of his seeming merriment and his habitual use of irony seem to have been the result of an almost compulsive desire to separate himself from the intensity of his own feelings, from a truly tragic involvement of his "moral sympathies" with the cruelty and folly and terror of life. In a revealing passage in his *Journal to Stella,* he wrote:

I say Amen with my heart and vitals, that we may never be asunder again ten days together while poor Presto lives————
I can't be merry so near any splenetic talk; so I made that long line, and now all's well again.[15]

It is not, perhaps, too much to say that Swift's comic satire often served the same function as this long dash. When he told Esther Vanhomrigh, "I fly from the spleen to the world's end,"[16] he was not speaking carelessly, and what he called his "rule" of life—*Vive la bagatelle!*[17]—was the product of a more compelling need than a simple and cheerful delight in trifling. How much of Swift's comedy arose from an intense, inward pressure to control and master stronger emotions may be surmised from this poetic self-portrait:

> Like the ever laughing Sage,
> In a Jest I spend my Rage:
> (Tho' it must be understood,
> I would hang them if I cou'd.)[18]

If comedy satisfied certain objective conditions for moral reform, it also had for Swift a *subjective utility* as well—a means of varying his angle of vision so that he would not care too much.

But, as he grew older, the "present turn" of Swift's "humour" seems to have concentrated increasingly upon the agony of life. A fundamental shift in focus has taken place between the acid but comic irony in *A Tale of a Tub,* where the motives of military conquerors are found to stem either from vapours or fistulas, and Gulliver's ironic and scarifying defense of modern warfare in "A Voyage to Brobdingnag." At the very heart of Swift's comic perception there is a tragic potentiality. For tragedy shares with comedy its concern with man's limitations, but differs from it, in one respect at least, in presenting these limitations as both disastrous and part of the ultimate configuration of life itself; tragedy, at its best and as distinct from mere pathos or melodrama, rests upon and implies a universal import in the structure of man's situation in the world. Now, Swift's comedy, as we have noted, is founded upon his perception of a disparity between reality and the ideal—a disparity of which mankind as a whole, he felt, was deceived into ignorance. Of all man's limitations, the one which most concerned Swift was man's self-deception, his wilful ignorance of his true worth. "There is a pedantry in manners, as in all arts and sciences; and sometimes in trades," Swift wrote; "Pedantry is properly the over-rating any kind of knowledge we pretend to."[19] If pedantry is the over-rating of knowledge, the ultimate stupidity of man is the over-rating of man's virtue. As Swift's reason increasingly universalized this tendency of mankind, finding it an apt description of a basic flaw not merely in particular persons but in human life itself, he approaches that generality of comment which gives tragedy its own unique dimension. Like the journey of Oedipus from ignorance to a tragic self-knowledge, so the rational journey of Gulliver was an experience which led him from the ignorant complacency of the typical Englishman towards an undeceived, though intensely bitter, knowledge of "reality." In this way, *Gulliver's Travels* can be said to assume a tragic significance. When Swift's eye was focused upon the absurdity of "man-deceived," he portrayed a comic affectation or self-delusion; but as he concentrated more upon the reality beneath, contrasting it with the surface deception, and as he attempted to shock men with graphic and concrete vividness into seeing how enormous was the disparity, what began in a comic spirit was liable to develop into a horror and disgust and loathing of life itself.

Swift's sense, therefore, of an ultimate tragedy in life was not solely the product of ratiocination, of logically extending a comic premise to a tragic conclusion. Instead, this developing awareness was motivated by an acute moral sensitivity to fraud and deceit and was sharpened by the circumstances of his own life which corroborated and seemed to verify these feelings. Even as a relatively young man and at the height of his power in England, as W. B. C. Watkins has reminded us,[20] Swift was deeply distrustful of life, and from an early age he often repeated the passage from Job, beginning: "Let the day perish wherein I was born, and the night in which it was said, There is a man child conceived." For Swift was unable through reason to justify God's ways to man, and he was forced to view God's purposes on earth as both inscrutable and terrible: "I hate life," he wrote after the death of Lady Ashburnham, "I hate life when I think it exposed to such accidents; and to see so many thousand wretches burdening the earth, while such as her die, makes me think God did never intend life for a blessing."[21] This moving and utterly genuine distrust of life as being incompatible with man's rational sense of justice gives Swift's passage in his *Thoughts on Religion* a poignant despair:

Although reason were intended by Providence to govern our passions, yet it seems that, in two points of the greatest moment to the being and continuance of the world, God hath intended our passions to prevail over reason. The first is, the propagation of our species, since no wise man ever married from the dictates of reason. The other is, the love of life, which, from the dictates of reason, every man would despise, and wish it at an end, or that it never had a beginning.[22]

What Swift was to call the "greatest unhappiness of my life ... I mean my banishment in this miserable country,"[23] began the final stage of his career, and his early general distrust of life seems now, in Keats's phrase, to have been "proved upon his pulses." His letters to his many friends in England—from 1713, when he was made Dean of St. Patrick's Cathedral, Dublin, until his physical ailments overwhelmed his articulate reason in 1742—are a painful witness to Swift's bitterness against a life which, at the mere change of a ministry, should disappoint all his worldly expectations and, even worse, separate him from his closest friends. In 1713, Swift wrote Esther Vanhomrigh about his first arrival in Ireland: "At my first coming I thought I should have died with discontent, and was horribly melancholy while they were installing me; but it begins to wear off, and change to dulness."[24] His sense of personal disappointment with the collapse of his career is eloquently summed up in a letter to Bolingbroke:

I never wake without finding life a more insignificant thing than it was the day before, which is one great advantage I get by living in this country, where there is nothing I shall be sorry to lose. But my greatest misery is recollecting the scene of twenty years past, and then all on a sudden dropping into the present. I remember, when I was a little boy, I felt a great fish at the end of my line which I drew up almost on the ground, but it dropped in, and the disappointment vexes me to this very day, and I believe it was the type of all my future disappointments.[25]

With the disappointment of his youthful ambitions, Swift was denied even the pleasure of his friends, and he wrote to Arbuthnot in 1714: "Writing to you much would make me stark mad; judge his condition who has nothing to keep him from being miserable but endeavouring to forget those for whom he has the greatest value, love, and friendship."[26] For some years, however, Swift retained one association which, in part, was able "to keep him from being miserable"; that is, with his friend Stella (Esther Johnson). But Stella, after a long illness, died in 1728 and how this event affected Swift may be surmised from a letter to Stopford in 1726, when Stella was very ill: "For my part, as I value life very little, so the poor casual remains of it, after such a loss, would be a burden that I must heartily beg God Almighty to enable me to bear";[27] and from another letter to Sheridan, a year later, when Sheridan informed him that Stella's death was imminent:

I am still in the same condition, or rather worse, for I walk like a drunken man, and am deafer than ever you knew me . . . These are the perquisites of living long: the last act of life is always a tragedy at best, but it is a bitter aggravation to have one's last friend go before one . . . What have I to do in the world? I never was in such agonies as when I received your letter, and had it in my pocket. I am able to hold up my sorry head no longer.[28]

How Swift's thoughts were filled during these terrible last years of pain, separation, and loss, is explicitly stated in two letters to Pope in 1733. In the first, Swift says: "As to mortality it hath never been out of my head eighteen minutes these eighteen years; neither do I value it a rush further than as it parts a man from his friends for ever, and that share of it I have suffered already, and am likely to suffer as long as I live"; and in the second, written only a month later, Swift says: "When I was of your age, I thought every day of death, but now every minute."[29] It is against the background of these assertions of Swift's that we may appreciate fully the significance of his earnest and honest assessment of man's situation in the world: "For life is a tragedy, wherein we sit as spectators awhile, and then act our own part in it."[30]

If Swift, then, viewed man's life as a "ridiculous tragedy," comic or calamitous according to his point of view at the moment, his moral sensibilities were too intense to permit him the luxury of separating himself from it. Commentators on Swift have often noted that the phrase on his epitaph, *saeva indignatio,* describes his most persistent reaction to the disparity he saw between the real world and his ideals. As Professor Sherburn has pointed out,[31] however, used as a label this phrase can be a misleading summation of Swift's "dominant mood," both because it may exclude other important aspects of his complicated personality and because it too often is interpreted narrowly as mere emotional and neurotic self-laceration. It is perfectly true that Swift's most moving satires were written under the pressure of a controlled fury: ". . . what I do is owing to perfect rage and resentment, and the mortifying sight of slavery, folly, and baseness about me, among which I am forced to live."[32] But this anger is complex. Two passages, which seem to throw most light upon Swift's savage indignation, deserve lengthy quotation here, even though to many readers they contain the most familiar lines in Swift's canon. Both quotations are taken from letters to Pope, written in 1725 only two months apart and shortly before the publication of *Gulliver's Travels:*

I like the scheme of our meeting after distresses and dispersions; but the chief end I propose to myself in all my labours is to vex the world rather than divert it; and if I could compass that design, without hurting my own person or fortune, I would be the most indefatigable writer you have ever seen, without reading . . . when you think of the world give it one lash the more at my request. I have ever hated all nations, professions, and communities, and all my love is toward individuals: for instance, I hate the tribe of lawyers, but I love Counsellor Such-a-one, and Judge Such-a-one: so with physicians—I will not speak of my own trade—soldiers, English, Scotch, French, and the rest. But principally I hate and detest that animal called man, although I heartily love John, Peter, Thomas, and so forth. This is the system upon which I have governed myself many years, but do not tell, and so I shall go on till I have done with them. I have got materials toward a treatise, proving the falsity of that definition *animal rationale,* and to show it would be only *rationis capax.*

Upon this great foundation of misanthropy, though not in Timon's manner, the whole building of my Travels is erected; and I never will have peace of mind till all honest men are of my opinion. By consequence you are to embrace it immediately. . . . I am daily losing friends, and neither seeking nor getting others. Oh! if the world had but a dozen Arbuthnots in it, I would burn my Travels.

Drown the world! I am not content with despising it, but I would anger it, if I could with safety . . . I desire you and all my friends will take a special care that my disaffection to the world may not be imputed to my age, for I have credible witnesses ready to depose, that it has never varied from the twenty-first to the f——ty-eighth year of my life; pray fill that blank charitably. I tell you after all, that I do not hate mankind: it is *vous autres* who hate them, because you would have them reasonable animals, and are angry for being disappointed. I have always rejected that definition, and made another of my own. I am no more angry with [Walpole] than I was with the kite that last week flew away with one of my chickens; and yet I was pleased when one of my servants shot him two days after.[33]

Two remarks may be made about these passages. In the first place, Swift was evidently unique among misanthropes. For his professed hatred of mankind—which he disclaims in the second letter—springs from the despair of caring too much, and unlike other haters of man, Swift's love for individuals was not only strong but enduring. Because he valued so highly certain moral and rational qualities of which man is capable, he responded fervently to the rare individual who exemplified these qualities, and he recoiled with horror from the great bulk of human kind which does not attain that high standard. In other words, Swift's "misanthropy," as he called it, did not prevent him from treasuring human excellence when he found it; but the idealism upon which these affections were based made him perceive the gap between what man is and what man can be with an acute and pained exasperation. In the second place, and this is especially important as it pertains to his literary work, Swift was not, as he himself says, "content with despising" the world, and his desire to "anger it" reflects his strong urge, even in the midst of his hatred, to reform humanity. Although he was convinced that most men were not, by nature, reasonable animals, and were, therefore, like the kite, basically unchangeable, even his most bitter attacks assume some element of corrigibility in man. This fundamental hope[34] is suggested, as late as 1737, in a remark to the Earl of Oxford that Ireland was a "cursed, factious, oppressed, miserable country, *not made so by nature, but by the slavish, hellish principles of an execrable prevailing faction in it.*"[35] As long as Swift could find vices and follies which were not ingrained in man by nature and which could therefore possibly be shamed out of existence, his satire had a place. At the same time, as his gloom deepened, his satiric intention tended more and more towards shaming men out of their vices not by *laughing at* but by *lashing* them. This tendency may be said to have reached its culmination in the fourth voyage of *Gulliver's Travels.*

With a fine irony, Swift wrote in *A Tale of a Tub* that, being "so entirely satisfied with the whole present Procedure of human Things," he had been preparing materials for *A Paneygyrick upon the World* and *A Modest Defence of the Proceedings of the Rabble in all Ages,* but that he had been forced to abandon this agreeable project because he found "my Common-Place-Book fill much slower than I had reason to expect."[36] Twenty years later, his notebook full, he completed his panegyric and published it under the innocent title of *Gulliver's Travels.* Kipling once said that Swift "ignited a volcano to light a child to bed," and certainly one of the high comedies of literary history has been the reception of this savage work as a children's classic. For Gulliver—whom Swift was to call a "prostitute flatterer . . . whose chief study is to extenuate the vices, and magnify the virtues, of mankind, and perpetually dins our ears with the praises of his country in the midst of corruption"[37]—Gulliver became the vehicle for Swift's most searching and impassioned criticism of mankind. It is significant, however, to the study of satire as a genre, to note that the same elements which make the early voyages often comic—namely, the projection of man's complacency and pride against the background of his real limitations—are raised in the final voyage by the very intensity of

Swift's concern into an art form which verges upon tragedy.
As this is Swift's most moving work, it is also, from one point
of view, his highest artistic achievement: it is the greatest
example in any language of what Dryden had called, referring
to the works of Juvenal, "tragical satire." Its aim is openly
didactic in its almost overwhelming attempt to shock and
disgust men out of one vice which Swift believed was still
corrigible: pride. The vision of an ideal perfection from
which Gulliver wakens, to find himself only a Yahoo after all,
has the breadth and passion and despair of tragedy. And yet
this "tragical satire" cannot, as some readers have urged, be
said to attain the same level as great dramatic tragedy. The
disjunction between the ideal Houyhnhnms and the Yahoos
is too complete. One recent critic, in a provocative introduction to Gulliver's Travels, has attempted to show that Swift's
"literary imagination transcended his professed misanthropy,"
and that in his concluding allegory he "has not so much condemned humanity as he has demonstrated two of its com-
ponent elements—animality and rationality."[38] This is partly
true; but the point is, that Gulliver—and Swift—identified
man's actuality with the Yahoos, and the sweet reasonable-
ness of the Houyhnhnms (even if not entirely faultless in
Gulliver's eyes) remains an unattainable and desirable ideal:
"expect no more from man," Swift wrote Sheridan, "than
such an animal is capable of, and you will every day find my
description of Yahoos more resembling."[39] The satiric form
and intention is insufficient to support the pressure of Swift's
personal involvement; Gulliver is pushed out as a creature of
irremediable limitations, without hope of achieving any real
dignity or worth beyond the recognition, in helpless sensitivity, of his own and mankind's defectiveness. In short, although resignation comes to Gulliver, it is the resignation
of an unwilling and bitter self-knowledge, without the grandeur which is a necessary quality for the true tragic catharsis.
The fourth voyage of Gulliver's Travels, therefore, is not a
tragedy, but satire pushed to the breaking point.

As a satirist, then, Swift's work ranges from the most delightful comedy to a profoundly moving and even tragic

despair. His techniques of writing, developed with remarkable virtuosity and effectiveness, cannot properly be separated from the ideals which defined his basic perception of life as both ridiculous and tragic. And if Swift's technical skill appears most brilliantly and abundantly on those occasions when his sense of the ridiculous overrides his sense of the tragic, still we are always conscious that our laughter may at any moment be converted into a deeper response. What, finally, gives Swift a just claim to high eminence as a literary artist, is that the disparity between the ideal and the actual has been a pressing and persistent problem to many men, and yet very few have equaled either the sustained intensity of Swift's purpose or the masterful artistic control with which he expressed this impassioned concern.

The Social Sense of Shame

Although Swift's insight and temper transcended his own period, and although his most bitter criticism was often directed against ideas and beliefs which are commonly thought typical of the Age of Reason, his literary expression was markedly influenced by the very age he attacked. It is probable, as we have already noted, that some unanimity on moral standards, considered as both rational and permanent, is a necessary precondition for any great satiric effort. If indeed, these standards are broadly conceived and reflect a high idealism, almost every human action may be viewed as a departure from the established norm; and these departures constantly tempt and provoke a desire to criticize them. From this point of view, it may be questioned whether great satire can be written in a period of grave anxiety, such as the present day. Whether or not this argument is valid, a causal connection between the general acceptance of normative values and the satiric impulse seems to be almost inescapable in the late seventeenth and early eighteenth centuries—a period whose general intellectual character must, if we may judge from the quantity and quality of its satire, have been highly favorable to this genre. If one believes in an absolute standard that is fixed, ideal, and knowable

through reason, then against the white light of that ideal the
actual conduct of man will stand out dark by contrast. There
is also a psychological effect subjoined to this. If too great
an effort is made to see man as reasonable and just, and as
part of a rational and fixed universal Nature, then man, as
he is in actuality, as he is in the flesh, will appear to depart
at every turn from the ideal, and he may even appear not
merely defective but monstrous. And of course it is precisely
this enormous discrepancy between the ideal and the actual
which so strongly cuts into the intense idealism of Swift.

If satire may be said to serve classical aims in its confident
reference to rational and objective standards, it is also essentially classical in that it can be given, and employed for,
a moral purpose. Indeed, some critics, notably Shaftesbury,
went so far as to insist that ridicule was an effective "test of
truth"; John Brown and others argued that the love of glory
and the fear of shame are universal passions which are exploited by satire for moral uses. In this sense, satire may be
viewed as an extension of the classical approach to comedy.
Hence, one has Dryden, in his *Discourse Concerning Satire,*
saying that satire "is of the nature of moral philosophy, as
being instructive." The didactic purpose of satire in the
English literature of this period was heightened by the post-
Restoration interest in reforming manners. Such a work as
*A Short View of the Immorality and Profaneness of the
English Stage* (1698), in which Jeremy Collier attacked the
current tendency of drama to encourage instead of to correct
vice, is characteristic of a growing discontent, both with the
laxness of the Restoration court and the reflection of these
manners and morals in the drama of the period. This interest in moral reform, which continues on in various ways
in the early eighteenth century, serving, for example, as the
guise under which Defoe writes such a novel as *Moll Flanders*
or, in a somewhat more refined form, as the aim of the
Tatler and *Spectator* papers—this localized concern to reform
manners further sharpens the general moral purpose which
classicism and neoclassicism assigned to satire.

With this moral sanction that was accorded satire, there

was consequently a good deal of critical interest in it—in addition to the actual writing of it. This critical discussion of satire—of its nature and aims, and of the various techniques it employs—is important as an indication of the desire in this period to turn satire both into an effective moral tool and at the same time into a fine art—into an accomplished form of literature. One finds writers stating with confidence that the aim of satire is to supply the defects of governmental legislation and even religious institutions. Civil laws cannot reach all follies and vices; divine laws are ineffective in this world unless men fear and obey them. But satire, by appealing to man's susceptibility to shame, sets up, as it were, a more reaching and immediately effective tribunal. That is, it increases man's moral sensibility, by goading him through shame and ridicule, and thus prepares the mind to accept more freely the dictates of religion. In addition to elaborate justifications of this sort, writers also discuss the proper tone and approach which the satirist should have. And on the whole, like Shaftesbury, they feel that ridicule and wit should be joined with good humour. It is partly in keeping with this feeling that Horace attained such popularity as a model of satiric writing. Dryden and other critics often contrast the good-natured banter of Horace with the somewhat stronger satire of the other Roman satirists, Juvenal and Persius. But in actual practice, the English genius for satire in both poetry and prose, from Dryden through Swift and Pope to the later eighteenth century, is perhaps closer to Juvenal: it probes more deeply than does mere good-humoured raillery. These theoretical and critical discussions of satire, then,—the justification of it as a moral and social weapon of reform, the emphasis on the proper approach and temper of the satirist, and also, of course, the discussion of the proper techniques of satire—all this critical interest in the subject deserves further analysis to indicate how consciously this period was approaching satire, and how it was making a deliberate effort to turn satire into an important kind of literature. In Swift, this effort achieves a success which reflects directly the critical tendencies and attitudes of his period.

"Do not the corruptions and villainies of men eat your flesh and exhaust your spirits?" Swift's question is couched in the agonized voice of the moral reformer. Like every moralist in every age Swift saw feelingly the gap between man's moral depravity and his ideals. But if this recognition of evil is common to all men passionately devoted to the cause of reformation, the methods adopted by the moralist must vary according to the structure both of his own values and those of the part of mankind he intends to reach. Writing as a Christian divine, Dean Swift explained to a young clergyman that the "two principal branches of preaching are first to tell the people what is their duty, and then to convince them that it is so." By duty Swift means here the whole body of traditional humane ideals as well as what he believed to be the limit and extent of man's necessary belief in the Christian revelation. Swift felt the latter demanded careful formulation in order to protect men from the enthusiasts who insisted that man must or can know more than Swift thought him generally capable of knowing. But Swift's own belief in the self-evidence and simplicity of man's moral virtues—in the ethical ideals towards which it is his duty to aspire—left him less concerned with the problem of demonstrating these ideals than in persuading men to live up to them.

Since Socrates, a principal method of moral persuasion had been to arouse in man a passionate love of the good—a love that might even be termed *eros,* as in Diotima's discourse in the *Symposium.* In the Christian tradition, this emotional appeal to the love of the good was supplemented by an equally powerful appeal to the fear of evil, and these two responses found a systematic expression in the belief in eternal rewards and punishments, in heaven and hell. The moralist was possessed with a weapon that could strike at the very heart of man's self-interest. As a moralist, however, Swift was more concerned with the rational than with the emotional appeal of Christianity. He eschewed these passionate appeals to man's emotionalism. ". . . I do not see," he wrote to the young clergyman, "how this talent of moving the passions can be of any great use toward directing Christian men in the con-

duct of their lives . . ." As long as the moralist is dealing with
"Christian men," with men who desire to know their Christian duty and need more to be reminded than to be instructed, then a "plain convincing reason" is sufficient to
persuade them to moral activity. This attitude, of course,
assumes both the *capacity* of the rational mind to perceive
and the *desire* of man to imitate the ideal. The most concrete
illustration of the kind of creature who could be thus reached
by plain convincing reasons was the noble race of Houyhnhnms: they were not only "endowed by nature with a
general disposition to all virtues" but they also possessed an
intuitional reason that "strikes you with immediate conviction."

But the Houyhnhnms remained to Swift an ideal, attain-
able or approachable perhaps, by John, Peter, Thomas, but
not by the generality of Yahoos whom Swift grew to detest as
being not rational animals but only beasts capable of reason.
Even in his letter of advice to the young clergyman, Swift
seems to doubt that in dealing with freethinkers "passion
should never prevail over reason." If man is bestial and not
rational, if his general disposition is to evil instead of good,
he cannot be "reformed by arguments offered to prove the
truth of the Christian religion, because," Swift goes on to say,

reasoning will never make a man correct an ill opinion, which by
reasoning he never acquired: for in the course of things, men
always grow vicious before they become unbelievers; but if you
would once convince the town or country profligate, by topics
drawn from the view of their own quiet, reputation, health, and
advantage, their infidelity would soon drop off: This I confess
is no easy task, because *it is almost in a literal sense, to fight
with beasts.*[40]

Swift's disillusionment in the rationality of man, his conviction that "the bulk of mankind is as well qualified for
flying as thinking,"[41] was the precondition for his method of
convincing the "bestial man" by the use of satire. In a letter
to his unfortunate friend, Sheridan, Swift said: "I do think it
is agreed, that all animals fight with the weapons natural to
them, which is a new and wise remark out of my own head,

and the devil take that animal, who will not offend his enemy when he is provoked, with his proper weapon; and though your old dull horse little values the blows I give him with the butt end of my stick, *yet I strike on and make him wince in spite of his dulness;* and he shall not fail of them while I am here . . ."[42] If one engages in a contest of strength against beasts one must employ the weapons that will subdue them; and satire was for Swift the best, perhaps the only, available instrument with which to make brutish men wince.

If the impetus behind Swift's satire was his perception of the bestial depravity of mankind, and the inability of sheer reason to improve him, a similar though not identical skepticism and disillusionment dominated the satire of his contemporaries. Indeed, neoclassic satire may be said to have arisen from the ruins of a traditional basis for morality—from a sense of the failure of traditional institutions and beliefs to improve mankind. Certainly the new philosophy that "calls all in doubt," the philosophy of skeptical inquiry and scientific experiment, had corroded men's collective faith in the absolute certainty of final judgment. Not that all men, or even most men, had lost their religious scruples. But as the foundation of Christianity, the Bible, became, like other historical documents, the subject of experimental scrutiny, and as the system of heavenly rewards and punishments lost its concreteness and became increasingly abstract, speculative and even doubtful, many thinking men tended to pin their faith upon the rewards and punishments of this world—a faith founded on the belief in the capacity of reason to bring heaven down to earth. Whitehead has described this fundamental shift in values as being from a faith based on reason to a reason based on faith—a "faith in the order of nature." From this new optimism, engendered by the possibilities of reason and scientific inquiry, emerged a "Religion of Reason," as Newman later described it, "A religion of civilized times, of the cultivated intellect, of the philosopher, scholar and gentleman." In this atmosphere of intellectual rather than religious culture, Newman says with specific reference to the doctrines of Shaftesbury, conscience becomes "self-respect" and "sin is not an offence against God, but against human nature." Wrong-doing is punished in the individual by a sense of social degradation; vice becomes ugly and deformed and ridiculous; the religious sense of remorse is swallowed up in the social sense of shame.

Swift, needless to say, hardly pinned his faith to the view of human nature described by Newman and most familiarly associated with the Earl of Shaftesbury. But it is equally evident that Swift joined other satirists in the belief that traditional religious, political, and rational standards had proved to be inadequate by themselves as means for the clarifying and improving of human morality. And if one result of the Religion of Reason was the moralist's appeal to man's shame, the result of Swift's skeptical antirationalism was a similar appeal to this social sense. "Graver divines," Lord Orrery said in praise of Dean Swift's *Argument Against Abolishing Christianity*,

threaten their readers with future punishments; Swift artfully *exhibits a picture of present shame*. He judged rightly in imagining that a small treatise, written with a spirit of mirth and freedom, must be more efficacious, than long sermons, or laborious lessons of morality. He endeavors to laugh us into religion; well knowing that we are often laughed out of it.[43]

Pope, an avowed antagonist to man's pride, found his own pride in an art which reached more men, more effectively, than law, religion or kingly mandate:

> Yes, I am proud; I must be proud to see
> Men not afraid of God, afraid of me:
> Safe from the bar, the pulpit, and the throne,
> Yet touched and shamed by ridicule alone.[44]

And Swift traced the origin of satire to the practical utility of this exhibition of present shame when all other methods of persuasion have failed:

. . . many great abuses may be visibly committed, which cannot be legally punished . . . I am apt to think, it was to supply such defects as these, that satire was first introduced into the world; whereby those whom neither religion, nor natural virtue, nor fear of punishment, were able to keep within the bounds of their duty, might be upheld by the *shame of having their crimes exposed to open view in the strongest colours, and themselves rendered odious to mankind.*[45]

Swift's long and active experience in public life seems to have confirmed this early (1711) conviction, and over twenty years later, while in almost the nadir of his disillusionment, he lent a willing ear to Pope's observation: "Let philosophy be ever so vain, it is less vain now than politics, and not quite so vain at present as divinity. I know nothing that moves strongly but satire, and *those who are ashamed of nothing else are so of being ridiculous.*"[46] This is not to argue that, for Swift, the recognition of vice was separable from religious belief, or that immorality ought to be viewed merely as social deformity and a departure from a norm of orderly politeness. But Swift refused, more strongly, perhaps, than any of his contemporaries, to accept the comforting illusion that either divine or civil law, however abstractly true or right, was a sufficiently effective moral stimulus; satire, he felt, was a method of reform adapted to the understanding of a corrupt humanity. Given the desire to force men to realize, or at least *attempt* to realize, the ideals of both Christian virtue and classical genius, he "Thought no Method more commodious,/ Than to shew their Vices odious."[47] The common critical misunderstandings of the fourth voyage of *Gulliver's Travels* result partly from forgetting Gulliver's claim to have written "for the noblest end, to inform and instruct mankind" through the moral device of making man "*ashamed of his own vices.*"[48]

A belief in the social utility of satire, then, is entirely consistent with Swift's own views of man. His delight and agreement with the maxims of Rochefoucauld—"who is my favorite, because I found my whole character in him"[49]— testifies to his assumption that self-love is man's most basic motivating force. And the appeal of shame is, of course, directly to self-love, for, as Newman recognized, the eighteenth-century gentlemanly fear of shame was the fear of social censure—the humiliation of pride that comes from being laughed at by society. Swift's *A Project for the Advancement of Religion* is founded upon this same recognition. Here Swift proposes to equate piety and virtue with social and political success, thus making men's secular self-interest demand at least the pretense of morality. Here again Swift is affirming that most men are moved to action neither by a rational recognition of the good nor by religious fear of eternal punishment or hope for divine bliss; the single possible way of completing the process of leading men to correct their vices and follies is to relate such a correction to their own secular ambitions. But Swift seemed convinced that the *Project* was doomed to failure even before he wrote it, and the essay remains among his works merely as a piece of delightful and trenchant wishful thinking. For princes are neither virtuous nor strong enough to reward only piety and virtue with favors; it is the satirist who alone must take over the task of making men's vices socially disagreeable.

Affectation: The Source of the "True Ridiculous"

In terms of its ethical aim, then, satire was conceived by Swift and many of his contemporaries as a means to arouse moral action through an appeal to "present shame." Unlike the Christian or rational moralist who attempts to picture an ideal of conduct and to persuade men to follow it, the satirist aims to expose men's vices in a shameful and ludicrous way. Accordingly, neoclassic satire tended to take on a rather restricted meaning and to become identified with ridicule. The subject of "ridicule" was much discussed in the period between Dryden's *MacFlecknoe* and Pope's *Dunciad,* and it was generally defined as the *perception* of the "ridiculous"— a perception of an objectively real discrepancy between what a thing actually was and what it pretended or appeared to be. And to ridicule a person, institution, or idea was thought to consist, at least in part, of the mere exposure of this discrepancy. In this sense, ridicule cannot properly be considered as a descriptive method; it is often thought of as a process of reporting objective facts. Some few writers, of course, in the eighteenth century, defined ridicule in terms of a witty and critical arrangement of words and ideas without reference to any universal standard of the ridiculous. To these writers "the ridiculous in itself is no jest; but the ingenious and acute presentation of it is such."[50] And, in a sense, this idea was reflected by John Brown and other anti-Shaftesburians who criticized ridicule because, as one writer said, "weak-minded" people "are apt to think everything to be ridiculous *in itself* which happens to be laughed at."[51] The conception of ridicule as being *merely* a device of rhetoric and a simple juxtaposition of seemingly unrelated objects to create surprise and laughter cannot, however, be accepted as a prevalent view in the period.

Indeed, it was generally admitted by most critics that "the ridiculous" had a real existence which it was the purpose of the satirist to discover and lay bare. We should recognize that there is a real distinction between the claim that all ridicule is an infallible test of an object's inherent ridiculousness and the conviction that some objects are in themselves truly ridiculous. Many, indeed the great majority, of the critics who rejected the former and Shaftesburian proposition, accepted along with Shaftesbury the latter and more classical belief. Plato defined the ridiculous as the exhibition in man of the quality: "know not thyself." The Socratic belief that virtue lies in true knowledge and vice in opinion or false knowledge resulted in his applying the word "ridiculous" to the vice of extreme self-delusion: "The ridiculous is in short the specific name which is used to describe the vicious form of a certain habit; and of vice in general, it is that kind which is most at variance with the inscription at Delphi." Socrates argues that "ignorance of self" is manifested in three kinds of "vain conceit": they are the pretenses of having more wealth, more beauty, and more wisdom than one has. And of these, Socrates insists, the pretense to wisdom is the affectation most practiced by men and the one which is most dangerous. If these pretenders are powerful, they are, Socrates says, "hateful and horrible"; but "powerless ignorance may be reckoned, and in truth is, ridiculous."[52] The real dichotomy between pretense to wisdom and actual ignorance, between the appearance of virtue and beauty and the reality of vice and deformity, was often considered in the eighteenth century to be a fixed and universal standard of the ridiculous. To ridicule an object may not be a proof that the object in fact exhibits this split; but wherever the chasm between the appearance of virtue and the reality of vice can be found, and by whatever means, there too the ridiculous has its residence.

The defenders, like Lord Kames, of Shaftesbury's theory of ridicule as a "test of truth" believed that no subject which in itself is "truly grave" and serious can, by any manipulation of comparisons and base allusions, be made to appear truly ridiculous. Both this group, however, and their severest opponents agreed that ridicule, properly employed, serves to *expose* the real imposture of pretense. Such words and phrases as "expose," "lay bare," "discover," "reveal," "detect," "unveil," and the like, as descriptions of the operation of ridicule, run through the writings of almost all these critics. For example, in his "prefix" to *Notes Upon Hudibras* (1752), Montagu Bacon praises the social utility of Butler's poem for "*unveiling* that dark Scene of Hypocrisy and Madness"; moreover, his assumption that men and nations commit horrors "the *Ridicule* of which is not perceived 'till a hundred Years afterward"[53] turns upon the idea that the ridiculous is a real monster, of such a ludicrous mien that to be laughed at, it needs but to be seen. To Hutcheson, the source of laughter is any incongruity which surprises the mind; but the ridiculous, which he called a subdivision of laughter, differs from its parent in presenting a special kind of incongruity: the separation of the appearance of moral worth and the reality of moral worthlessness, both adhering to the same object. "This contrast between ideas of grandeur, dignity, sanctity, perfection, and ideas of meanness, baseness, profanity," seemed to him to be the essence of the ridiculous, "and the greatest part of our raillery and jest is founded upon it."[54] It was upon this conception of ridicule as being directed towards an existing phenomenon in the external world that many critics defended ridicule against the charge of personal

malice. For the vices which satire exposes are not created by
the satirical mind; they are, rather, the "real Follies" of "real
Life."[55] It was "benignant heaven," itself, Akenside said in
The Pleasures of Imagination, which had stamped

> The glaring scenes with characters of scorn,
> As broad, as obvious to the passing clown,
> As to the letter'd sage's curious eye.[56]

"If Satire should exalt herself," another critic, at the end of
the century, said in praise of Pope,

and if her language should become bold and of ancient potency,
it is unjust to attribute it to ill-nature or to malignity. It is the
deliberate, keen sensation of a mind feeling for the human
nature and the human character, for the ruin, the degradation,
the confusion, or the disturbance of a well-ordered state, and of
that morality, and of those principles which can alone uphold it.
It must then be regarded . . . "not as malice, but indignation and
resentment against vice and wickedness."[57]

The specific kind of ruin, degradation and confusion which
most frequently struck the eye of the eighteenth-century
satirist seems to have been an "artificial colouring"; by the
influence of fashion, custom, or enthusiasm objects "acquired
a degree of veneration" to which naturally they were not
entitled.[58] Some critics held that it was not merely enough
for the appearance of an object to differ from its reality in
order for it to become ridiculous; the appearance must masquerade its essential baseness for the purpose of gaining our
veneration. Akenside developed this dichotomy into the definition of the ridiculous as being the "incongruity" which
exists between a false claim to our praise and esteem "and
those latent circumstances" which show the claim to be
spurious. The echo of Plato's "know not thyself" finds a
habitation and a name in Akenside's observation that ". . . the
first and most general source of ridicule in the characters
of men, is vanity, or self applause for some desirable quality
or possession which evidently does not belong to those who
assume it." To Akenside, *vanity* arose from a dispropor-
tionate evaluation of a thing or quality possessed; founded

upon ignorance of true value, this false evaluation appeared estimable to the person holding it and was offered also to the world for its applause.[59] Although he was on a different side of the Shaftesbury fence, John Brown's definition of the object of ridicule agrees with that of Akenside. Brown considered folly, not dangerous and powerful vice, to be the proper "known Falsehood" which it is the business of the satirist to expose; and folly, he says, consists chiefly of affectation which "arises from a false Pretense to *Praise*."[60]

This positing of affectation or vanity as the distinctive kind of pretension and falsehood underlying the ridiculous received its best clarification from Henry Fielding. His definition, in the preface to *Joseph Andrews,* of the ridiculous is more exact and more comprehensive than those attempted by most of his contemporaries. It differs from theirs, however, chiefly in this greater precision; the point of view from which it is written, the basic assumptions upon which it rests, and the practical application to which it was put in his writings, typify the prevailing critical attitude toward the real nature and existence of the ridiculous. "The only source of the true Ridiculous (as it appears to me)," Fielding said, "is affectation."

Now affectation proceeds from one of these two causes, vanity or hypocrisy; for as vanity puts us on affecting false characters, in order to purchase applause; so hypocrisy sets us on an endeavour to avoid censure, by concealing our vices under an appearance of their opposite virtues. . . . Affectation doth not imply an absolute negation of those qualities which are affected; and therefore, though, when it proceeds from hypocrisy, it be nearly allied to deceit; yet when it comes from vanity only, it partakes of the nature of ostentation.

The avaricious miser, who pretends to be philanthropic and tries to deceive the world into applauding him for a virtue which he does not possess, is a hypocrite; the man who is proud of his generosity and pretends to himself and the world that he has more of that virtue than actually he has, such a man is vain. Hypocrisy, Fielding says, creates more surprises and pleasure, because it is more ridiculous in the width of the chasm between appearance and reality, than vanity; but both are comic and the satirist need not deviate from nature in describing them. "Life everywhere furnishes an accurate observer with the ridiculous." [61]

Undoubtedly, much of the satiric writing and criticism of this period, as in any era, developed immediately out of the personal spleen and spite of the satirist. Undoubtedly, too, some defenders of satire who were most vehement in their abuse of the affectations of the age and most insistent upon their own virtuous indignation when confronted by these same affectations, often pretended to a virtue as hypocritical as any folly they attacked. Satirists are not immune to the vices of mankind. But if no other period in English literary history has produced greater satirists than did the eighteenth century, perhaps this is because no other period has achieved a more united front against the sham and pretense and imposture of men masquerading as angels. It was to ridicule that men turned, then, to demonstrate the inanity and absurdity of "splendid trifles passing for matters of importance, show and form for substance, and superstition or enthusiasm for pure religion." [62]

"Gay Contempt"

Swift and the neoclassic critics of his day did not, however, limit their interest in ridicule to a determination of the proper objects of satiric attack; with considerable subtlety and penetration, many of these writers analyzed the psychological responses which the satirist should elicit from the reader in order to accomplish most effectively a moral intention. If the purpose of exposing the vicious separation between appearance and reality was to arouse in man a fear of social ostracism and to shock mankind from complacency, this purpose could, of course, be best achieved by an appeal to those emotions that best arouse shame. Accordingly, ridicule was thought to be most effective, indeed only effective, when it excited the reader simultaneously to *laugh at* and also to *contemn* the described vices and follies of men. A confidence in the power of laughter to effect moral reform is more comprehensible when we recall Hobbes's famous theory of laughter and its basis in the primary human motivation of self-interest. Hobbes, in the *Leviathan,* had concluded that the "passion of laughter is nothing else but *sudden glory* arising from some sudden conception of some eminency in ourselves, by comparison with the infirmities of others, or with our own formerly."[63] The idea that laughter can go beyond a mere undirected and capricious spirit of play was as old as Plato's theory that laughter is a mixture of pleasure and pain, and that it is closely allied with envy. But Hobbes's phrase, "sudden glory," stuck like a burr to the theory of comedy; in fact it has not yet been completely dislodged, and its implications have never been effectively refuted. This conception of laughter, which emerges from the debatable general premise that all actions are motivated by self-interest, provided many critics with a ready explanation for the pleasures of satire. Even Hutcheson, who devoted a treatise to the refutation of Hobbes's theory of laughter, admitted reluctantly that ". . . in this species [of laughter, ridicule,] there may be some pretense to allege that some imagined superiority may occasion it."[64] A less equivocal and timid assertion of the motivating force of satire and ridicule was later made by Lord Kames: "Ridicule, which chiefly arises from pride, a selfish passion, is at best but a gross pleasure." And although Kames was an ardent supporter of the doctrine that ridicule should be used even on grave subjects, he insisted that ridicule

. . . swells the good opinion we have of ourselves. This contributes, more than any other particular, to the pleasure we have in ridiculing follies and absurdities; and accordingly, it is well known, that those who have the greatest share of vanity, are the most prone to laugh at others.

The assumption of sudden glory arising from superiority which underlies these explanations of the popularity of ridicule, was equally operative in explaining its social usefulness. If it is pleasurable to ridicule others, "it is painful," Kames said, "to be the subject of ridicule."[65] This pain arises when man's natural and innate desire for superiority is thwarted; the love of glory and the fear of shame, said John Brown, are universal passions in man. It is by the appeal to the "ruling passion" of this sense that "Satire's shaft can pierce the harden'd breast:/She *plays* a *ruling* passion on the rest."[66] Critics who were fond of planting new senses in man in order to harvest explanations of his complexity were not slow to find that nature has implanted in us a sense which tends to correct our disposition, where law and religion are seen to have no power. This sense is the desire of public estimation. It was this "susceptibility to shame and infamy"[67] which gave to ridicule a force and application denied to other forms of moral correction. The aim of the satirist was not to display to men their vices in terms of ultimate punishment in the next world; it was to strike at men through the Achilles heel of their vanity and love of superiority. "If, therefore, the Pen of the Satirist effectuates an attention to public appearance and decorum, it answers a very good and consequential design, by lessening the contagion of bad example."[68] The concern of the satirist was the vice and, especially, the affectation, which attended men in their daily active lives; the satirist, accordingly, considered himself as a practical, rather than a speculative or abstruse moralist.

The comic attitude which was thought to be unique in ridicule and the most efficacious method of practical reform consisted of a mixed emotion, and in *The Pleasures of Imagination* Akenside embodies in a phrase this conception which was so common in Swift's day:

> Ask we for what fair end, the almighty fire
> In mortal bosoms wakes this *gay contempt,*
> These grateful stings of laughter, from disgust
> Educing pleasure, Wherefore, but to aid
> The tardy steps of reason . . ? (Bk. III, ll. 259-263; my italics).

Neither the subject of ridicule nor the method of describing it elicits or exhibits the exclusive reaction of laughter or contempt, of pleasure or disgust; when either side of the balance is tipped, ridicule expires. "In producing Portraits of Mankind," wrote Arthur Murphy, it is not enough to display Foibles and Oddities; a fine Vein of Ridicule must run through the whole, to urge the Mind to frequent Emotions of Laughter; otherwise there will be Danger of exhibiting disagreeable Characters without affording the proper Entertainment.[69]

Murphy, who had accepted Akenside's definition of ridicule, suggests here the heart of the matter; if ridicule is to succeed in amending the manners of men, it must not only teach but please. This attitude toward the *utile et dulce* of ridicule was, of course, ingrained in neoclassic principles concerning the end of all writing. If one vilifies men's major and dangerous vices which, as Plato had said, are only "hateful" and "detestable," there may be an element of *utile,* but the *dulce* is apt to fade into mere scorn and disgust. The fusion of disgust and laughter into what Akenside called "gay contempt," however, is possible and necessary in dealing with minor vices.[70]

If the objects of ridicule differ from those which are merely contemptible they also differ from those which are simply risible; Lord Kames concludes his series of distinctions with a happy self-assurance:

A ridiculous object is improper as well as risible; and produceth a mixt emotion, which is vented by a laugh of derision or scorn. Having therefore happily unravelled the knotty part, I proceed to other particulars.[71]

Since Ben Jonson, it had been fashionable for English satirists to maintain that they sported "with follies, not with crimes." A similar emphasis is continued throughout the eighteenth century. Thus Fielding, for example, is in favor of teaching men the "good-nature to laugh only at the follies of others, and the humility to grieve at their own."[72] Indeed, the critical consensus seems to have been that the proper object of ridicule was not what Gerard called "enormous vice,"[73] but rather the slighter errors of men—the appropriate reaction to great offenses being anger and indignation:

> Dart not on Folly an indignant eye:
> Who e'er discharg'd artillery on a fly?[74]

Satire directed at large failings and serious vices—where indignation of an intense sort is almost inevitable—often fails to maintain, moreover, the detachment necessary for successful comedy. If it does not lapse into direct abuse or vituperation, it is ineffective for other reasons. Most important, it will probably not be read with aroused pleasure and interest, as Hume acutely implied; "delicate satire" is more penetrating than "scurrility" simply because the latter "revenges us in a manner for the injury at the very time it is committed, by affording us a just reason to blame and contemn the person who injures us."[75]

Since the "ridiculous" is found only in circumstances which are simultaneously laughable and disgusting, there arises the belief that both the manner and the matter of ridicule should be limited. Not only should ridicule not excite a simple emotion of disgust, it should also refrain from exciting other deeper emotions. Akenside disagreed with Aristotle's dictum that the ridiculous was never accompanied with pain; at least he amended Aristotle's doctrine by saying that when the ridiculous arouses painful feelings, "violent emotions," the mind ceases to perceive the object as ridiculous. An emotion which lies too deep for laughter and contempt, an emotion which involves man's passions on a level of deep or sustained intensity, cannot be ridiculous. To Akenside, the ridiculous could exist on either of two levels: it either resided absolutely in the object itself as an incongruity between real "deformity" and apparent excellence or beauty, or else "the inconsistent properties existing . . . in the apprehension of the person" who observed the object. In either case, however, this sense of incongruity should excite "no acute or vehement emotion of the heart."[76] The implication here is that if the object itself arouses "vehement emotion" it is not ridiculous; or, if the person apprehending the object is violently moved, regardless of what may seem to others to be the slight grounds of his emotion, then, too, there is no ridicule. The satirist must not only choose subjects which in themselves are incapable of arousing deep feeling, he must also preserve in himself that detachment and objectivity which prevents the vehement emotion of his own heart.

In these observations of Akenside, one may note an attitude that anticipates the thesis argued in the present century by Henri Bergson. To Bergson, the comic is possible only when it is accompanied by "a momentary anesthesia of the heart."[77] According to Akenside's view, which was widely accepted in the eighteenth century, nothing "that is full of Grief, Terror, Pity or other Tragical Passions," as John Brightland put it, is "the Subject of Satire."[78] The comic and pleasurable aspect of satire is overpowered by these strong emotions which arouse the "tragical passions."

In the light of the critical attitudes mentioned, the significance of Swift's remarks on satire and ridicule in his *Epistle to a Lady* can be better appreciated. In refusing to adopt the heroic style as his own, he argues that

> I, as all the Parish knows,
> Hardly can be grave in Prose:
> Still to lash, and lashing Smile,
> Ill befits a lofty stile,
> From the Planet of my Birth,
> I encounter Vice with Mirth.
> Wicked Ministers of State
> I can easier scorn than hate:
> And I find it answers right;
> Scorn torments them more than Spight.

And Swift's purpose and method are not to arouse anger or the "tragical passions," but to excite the laughter of the reader at the expense of the satiric object:

> I, who love to have a Fling,
> Both at Senate-House, and—
> That they might some better Way tread,
> To avoid the publick Hatred;
> Thought no Method more commodious,
> Than to shew their Vices odious:
> Which I chose to make appear,
> Not by Anger, but a Sneer:
> As my Method of Reforming,
> Is by Laughing, not by Storming.

If the "reform" is attained "by laughing, not by storming" it is because the effectiveness of the moralist must be measured in terms of the emotional response towards vice and folly that he is able to elicit from his readers. Just as Akenside and Brightland had perceived the ineffectiveness of unmitigated angry abuse, so Swift recognized that his desire to move the emotions of his readers could best be accomplished by laughter. And he adds, in the same poem:

> For, as
> It is well observ'd by Horace,
> Ridicule has greater Pow'r
> To reform the World, than Sour.
> Horses thus, let Jockeys judge else,
> Switches better guide than Cudgels.
> Bastings heavy, dry, obtuse,
> Only Dulness can produce,
> While a little gentle Jerking
> Sets the Spirits all a working.
> Thus, I find it by Experiment,
> Scolding moves you less than Merriment.
> I may storm and rage in vain;
> It but stupefies your Brain.
> But, with Raillery to nettle,
> Set your Thoughts upon their Mettle:
> Gives Imagination Scope,
> Never lets your Mind elope:
> Drives out Brangling, and Contention,
> Brings in Reason and Invention.[79]

It is significant, I think, to understand the extent to which Swift stresses here the necessity of moving the emotions of the reader. The neoclassic critical principles of clarity and precision, in both poetry and prose, have been much emphasized and illustrated. In particular the kind of poetic exactness practiced by Pope has been called the "poetry of statement," and the prose of the period has been discussed generally as a declamatory, rational, and above all unemotional and sensible medium of communicating clear ideas. This view of neoclassic English literature has much truth in it, but it has tended towards an extreme. At least, it has helped the belief that the reader of eighteenth-century litera-

ture need only absorb in a passive way the sound good sense
of the writer. Such a belief continues, though in other terms,
the romantic assumption that "imagination" subsided after
the mid-seventeenth century. In this case, the form of the
assumption is that in neoclassic—as distinguished from "metaphysical"—wit the element of emotion has largely evaporated.
Actually, of course, the distance between Donne and Pope
is usually made to seem far greater than it is. In Pope's revi-
sions of Donne's satires, for example, we may detect a conscious attempt to retain the imaginative impact of the wit
while "correcting" Donne's obscurity of diction and irregu-
larity of line. The imaginative appeal of Swift is, perhaps,
even greater. It is doubtful whether any author in the history
of English literature was more intent upon arousing the feelings of his readers than was Swift. Although he urged a style
which was "like a Shrewsbury cake, short and sweet upon
the palate," his intention was always to persuade with this
unaffected style a highly directed emotional response; it was
not only to portray the distance between appearance and
reality, between reality and the ideal, but, by arousing laughter at the cosmic absurdity of this affectation, to make men
ashamed of the disparity. Thus we see that one essential
purpose of Swift's satiric technique is to stimulate an
awakened and indeed a poetic awareness in the reader's
mind—an awareness dulled by traditional and heavy-handed
moralizing—of the vicious limitations of man.

This defense and justification of satire urged by Swift and
supported by a sizable number of the writers and critics of
his day is, in other words, an appeal to the moral usefulness
of this minor genre. The person satirized is exposed to the
"gay contempt" of a polished society where, as Swift himself
observed, "the consequences of contempt are fatal." Although
in the early part of the century Queen Anne could, in a
message to Sir Robert Walpole, refer to herself as "the fat
bitch," the tendency of English society in the eighteenth century was towards the development of a more polite and
gracious form of social intercourse. As this development continued, the Christian gentleman seemed often to forget his

Christian principles in pursuit of a French and Chester-
fieldian elegance of manner; and "ridicule" became both
desirable and respectable. In such an atmosphere, the "man
of taste" could become the moral as well as the social arbiter,
and to occasion a social sense of shame was deemed to be
more effective, more conducive to moral reformation, than
the urgencies of any direct and unvarnished attack. If "the
content of satire," as David Worcester sensibly remarked, "is
criticism,"[80] the content of *effective* satire, of ridicule, was
thought to be a derisive and laughing criticism. A direct
attack upon an individual or institution creates an answerable argument, one that admits disagreement or defense; but
ridicule, because it "drives out brangling and contention,"
also deprives the object of any effective vindication. Moreover, if ridicule is most effective in its impact on the person
satirized, it is also most pleasing to the reader. For the reader
—and Swift realistically and somewhat hopelessly recognized
that few readers would include themselves among the objects
of ridicule—is quickened to an awareness of the vicious
disproportions of the world more by laughter than by
solemn and direct moralizing. In this sense, then, if ridicule
aims to deflate men's vanity by shaming their self-love, it
also aims to excite the reader's interest by appealing to his
own sense of superiority. Quite properly, then, Swift could
claim for satire both *utile* and *dulce*.[81]

II

Satiric Detachment: Invective, Diminution, and Irony

Invective

The author-reader relationship is nowhere a more delicate and sensitive affair than in satire. For the success of satire depends very much upon the author's ability to involve his readers on his side of a moral issue—to make them share his condemnation. In order to achieve and then maintain this subtle relationship, the satirist must allow himself neither to relax into an uncritical and laughing amusement nor to lose his temper. There is abundant evidence to show that Swift could delight in comedy for its own sake, as, for example, in his punning mock Latin poem, "A Love Song":

> Apud in is almi des ire,
> Mimis tres I ne ve re qui re.
> Alo veri findit a gestis,
> His miseri ne ver at restis.[1]

But Swift's general tendency of mind was to vent his deep, bitter, and disillusioned anger against the proud fraud of human effort. Perhaps the ultimate difference between the satire of Swift and that of most of his contemporaries—both in England and France—is that Swift really cared. However, revealed intensity of feeling, as Swift recognized early in his writing career, is incompatible with the comic spirit; and both consciously and perhaps unconsciously—with a self-protective need—he developed a variety of techniques which dissociated himself, and consequently his feelings, from any direct *vis-a-vis* relationship with his object. In satire, as much as and perhaps more than in any other literary genre, an apparent *detachment* from too intense a personal involvement is the necessary precondition to greatness.

It is useful to remember that Dryden in his *Discourse Concerning the Original and Progress of Satire* accepts the "general signification of the word," satire, to be an "invective," or a "reflection, as we use that word in the worst sense; or, as the French call it, more properly, *médisance*." Whether good or bad, general or particular, true or false, savage or humorous, prosaic or poetic—any literary attack upon the vice or folly of men and manners may be contained under the general word satire. This general definition implies, of course, no evaluation of the different kinds of satire. Dryden supplies this qualitative distinction when he insists that "the best and finest manner of satire" appears in "laughing a fool out of countenance." The laughter of good satire arises from that "fine raillery" which attacks its object from the flank with wit and technical skill, rather than crudely and brutally from the front. Dryden summarizes this distinction in saying:

. . . there is still a vast difference betwixt the slovenly butchering of a man, and the fineness of a stroke that separates the head from the body, and leaves it standing in its place. A man may be capable, as Jack Ketch's wife said of his servant, of a plain piece of work, a bare hanging; but to make a malefactor die sweetly, was only belonging to her husband.[2]

Here Dryden suggests an important and fundamental distinction between the direct criticism of invective and the fine stroke of ridicule. If all satire is criticism, then invective, at its lowest level of "butchery," is merely that criticism in which the author vilifies an object directly and openly without recourse to wit and with no attempt to arouse the comic spirit. It is a frontal attack, and its abuse is not mingled with sufficient wit or technical ingenuity to evoke any response lighter than the "vehement emotions" of anger and rage. The substance of this kind of satire is outright denunciation. It not only proceeds from the conviction that the object is evil, hateful, and probably dangerous, but it also expresses this belief overtly in vilification and vituperation. Its tendency, therefore, is towards the expression of an emotional extreme: it tends to magnify and exaggerate the viciousness of the object and it finds its vocabulary in the lexicon of hyperbole and billingsgate.

When Saint Paul castigated the Gentiles, he expressed himself in the direct abuse of invective, damning a whole people as sinners

. . . filled with all unrighteousness, fornication, wickedness, covetousness, maliciousness; full of envy, murder, debate, deceit, malignity; whisperers, backbiters, haters of God, despiteful, proud, boasters, inventors of evil things, disobedient to parents, without understanding, covenantbreakers, without natural affection, implacable, unmerciful: [3]

This powerful catalogue of vices exemplifies (if considered as satire) the limitations of invective when a writer directly communicates his anger through a series of exact verbal equivalents of the object attacked. Indeed, the passage is a "plain piece of work, a bare hanging." The technique itself is a kind of *amplification,* that traditional figure of rhetoric which, as Thomas Wilson defined it, "consisteth in heaping and enlarging of those places, which serve for confirmation of a matter."[4] As invective, this passage expresses Paul's rage with painful clarity; as ridicule, however, which is not content with self-expression but aims to *persuade and direct the reader's own responses against the criticized object,* the passage is less successful. The relation between the author and the object of attack is, in this case, so intense and monocular, and expressed with so much direct anger, that the reader tends to *withdraw* his sympathy from Paul and to conclude, perhaps, that the abuse is a feverish exaggeration. "Anger does not beget anger," David Worcester has observed; when we see a man in a furious passion, instead of feeling *with* him we are likely to protect ourselves from sharing his painful emotion by laughing *at* him—even to the point of ridiculing him as a "lobster-faced baboon in a fit."[5]

An antipodal contrast to this passage may be found in Rabelais: "The cake-bakers . . . did injure them most outrageously," Rabelais tells us,

. . . calling them prating gablers, lickorous gluttons, freckled bittors, mangy rascals, shite-a-bed scoundrels, drunken roysters, sly knaves, drowsy loiterers, slap-sauce fellows, slabberdegullion druggels, lubbardly louts, cousening foxes, ruffian rogues, paltry customers, sycophant varlets . . . (Book I, Chap. 25)

and so on for half a page. This abusive catalogue is also an invective, but its effect upon the reader is to stimulate neither anger nor withdrawal, but laughter. The reason seems to be that the technique of exaggeration is here contrived to be amusing in itself. Moreover, not only is the author himself *detached* from any real anger, but the anger of the cake-bakers, too, is without real virulence. It is not the emotion of Rabelais or the bakers which affects the reader; it is the remarkable variety and exaggerated exuberance with which it is expressed. As in the passage I have just cited from the Bible, this Rabelaisian invective diverts the reader's attention from the object attacked, but in this case to the technique of its expression. Similarly, too, this direct abuse is unsuccessful satire, although for somewhat different reasons. Not only is the satiric object here obscure (do we contemn the cake-bakers' vulgar invective or sympathize with the cake-bakers' contempt for Gargantua's party?); but, unlike that in the Bible, the seeming content of criticism is not *criticism* at all. At least the reader recognizes that most of the bakers' anger is harmlessly expended in verbosity; where there is such a plethora of metaphor, and where the words have so slight an accuracy of denotation, the content of criticism is overshadowed by the humour of word-play. In short, whereas Paul's invective nullifies itself in its excessive contempt, that of the cake-bakers spends itself in a humour almost devoid of criticism.

Of the Rabelaisian kind of direct invective, which sports playfully with words, there seems to be remarkably little in

Swift's prose satire. Occasionally, however, Swift's strongly developed sense of play found release in subordinating satiric criticism to his delight in sheer verbal ingenuity. In *A Tale of a Tub,* for instance, he describes Peter's Bulls in terms which are reminiscent of the extravagant gusto of the cake-bakers: ". . . they would *Roar,* and *Spit,* and *Belch,* and *Piss,* and *Fart,* and *Snivel* out *Fire,* and keep a perpetual *Coyl,* till you flung them a Bit of *Gold*" (p. 112). Although the description has considerable satiric direction, the piling up of these Anglo-Saxon and vulgar monosyllables gives an exuberance and gaiety to the satire which takes the edge off Swift's latent savage intensity. Perhaps an even better example of the comic technique taking precedence over the satiric content may be seen in the catalogue of medical remedies which a Laputan projector offered as cures for politicians:

This doctor therefore proposed . . before the members sat, [to] administer to each of them lenitives, aperitives, abstersives, corrosives, restringents, palliatives, laxatives, cephalalgics, icterics, apophlegmatics, acoustics, as their several cases required; and according as these medicines should operate, repeat, alter, or omit them at the next meeting.[6]

Unlike the Rabelaisian abuse of the cake-bakers, there is no doubt here about Swift's satiric intention both to ridicule politicians and the jargon of the physician's trade. But seen in its effect upon the reader, this catalogue of medical terms stimulates through its very exaggeration our laughter as much as our contempt. A similar Rabelaisian sporting with words informs Swift's satiric thrust at contemporary poets: ". . . for although we have not one masterly poet, yet we abound with wardens and beadles, having a multitude of poetasters, poetitoes, parcel-poets, poet-apes and philo-poets, . . ."[7] These passages share with much of the humour of Rabelais a preponderance of the sense of comedy over the sense of direct satire.

If Swift rarely relaxed into Rabelais' easy chair, he almost never donned the hair shirt of an angry Saint Paul—not because he felt less intensely but because he organized his anger into an artful rhetoric. When Swift employs invective,

he generally includes some sly indirection of technique which
relieves and interrupts the pattern of his contempt. In such
cases, the readers' emotions are, for a moment, intellectual-
ized, and this temporary relief allies us with Swift and makes
possible a coalescence of contempt and laughter. Even in the
final voyage of *Gulliver's Travels,* which is as savage an indictment of humanity as has ever been written, Gulliver's most
violent diatribe against his own society is not without an
element of technical indirection:

I wanted no fence against fraud or oppression; here was neither
physician to destroy my body, nor lawyer to ruin my fortune; no
informer to watch my words and actions, or forge accusations
against me for hire: here were no gibers, censurers, backbiters,
pickpockets, highwaymen, housebreakers, attorneys, bawds, buffoons, gamesters, politicians, wits, splenetics, tedious talkers,
controvertists, ravishers, murderers, robbers, virtuosos; no leaders
or followers of party and faction; no encouragers to vice, by
seducement or examples; no dungeon, axes, gibbets, whipping-
posts, or pillories; no cheating shopkeepers or mechanics; no
pride, vanity, or affectation; no fops, bullies, drunkards, strolling
whores, or poxes; no ranting, lewd, expensive wives; no stupid,
proud pedants; no importunate, overbearing, quarrelsome, noisy,
roaring, empty, conceited, swearing companions; no scoundrels,
raised from the dust for the sake of their vices, or nobility thrown
into it on account of their virtues; no *lords, fiddlers, judges, or
dancing-masters.*[8]

Even if we make Gulliver a surrogate for Swift (an identification not entirely plausible), we see at once that he is able,
in spite of the intensity of his feelings, to conclude his invective with a witticism which immediately detaches him from
mere violence: "No lords, fiddlers, judges, or dancing-masters." What makes invective poor as satire is the excess of
expressed feelings; what rescues this passage from the over-
heated venom of mere abuse is the "economy," to use Freud's
word, of its final witty juxtaposition. Gulliver had his eye
not only on his hated England, but also on the technical
virtuosity with which he could express his contempt. The
reader is able to sympathize with Gulliver and to join with
him in his equation of lords and judges with fiddlers and
dancing-masters.

Diminution

The witty juxtaposition and, by inference, equation of dignified with admittedly undignified professions reflect a tendency fundamental to all satire: professions and actions to which custom has allowed authority and importance are, in Kenneth Burke's phrase, "converted downwards."[9] The mixed catalogue is a convenient device by which to show this tendency at work. Swift's *A Serious and Useful Scheme to Make an Hospital for Incurables* contains nearly fifteen pages of listed "incurables." Although we are never unaware of Swift's misanthropic intention to damn mankind in general, we are also continually surprised out of anger by the wit of the juxtapositions. For example, when Swift lists those incurables who "lie for their interest," he includes in one list "fishmongers, flatterers, pimps, lawyers, fortune-hunters, and fortune-tellers." Similarly, Swift herds together such incurables as "attorneys, solicitors, pettifoggers, scriveners, usurers, hackney-clerks, pickpockets, pawn-brokers, jailors, and justices of the peace," as well as "hounds, horses, whores, sharpers, surgeons, tailors, pimps, masquerades, or architects."[10] This device is an important one among the almost infinite variety of techniques used in *A Tale of a Tub* to degrade professions in general: Swift mixes "Eves-droppers, Physicians, Mid-wives, small Politicians, Friends fallen out, Repeating Poets, Lovers Happy or in Despair, Bawds, Privy-Counsellours, Pages, Parasites and Buffoons"; he joins in a single list *"Parliament-, Coffee-, Play-, Bawdy-houses";* and *"Beaux, Fidlers, Poets, and Politicians"*[11] are huddled together in an uneasy equality. In all these catalogues the element of witty surprise is strong enough to startle the mind from the sense of total contempt and, although the critical content is manifestly present, it coalesces with the reader's recognition of the technique itself.

Now, in any angry invective against specific abuses or general actions, we may sense fear as well as scorn. If the object attacked is great enough or dangerous enough to be feared, it may often acquire a compelling attractiveness, possibly even a certain magnificence. The most prominent example is that of Satan in *Paradise Lost*. The very scope and dimension of the evil he represents could, in the eighteenth century, be felt as "sublime." Blake was not alone in feeling that perhaps Milton himself was of Satan's party. One may, indeed, "first endure, then pity, then embrace" a monster as fearful as Satan; both his evil and his punishment exist on so cosmic a level as to arouse our respect. The effectiveness of the satirist, however, must be measured by the extent to which he is able to arouse contempt unmixed with any such incipient admiration. Joseph Conrad's sense of the dimly perceived evil lying behind the appearances of life led him in at least one story, *The Heart of Darkness,* to distinguish sharply between the cosmic evil of an ultimate horror and what he called the "flabby devil" of man's ordinary vice. Between the grandeur of Milton's Satan and the mere vulgarity of Conrad's "flabby devil" has fallen the shadow of satiric diminution. If Satan inspires us with a secret pity and terror, Conrad's "papier-mâché Mephistopheles" is not worth the powder to blow him up.

This technique of rendering devils flabby is a common literary device which was discussed in rhetorical handbooks under the Greek title, *meiosis,* meaning, literally, "belittling" or "diminution."[12] Diminution may be described briefly as the use of any "ugly or homely images" which are intended to diminish the dignity of an object. In a sense, of course, nearly all satire might be included within this broad definition. But a more specific meaning is suggested when we recall Puttenham's description of it as the "disabler," a figure useful to express "derision and for a kind of contempt." Specifically, then, diminution is any kind of speech which tends, either by the force of low or vulgar imagery, or by other suggestion, to depress an object below its usually accepted status. Diminution may be accomplished in a variety of ways. A similarity may be drawn between an object and one which is universally acknowledged to be inferior; the comparison results, of course, in the primary object absorbing the contemptibility of the secondary object. Diminution may also be effected by dwelling upon certain physical characteristics of a person and then, by synechdoche, equating the whole object with that one part. Diminution may be expressed in innumerable other forms; it may appear as direct abuse, irony, litotes, and so on. The following paragraphs touch primarily on some types of diminution which Swift used in direct satire.

One of Swift's most expert devices of direct diminution was the attribution of *failure and impotence* to an opponent. In Puttenham's sense, this was to "disable" an opponent by showing him to be not dangerous but merely offensive and disgusting. This kind of attack appeals to no logic of argument; it is aimed solely at degradation through contrasting an opponent's attempt to be powerful with his actual failure. Sometimes he joins the idea of failure with a comparison to an animal which may offend our senses, but is too weak to inspire our terror. A characteristic example of this kind of direct diminution is seen in Swift's attack upon Tindal's "The Rights of the Christian Church . . .":

But still there is the same flatness of thought and style; the same weak advances toward wit and raillery. . . . And, lastly, the same rapid venom sprinkled over the whole; which, like the dying impotent bite of a trodden benumbed snake, may be nauseous and offensive, but cannot be very dangerous.[13]

The passage arouses no loud laughter, but the author's seeming detachment from anger and his skillful deflating of Tindal's pretensions create a sense of the ridiculous without the admixture of stronger emotions. Similar diminution through the use of debasing imagery, joined with the content of impotence and failure, is developed indirectly throughout *A Tale of a Tub*. A remarkable illustration of Swift's use of direct diminution in that work, is found in the passage:

May their own Dullness, or that of their Party, be no Discouragement for the Authors to proceed; but let them remember, it is with *Wits* as with *Razors,* which are never so apt to *cut* those they are employ'd on, as when they have *lost their Edge*. Besides, those whose Teeth are too rotten to bite, are best of all others, qualified to revenge that Defect with their Breath (p. 49).

By debasing metaphors Swift shows his critics to be dangerous only in their dullness, and then shows this to be no real danger at all but, rather, something merely shameful and unpleasant. A sexual analogy may well underlie the basic humour of the device—the analogy involving sexual incapacity. And Swift often arouses an amused contempt by the indirect equation between a man's intellectual failures and his sexual life. Alexander Pope, whose own variety of satiric methods includes many in common with Swift, availed himself of the disgraceful connotations of sexual incapacity when, in the familiar Sporus passage, in the *Epistle to Dr. Arbuthnot,* he characterized Lord Hervey's rhetoric as "florid impotence" (l. 317). Impotence of any sort is a possible subject of ridicule, and Swift makes frequent use of it.

A more direct, less subtle method of diminution is attained through comparisons with lower animals. Swift was alert to any method of arousing contempt, and he often appealed to the associations with human vice traditionally acquired by many lower animals. A few examples here are sufficient to illustrate his use in direct abuse of what we may call "bestial diminution." In the passage quoted above, the satiric effect of Swift's disdain for Tindal's wit depends in part upon the graphic image of "the dying impotent bite of a trodden benumbed *snake.*" Swift here gives a local habitation and a name to Tindal's weakness of thought. The abusive ideas which, in the abusive catalogue, remain simply as abstractions, are here attached to a concrete image. Death, impotence, and insensitivity lose their abstract generality when thus associated with a creature to which the mind brings already existing attitudes of disgust. Accordingly, this bestial comparison gives a compression to Swift's contempt which is absent in more general abuse. This compression is similarly attained in Swift's direct satire (which follows a series of indirect and ironical attacks) upon the "True Criticks" in *A Tale of a Tub:*

The *True Criticks* are known by their Talent of swarming about the noblest Writers, to which they are carried meerly by Instinct,

as a Rat to the best Cheese, or a Wasp to the fairest Fruit. . . .
A *True Critick,* in the Perusal of a Book, is like a *Dog* at a Feast,
whose Thoughts and Stomach are wholly set upon what the
Guests *fling away,* and consequently is apt to *Snarl* most, when
there are the fewest Bones (pp. 103-104).

Not only do the series of comparisons degrade the critic, they
also serve to place his ignominy in sharp contrast with the
nobility of the works criticized. It is evident that this device
may be among the easiest possible in satire; even the abusive
catalogue, when it is performed through amplification, requires some breadth of vocabulary. But all that is necessary
to simple bestial diminution is the recognition that certain
animals have absorbed different human and unpleasant
associations. Swift's use of this device, however, is rarely
overworked and when it appears it comes as a shock. Moreover, Swift often complicates the device by setting up a contrast between animals which have pleasant, and those which
have unpleasant, associations. In a sense, this use of bestial
comparisons becomes almost allegorical with each animal
standing for a specific quality. An example of an extremely
effective and surprising contrast is found in Drapier's question: "It is no loss of honour to submit to the lion, but who,
with the figure of a man, can think with patience of being
devoured alive by a rat?"[14] Much of this effect results, also,
from opposing the passive idea of "submission" to the lion
and the activity of "being devoured alive" by the rat.

Invective, when coupled with an un-Rabelaisian sincerity,
may declare outrage, but as a method of satire, of making
men uncomfortable in their vices, it fails in almost direct
proportion to the honesty of its expression. It fails to communicate that artistic *control* which is so essential to literary
craftsmanship, because, without it, the outraged moralist
will fail to arouse belief. Diminution, on the other hand, is
the very heart of satire. It can, of course, be so direct and
vituperative that, in the process of reducing an object to
what is disgusting and loathsome, it loses the control and
guidance of its literary purpose. But when diminution is
effected by a skillful and organized artistic effort, when wit

is employed to relieve the naked intensity of indignation, satire approaches its neoclassic aims. Swift recognized, however, that diminution, no matter how witty, could never be completely transmitted by direct attack. And it was partly to preserve his own personal detachment and partly to increase the distance between himself, as moralist, and his audience, that Swift developed the techniques of irony with an unrivaled brilliance.

Irony

Irony has accumulated so many meanings in its long history that the word justifies Otto Ribbeck's description of it as *proteusartig*. How many shapes it has assumed is suggested when we recall the distinctions, to name only a few, that have been drawn among Socratic irony, dramatic irony, Romantic irony, irony of understatement; irony has been studied as a rhetorical device and has been extended to include a whole mode of behaviour. It is certain, however, that the first great ironist was Socrates, although, as G. G. Sedgewick reminds us in *Of Irony, Especially in Drama,* the term "eiron" was first applied to Socrates as a term of abuse—meaning something like "sly-foxery," tinged, perhaps, with connotations of "low-bred." The most influential definition of the word appeared in Aristotle's *Nichomachean Ethics* where for the first time irony was associated with "understatement." Aristotle, in describing the honesty of "truthful man" places it as a mean between *alazoneia,* the boastful man's tendency to exaggerate, and *eironeia,* the "mock-modest" man's tendency to understate the truth. Using Socrates as his example, Aristotle somewhat uneasily praises the ironist as being "more attractive" than the braggart because understaters "speak not for gain but to avoid parade." As Sedgewick emphasizes, however, Aristotle's idea of the Socratic *eironeia* meant more than a mere rhetorical device of understatement: "In the *Ethics, eironeia* is a pervasive mode of behaviour, a constant pretence of self-depression—of which understatement is only one manifestation."[15] The very essence of the word, whether considered as a rhetorical trope (along with synechdoche, metonomy, and hyperbole) or as a whole way of life, is *dissimulation:* the ironist appears to say or to be one thing while making it apparent to his audience that he means or is something quite different.

It was as a technique of satiric utterance that Swift seems to have viewed irony which, he said in his *Verses on the Death of Dr. Swift,* "I was born to introduce,/ Refin'd it first, and shew'd its Use" (ll. 57-58). The "use" of irony lies preëminently in its capacity to create the appearance of the satirist's emotional detachment. When Aristotle discusses irony in his *Rhetoric,* he notes that the "ironical man jokes to amuse himself," (1419b) and it is in this spirit that Swift writes in defense of his own ironic *"laughing with a few friends in a corner."*[16] As we have seen, the limitations of invective lie in its display of an excess of concern—the reader may distrust violence in a moralist and the person attacked may congratulate himself on his own importance. On the other hand, ironic laughter from the corner is, perhaps, the most effective form of diminution at the satirist's disposal. By disdaining to exert himself directly against an opponent, the ironist preserves a status of *superiority* to what he attacks and invites the reader to join him (and his coterie of select and privileged souls) on the mountaintop of truth.

Praise-blame Inversion   The first use of the word "irony" in English appeared in 1502 when, as the *New English Dictionary* tells us, Wynken de Worde spoke of "yronye of grammar, by the whyche a man sayth one and gyveth to understande the contrarye." In *The Arte of English Poesie* (1589), Puttenham called irony a "dry-mocke," and, by the end of the eighteenth century, it was taken for granted that irony fused both dissimulation and mockery. Accordingly, Bailey's *Dictionary* (6th ed., 1733) defined the word as " a Figure in *Rhetorick,* by which we speak contrary to what we think, by Way of Derision or Mockery to him we argue or talk with." Now, the satirist is concerned with both evaluating the world and communicating these judgments to his readers. The simplest form of satiric irony, by which the satirist can "speak contrary to what he thinks," is through the *inversion* of these judgments: the satirist pretends *to praise what he means to condemn* or he pretends *to condemn what he means to praise*. It is of this inversion that Quintilian speaks when he says *laudis adsimulatione detrahere et vituperationis laudare*.

In *A Tale of a Tub* Swift first displayed his remarkable talent as a mock eulogist. Indeed, the whole tale is ironically organized as a panegyric upon the moderns, written by a modern and for the moderns. The reader is introduced to the panegyrical intention of the essay at the very outset when he reads the list of titles, written by the same "author," which will be "speedily published." These include the extremes of both a *Panegyrick upon the World* and a *Panegyrical Essay upon the Number Three*. In a masterful account of the reasons why the former treatise had not yet appeared in print, Swift in the "Preface" gives a further twist of diminution to his inverted praise: ". . . I am so entirely satisfied with the whole present Procedure of human Things, that I have been for some Years preparing Materials towards *A Panegyrick upon the World;* to which I intend to add a Second Part, entituled, *A Modest Defence of the Proceedings of the Rabble in all Ages.* Both these I had Thought to publish by way of Appendix to the following Treatise; but finding my Common-Place-Book fill much slower than I had reason to suspect, I have chosen to defer them to another occasion" (pp. 53-54).[17] This encomiastic intention, however, is not thwarted in other matters and he pursues his joyful praise of the moderns throughout the remainder of the tale.

Swift's ironic tendency to exaggerate praise into a paean of indirect damnation can be illustrated in almost every satire he ever wrote. How easily and naturally he adopted the indirection of ironic eulogy may be seen in his marginalia, written in longhand on his own copy of Dr. Gibbs's translation of fifteen psalms of David; the comments were evidently intended not for publication but simply for Swift's own private amusement. In the midst of other remarks which specifically ridicule or parody Gibbs's logic, diction, rhymes and so on, Swift includes encomiums upon the poetry: "Admirably reasoned and connected!" he exclaims over one stanza which says that if God is angered by his foes then those are happy who have confidence in Him; to Gibbs's line that men should "with *fear*/His joyful praise proclaim," Swift gives his bland approval: "Very proper to make a joyful proclamation with fear"; Swift lauds another foolish idea with the praise: "A good principle!"; and to the lines,

> O Lord, how glorious are the ways
>   Of Thy good Providence!
> Thou, Lord, Whose blessed Name I praise,
>   True justice dost dispense,

Swift notes in the margin: "Do not these verses end very sublimely?"[18] The irony of this praise is at once apparent. Not only are the comments imbedded among other remarks more directly contemptuous and slighting, but the praise sends our eye to the text of Gibbs's version, and Swift is confident that the text will damn itself. The device, then, provides one more kind of detachment in which the values of an object are presented in such a way that they seem to ridicule themselves, and Swift can eliminate the personal element of his own critical intervention.

A device so simple and obvious might be expected to dull itself with repetition, but Swift avails himself of a variety of other techniques with which to diversify the basic pattern of inverted eulogy. Two passages drawn from *A Letter to the Bishop of St. Asaph* will serve as example. The Bishop, William Fleetwood, who was a favourite of Queen Anne, was also a Whig in politics and an advocate of Low Church principles in religion. He published four of his sermons with a preface attacking Harley's Tory administration, and the Whigs of the Kit-Cat Club inserted the preface as a party pamphlet in the *Spectator*. In his *Letter* answering the preface, Swift characteristically denies any need for praising Fleetwood: "Nor need I run riot in encomium and panegyric," he says to the Bishop, "since you can perform that part so much better for yourself." Nevertheless, the *Letter* is a riot of praise for the Bishop, his ideas, and even his prose style:

Here, your lordship rises, if possible above yourself: Never was such strength of thought, such beauty of expression, so happily joined together. Heavens! Such force, such energy in each pregnant word! Such fire, such fervour, in each glowing line! One would think your lordship was animated with the same spirit with which our hero fought. Who can read, unmoved, these following strokes of oratory? "Such was the fame, such was the reputation . . ." &c. O! the irresistible charm of the word "such!" Well, since Erasmus wrote a treaty in praise of Folly, and my Lord Rochester an excellent poem upon Nothing, I am resolved to employ the "Spectator," or some of his fraternity, (dealers in words) to write an encomium upon Such.[19]

This is "gay contempt" at its very best. The contrast and incongruity between the exaggerated praise and the foolishly diminutive word "such" tends to reduce the word below even its usual status. From something innocuous, the word has been "converted downward" to something contemptible through mere excess and exaggeration. Moreover, the whole passage is a parody of the very fault it satirizes; Swift's own use of "such" as a means to exaggerate praise turns the passage into dramatic irony: the reader (audience) is detached from the satirist's position and perceives for himself that the appearance of vigor created by the word "such" is in fact the merest verbiage. The level of ironic detachment created by this dramatic representation of the folly which Swift is attacking is paralleled by another level of conscious ambiguity. The praise of Fleetwood's rising "if possible above yourself" contains not only a logical impossibility in the physical world, but all the suppressed connotations which Swift brought to the idea of soaring above matter and good sense. In addition, there is an immediate ambiguity in Swift's identifying the happy junction of Fleetwood's thought and expression; the parody of the latter reflects by association upon the former. And the word "unmoved" is charged with the *double-entendre* of our being "moved" either to praise or to laughter by those "strokes of oratory."

Swift's cleverness in mingling ambiguity with exaggerated praise may be even more clearly illustrated in another passage from this vigorous and comic satire. Instead of focusing upon details of diction or rhetorical devices (Swift had also praised the "expressive dash," or aposiopesis, through which this "consumate orator" showed that his "very silence is thus eloquent"), Swift praises the essay as a whole:

I cannot but observe with infinite delight, that the reasons your lordship gives for reprinting those immortal pieces, are urged with that strength and force, which is peculiar to your lordship's writings, and is such, as all who have any regard for truth, or relish for good writing, must admire, though none can sufficiently commend. In a word, the preface is equal to the sermons, less than that ought not, and more cannot, be said of it.[20]

Swift creates the impression of praise with very few words which state approbation. The only standard of reference he supplies is the rest of Fleetwood's writings; the preface is said to reflect that "peculiar" strength and force which mark all his works, and the concluding sentence with its distinction between "can not" and "ought not" is loaded with the possibility of two meanings. And even the commendatory words are chosen with care for their suggestive implications; whether Swift takes "infinite delight" (he cannot be "unmoved") in the excellence of these writings or in their *absurdity* is equally possible, and whether Swift's "admiration" is directed towards Fleetwood's truth and good style or towards his departure from them is likewise left to the reader to determine. The ambiguity of "admire" is even more sharply seen when we recall the pejorative connotations of the word in the early eighteen century. The pieces could be equally "immortal" as monuments of stupidity as of wisdom, and the phrase "none can sufficiently commend" might well mean that no commendation is possible where there is no excellence.

The converse of this ironical technique is, of course, *to condemn what we mean to praise.* A characteristic example is to be found in Swift's defense of Carteret, who was among the very few men sent from England to govern Ireland for whom Swift had any respect. Carteret became the Lord Lieutenant of Ireland, and it was to him that Swift made the famous remark: "What, in God's name, do you do here?

Get back to your own country, and send us our boobies again." Even in praise Swift was oblique and the remark recalls his practice in his letters of couching his highest compliments in terms of abuse. When a number of Whigs led by one Richard Tighe attempted to discredit Carteret on the grounds that he had favoured Tories, Swift jumped to the defense and wrote *A Vindication of his Excellency the Lord C———t*. Swift introduces his essay with an elaborate presentation of Carteret's "faults." Well educated at Oxord, Carteret "could never wipe off the stain, nor wash out the tincture of his University acquirements and dispositions," Swift laments. He then proceeds to particularize upon these grievous faults:

To this another misfortune was added; that it pleased God to endow him with great natural talents, memory, judgment, comprehension, eloquence, and wit. And, to finish the work, all these were fortified even in his youth, with the advantages received by such employments as are best fitted both to exercise and polish the gifts of nature and education. . . . I cannot omit another weak side in his Excellency, for it is known, and can be proved upon him, that Greek and Latin books might be found every day in his dressing-room, if it were carefully searched. . . . I have it from good hands, that when his Excellency is at dinner with one or two scholars at his elbows, he grows a most unsupportable, and unintelligible companion to all the fine gentlemen around the table.[21]

Thus Swift "freely acknowledges" the "failings" of Carteret and succeeds in constructing by indirection a positive portrait of the idealized educated gentleman and man of affairs.

This dissimulation of moral attitude is the method underlying most of Swift's irony and it is readily seen to be a technique of the practiced orator. That is, the speaker addresses his audience directly but varies his discourse by appearing to say one thing when in reality he is communicating the contrary. Shakespeare provides us with a classic expression of the effectiveness of this venerable technique in Antony's praise of Brutus as "an honourable man." But Swift, although profoundly influenced, as I will emphasize later, by the classical tradition of rhetoric, extended his irony far beyond the potentialities of spoken oratory. His irony achieves its most compelling power when "dissimulation" ceases to be the technique of an advocate and becomes instead subordinated to a more complex artistic intention. That is, at its best, Swift's irony becomes *dramatic;* the disparity between appearance and reality no longer exists as a device of the speaker but is itself embodied in an objective situation. Swift's tendency away from invective and towards a more fully developed artistic detachment completes itself in dramatic characterization.

Ironic Masks   In the above examples of simulated panegyric, Swift's own voice is heard directly only in his marginalia on Dr. Gibbs's paraphrase of the psalms. But in the other essays, he has developed a *fictitious author* who acts as a vehicle for the irony. The full title, for example, of the eulogy on Fleetwood reads: *A Letter of Thanks from my Lord W ... n to the Lord Bp. of S. Asaph in the Name of the Kit-Cat Club* and the piece is signed by "the greatest (next yourself) of your lordship's admirers, Wharton."[22] Not only must the reader convert seeming praise into actual condemnation, but he also perceives that the supposed author, Wharton, dramatizes a new dimension of satiric attack. As Maynard Mack has observed, "an assumed identity, a *persona,* a mask," was a "specialty of the Augustan Age," and although it is not "fatal" to identify Wordsworth with the "speaker" of the "Ode on Intimations of Immortality," in Augustan satire "this identification is very often fatal."[23] When, in the *Dunciad,* Pope apostrophized Swift by "Whatever title please thine ear/ Dean, Drapier, Bickerstaff, or Gulliver" (Bk. I, ll. 19-20) he listed in a pentameter line's narrow room but a small fraction of Swift's assumed identities. Included among these *personae* are Simon Wagstaff, the Examiner, Gregory Misorarum, Sieur de Baudrier, Ebenezer Elliston, Thomas Hope, "A Person of Quality," "A Friend of the Author," and a host of anonymous projectors, politicians, freethinkers, atheists, and Grub Street hacks. Obviously, Swift had a practical reason for concealing himself behind many of these assumed

identities: the penalties for sedition were severe and Swift's
pamphlets were more than once condemned as both libelous
and seditious. In 1714, a reward of £300 was offered for the
discovery of the author of *The Publick Spirit of the Whigs,*
and in 1724 a similar reward was posted for the disclosure of
M. B. Drapier's identity as author of *A Letter to the Whole
People of Ireland*—although, in the latter case, Swift's identity
was generally known and his safety lay in the strength of an
aroused public opinion directed against Wood's patent and
in favour of Swift as the saviour of Ireland. Far more important, however, than these practical and political reasons for
concealing his identity was the more fundamental reason that
Swift could partially conceal behind ironic masks the intensity
of his personal involvement—and thereby, of course, at the
same time energize his readers into a greater intensity of
imaginative awareness than would be possible with a more
direct approach.

Amidst the variety of fictitious authors presented by Swift,
we may distinguish two major kinds of *personae*. The first,
and least complex kind, is the mask of what we may call "the
detached observer." This mask is similar to that of the typical
Augustan figure, the Spectator, and in Swift's writing differs
mainly in the variety of its guises. In such essays as Swift's
*A Letter to a Young Gentleman Lately enter'd into Holy
Orders,* and *Of the Education of Ladies,* as well as in his
contributions to *The Examiner,* we perceive him assuming
the role of a speaker who, though not Swift himself, nonetheless expresses with only slight dissimulation Swift's own
moral attitudes. In *A Letter to a Young Gentleman,* for example, he offers genuine and thoughtful advice on the learning, rhetoric, and rationality proper to a pulpit orator. He
writes, however, not as the Dean of St. Patrick's, but as "A
Person of Quality"—his initialed signature is "A.B."—and
he delivers his advice from the point of view of a well-
informed and intelligent layman whose opinion reflects that
of "the generality of mankind" and of those "who are hearers"
and not preachers.[24] By appearing as an objective and dis-
interested commentator on the more frequent abuses in the

pulpit, Swift creates an atmosphere of veracity and his arguments convince because they avoid the "enthusiasm" of special pleading.

There is probably no science which seems to be more detached from human emotions than is mathematics. And although abstract Cartesian rationalism was a constant thorn in Swift's side, he himself made frequent and effective use of the *impersonality* of arithmetic. There is a distinct difference in effect between saying "all men are fools" and saying "after careful count, I find that thirty-nine out of forty men are fools." The distinction is less in the actual proportion— which is within one man of being the same—than in the pretended detachment of the author, who claims to have made an actual computation and who presents only the objective statistics of his observation. Swift habitually used this device of computation in sustaining his role of detached observer, as may be seen in *A Project for the Advancement of Religion* where he solemnly attempts to prove that the wickedness of the age is not merely a "form of speech" but is an "undoubted truth":

For, first; to deliver nothing but plain matter of fact without exaggeration or satire; I suppose it will be granted, that *hardly one in a hundred* among our people of quality or gentry, appears to act by any principle of religion. . . . Then, it is observed abroad, that no race of mortals hath so little sense of religion, as the English soldiers; to confirm which, I have been often told by great officers in the army, that . . . they *could not recollect three of their profession,* who seemed to regard or believe one syllable of the Gospel.[25]

The tone of this whole passage is one of unbiased calm. The objectivity is produced partly by the computation itself and partly by the denial of exaggeration, the appeal to what readily "will be granted." As to computation itself, part of its effect lies in Swift's use of negatives: "hardly one in a hundred" and "could not recollect three." Swift suggests that the numbers are the absolute maximum and that, in fact, if his personal opinion were consulted, he would put them much lower. In the fragmentary essay, *Of the Education of*

Ladies, Swift enters into a long and brilliantly effective computation of the numbers of educated younger brothers of the gentry:

Of this kind, I reckon, by *a favourable computation, there may possibly be found, by a strict search* among the nobility and gentry throughout England, about five hundred. Among those of all other callings or trades, who are able to maintain a son at the university, about treble that number. The sons of clergymen bred to learning with any success, must . . . be very inconsiderable . . . I shall therefore count them to be not above fourscore. But, *to avoid fractions,* I shall suppose there may possibly be a round number of two thousand male human creatures in England (including Wales), who have a tolerable share of reading and good sense. I include in this list all persons of superior abilities, or great genius, or true judgment and taste, or of profound literature, who, I am confident, we may reckon to be *at least* five-and-twenty.

Thus, Swift supposes that out of fifteen thousand families "one in thirty" may be tolerably educated; but he then fears the censure that this number is too high, and "upon cooler thoughts, to avoid all cavils," he reduces his computation to one thousand. The enumeration helps to detach Swift from his own emotional contempt for the general ignorance of the English gentleman. The atmosphere of detachment and objectivity which gives to the passage its humourous flavor is created by Swift's care in avoiding any personal assessment of his own. "There may possibly be found, by a strict search," not only suggests that the figures could be arrived at by any objective statistician but that these figures are an absolute maximum. Similarly, the phrase, "at least," which Swift often used to connote the minimum number possible is here used with an ironic twist; the number is so low that to think of it as a possible minimum is to feel again the almost complete absence of learning. Finally, the effect of this cool appraisal of the numerical deficiency of learning is increased by Swift's ironic fear that others will think him too generous, and his "cooler thought" makes him halve the number.[26]

    The dissimulated urbanity and objectivity of this kind of irony brings us to Swift's most complex masks. When writing in the guise of a detached observer, Swift may be said to be dramatizing himself, in the sense that he appears to be more dispassionate than in fact he really is—a disparity he manages to communicate with great subtlety and ingenuity. This distinction between the appearance and the reality of Swift's expression may be carried one step further. Instead of dramatizing himself as an observer meticulously and often ingenuously noting the folly of mankind, he dramatizes this folly in action. That is, Swift relinquishes his role as commentator and his satire becomes an *imitation,* in the classic sense, of what he means to condemn. In short, Swift's most powerful satires exemplify *dramatic irony* and appeal to an intellectualized concept of irony more profound than mere rhetorical dissimulation.

A succinct definition of dramatic irony has been given by Sedgewick, who calls it "the sense of contradiction felt by spectators of a drama who see a character acting in ignorance of his condition." In irony of this kind, it is a situation and the character's part in that situation which create irony. The character enjoys the felicitous "possession of being well deceived" by appearances while remaining blissfully ignorant of the reality of the situation; at the same time, the spectator apprehends both the appearance and the reality and knows how the actor ought to be responding. In Swift's satire, the character's "ignorance" is generally of a particular kind: he is ignorant of the correct evaluation of his own moral nature. Accordingly, Gulliver's reflections on the discrepancy between man's real nature and man's false evaluation of himself may be taken as the foundation of Swift's own perception of ironic contradiction:

I am not in the least provoked at the sight of a lawyer, a pickpocket, a colonel, a fool, a lord, a gamester, a politician, a whoremaster, a physician, an evidence, a suborner, an attorney, a traitor, or the like; this is all according to the due course of things: but when I behold a lump of deformity, and diseases both in body and mind, smitten with *pride,* it immediately breaks all the measures of my patience; neither shall I be ever able to comprehend how such an animal and such a vice could tally together.[27]

advent of self-knowledge; and when that knowledge is a terrifying insight into evil and is accompanied by all the bitterness of a profound disillusionment, irony passes the threshold of tragedy. The tragic overtones of earlier voyages were relieved by the reader's perception of the ridiculous contradiction between Gulliver's complacency and man's actual worth. But with Gulliver's new insight into things as they are, the contradiction evaporates and we are brought face to face with one man's despairing vision of his own limitations. In the process of this final awakening, the mask of Gulliver slips and it is hard not to hear the voice of Swift himself and not to find in the dramatized tragedy of Gulliver the personal tragedy of Swift's own exasperated awareness. Some recent criticism has attempted to show that, contrary to more traditional interpretations, Swift in no way identified himself with Gulliver and that, in the fourth voyage, Gulliver is "at a still greater remove than in earlier books from Swift the narrator." [34] According to this point of view, the Houyhnhnms do not represent Swift's ideal of reason but a false ideal of a cold and abstract rationality which Gulliver foolishly attempts to emulate as the highest good; [35] similarly, Gulliver's identification of man with the Yahoos is said to reflect an opposite extreme of misanthropy which Swift also intended to ridicule. This provocative critical idea is summarized in Professor Mack's observation: "Though Gulliver makes the error of identifying himself and other human beings completely with the Yahoos, we and Swift do not. Nor do we take the ideal life for man, as Gulliver does, to be the tepid rationality of the horses . . . For the truth, as we are meant to realize, is that man is neither irrational physicality like the Yahoos nor passionless rationality like the Houyhnhnms . . . but *animal rationis capax*." [36] This is a valuable interpretation and serves as a useful reminder that Swift does not idealize Gulliver's isolation from mankind regardless of individual excellence. Nevertheless, we must also remain aware that "A Voyage to the Houyhnhnms" is not a cool analysis of a philosophic problem—a dispassionate study of the dualism in man's nature. For it is rather the culmination and climax of an attack on man's *pride* in deceiving himself into the belief that he is rational and virtuous when, in reality, he has not developed his reason, and his virtue is merely appearance. In other words, the focus of the last voyage is not upon a description of the dualism of man's nature, but upon the disparity between what man is and what Gulliver had thought man to be. Accordingly, Swift avails himself of the most extreme symbols with which to startle and shock his reader out of complacency; and as Gulliver's self-revelation increases, as he becomes aware of his own deluded evaluation of mankind, his devastating disgust with the hypocrisy and self-delusion of his own species is uttered in the voice of his creator. To read *Gulliver's Travels* as a treatise on human psychology is to miss entirely the intensity of Swift's anger and despair at the disparity, so lately discovered by Gulliver, between man's opinion of himself and the reality of man's limitations.

Through his irony and especially his ironic masks, Swift achieved a high degree of artistic detachment. But what gives the explosive power to this irony is the reader's recognition that Swift's seeming detachment is the artifice of a creative mind controlling, forming, and channeling the most intense personal involvement. Swift's detachment, that is to say, is not the product of any withdrawal from responsibility. Swift has no connection with any romantic view of the artist as a vagrant whose art expresses his desire to burst conventions and soar unfettered over circumstance. Nor has Swift any kinship with that romantic writer described by Santayana as a "solipsistic poet, proud of his every mood, and sure only of his present sensations." Swift's satire testifies repeatedly to his attempt to subject the intensity of his "present sensations" to the discipline of an artistic form with a social purpose. But his feelings always lurk somewhere just below the surface of his irony, and the effort of will he seems to manifest in controlling these emotions intensifies the reader's own awareness of Swift's real and profound *attachment* to life.

Without the discipline of a highly developed artistic conscience Swift's satire would have expressed his true *saeva indignatio* "in Timon's manner"—as Gulliver finally does; through irony, however, and the technique of dramatizing his deepest convictions in objective equivalents, Swift's satire attains that aesthetic beauty which, in Coleridge's phrase, derives from the "union of the shapely and the vital."

III

The Rhetoric of Satire

Swift's Razor

"True satire," writes G. K. Chesterton, "is always, so to speak, a variation or fantasia upon the air of pure logic." Although the word "always" gives to this definition an undeserved inclusiveness (like most definitions of satire and humour), the remark is a suggestive commentary upon much of Swift's satire. The "air" of logic is that of detachment and objectivity, of conclusions deduced calmly from proper premises and of argument supported by convincing proof. Swift's satirical variations upon this air retain the appearance of detachment and the external forms of argument, but the logic is no longer directed towards truth and the conviction of the reason, but towards contempt and the persuasion of the emotions. The logic of the "palpably absurd," which gravely argues and proves a conclusion of outlandish impossibility, has been a device often used by humourists. We laugh to see the discrepancy between the sage and serious appearance of some logical form producing real effects of manifest absurdity. As a tool for the satirist, however, who aims to combine simple gaiety with critical contempt, the use of the logic of rhetoric has a less casual and more pointed function than for the humourist. Laughter in Swift is generally laughter directed *at* something, and the logic of debate and argument appears in his writing as a peculiarly effective and individual method of ridicule.

It should be remembered that, from the time Swift was in college, as Orrery remarked, "he held logic and metaphysics in the utmost contempt."[1] The reasons for contemning logic as a formal science are not difficult to determine; they had been advanced by many writers since Aristotle's domination of learning had been weakened by analysis and the rise of the "new philosophy." Both logic and metaphysics were considered, in the phrase of Cornelius Scriblerus, as "polemical arts," not devoted to the pursuit of truth but to the confusion of truth in a maze of abstraction and verbal trickery. As such, formal logic was frequently thought to be merely "a civil war of words," as John Webster exclaimed in his *Academiarum Examen* (1654),

a verbal contest, a combat of cunning, craftiness, violence and altercation, wherein all verbal force, by impudence, insolence, opposition, contradiction, derision, diversion, trifling, jeering, humming, hissing, brawling, quarreling, scolding, scandalizing, and the like, are equally allowed of . . . and if they can entangle or catch one another in the Spider Webs of *Sophistical* or fallacious argumentations, then their rejoicing and clamour is as great as if they had obtained some signal Victory.[2]

In addition to the tendency of logicians themselves to be contentious and splenetic, the entire basis of logic, the formal syllogism, was attacked as being sterile and incapable of advancing knowledge. If we except Bacon's, the most famous of many attacks on the scholastic use of the syllogism appears in the late seventeenth century, in Locke's *An Essay Concerning Human Understanding*. The syllogism, said Locke, is incapable of disclosing new truths. It can only marshal into another arrangement what we already know: "A man knows first, and then he is able to prove syllogistically . . . Syllogism, at best, is but the art of fencing with the little knowledge we have, without making any addition to it." One may assume Aristotle's greatness, and esteem his "large views, acuteness, and penetration of thought and strength of judgment," without following the complete trust of his commentators in his theoretical science of logic as being an infallible "method" of arriving at truth.[3] The prevalent substitution of artificial "rules" and "methods of syllogizing" for the natural reason working upon concrete particulars, this giving priority to what Swift (referring to the Parisian manners of the eighteenth-century drawing room) called the "bigotry of forms,"[4] provided Swift with a constant object of ridicule.

It was in the flexible, empirical spirit, then, of Bacon, Locke, and of seventeenth-century thought that Swift, in *A Tale of a Tub,* ridiculed Aristotelian logic, as it appeared in the *"Aristotelis Dialectica,* and especially that wonderful Piece *de Interpretatione,* which has the Faculty of teaching its Readers to find out a Meaning in every Thing but it self."[5] The "meaning" that Lord Peter proceeded to deduce from his father's Will with the aid of these logical instruments was, of course, quite contrary to the plain and obvious meaning of that document. To Swift, logic so employed—and it could only too easily be employed for this end—became merely a tool in the service of the "converting imaginations" of scholastic sophists. The *reality,* that is, of the father's intentions, clearly and simply expressed in the Will, had been twisted by logic into an *appearance* consistent with the brother's own subjective desires. Moreover, the assumption—presented in this passage as sheer hypocrisy—that a system invented by man can supplant the clarity of "nature," of what really *is,* provides a characteristic instance of pedantry—the pride of man's "over-rating any kind of knowledge we pretend to."[6] It is this attitude towards systematic logic, also, that informs Swift's recurrent attacks upon the false logic of "strong reasoners,"[7] the "false reasoning" of atheists,[8] the "impudent sophistry and false logic" of Tindal's deism,[9] the spurious refinements of the "logician" who "might possibly put a case that would serve for an exception,"[10] the illogical logic of wits "who upon a thorough examination of causes and effects, and by the mere force of natural abilities, without the least tincture of learning, . . . made a discovery, that there was no God . . ."[11] In short, the whole "affectation of forming general rules upon false and scanty premises"[12] became one of the most important intellectual aberrations attacked by Swift.

With his propensity to ridicule the pretensions and the performance of logicians and "strong reasoners," it is not surprising that Swift should also condemn rhetoric as a specious art. For rhetoric, as it was first formulated by Aristotle[13] into a systematic study, was considered as "the counterpart of Dialectic" (1354a), and Aristotle defined it simply as the "faculty of observing in any given case the available means of persuasion" (1355b). In so far as a rhetorician is concerned strictly with his own art, with the several "modes of persuasion" (1355a), his moral purpose is irrelevant—that is, a man may be persuasive though his cause is of dubious value. The proper pursuit of rhetoric, as such, concerns itself solely with discerning the "real and the apparent means of persuasion" (1355b). Aristotle proceeds to outline the three modes of persuasion: (1) the kind that depends upon the effect of the speaker's character upon his hearers; (2) the kind that depends upon the emotions aroused in the audience; and, finally, and most important, (3) "the proof, or apparent proof, provided by the words of the speech itself" (1356a). Although Aristotle considers in detail the nature and quality of the first two modes, his principal interest is in the last, because "we are most fully persuaded when we consider a thing to have been demonstrated" (1355a). Indeed, it is evident that the orator's concern with his "character" and with the emotions of his hearers is entirely for the purpose of guiding and stimulating in them an agreement which is his aim to arouse. And it is the enthymeme, the "orator's demonstration" and the rhetorical counterpart of the syllogism, which Aristotle discusses at great length as the "most effective" of the three modes. Because rhetoric is, in itself, not concerned with the pursuit or even communication of truth but solely with persuasion—"the whole business of rhetoric," he reminds us, "being concerned with appearances" (1404a)—, not only true enthymemes, legitimate demonstrations, but also spurious enthymemes are included in the *Rhetoric* as proper subjects for the attention of the orator. Accordingly, we find Aristotle concluding his analysis of the demonstrative aspect of rhetoric with a series of fallacies by which "it is possible to gain an advantage" (1402b) and which illustrate

what is meant by making the worse argument seem the better. Hence people were right in objecting to the training Protagoras undertook to give them. It was a fraud; the probability it handled was not genuine but spurious, and has a place in no art except Rhetoric and Eristic (1402a).

Against the background of this conception of rhetoric—derived from Plato and extending through the Roman orators into the Renaissance and the eighteenth century—as including a strong potentiality for fraud and delusion and being, at best, "concerned with appearances," we can appreciate the force of Swift's attack upon oratory in *A Sermon upon Sleeping in Church:*

Nor, lastly, are preachers justly blamed for neglecting human oratory to move the passions, which is not the business of a Christian orator, whose office it is only to work upon faith and reason. All other eloquence hath been a perfect cheat, to stir up men's passions against truth and justice, for the service of a faction, to put false colours upon things, and by an amusement of agreeable words, make the worse reason appear to be the better.[14]

If formal logic could delude by presenting an *appearance* of reason inconsistent with experience, rhetoric, with its systematic appeal to emotion could be viewed with even more suspicion.

For all this, however, it was Swift himself who recognized that "eloquence, smooth and cutting, is *like a razor whetted with oil.*"[15] And the smoothest and most cutting blade in Swift's varied collection was one which had been tempered in the principles of Aristotelian logic and rhetoric. Indeed, Swift exploited the possibilities of these two disciplines to an unequaled extent; and we must bear in mind that Swift's attack upon Aristotle's *Dialectica* was not so much aimed at Aristotle as at the mechanical and subjective use to which his commentators and followers had put his analysis. It is significant that Swift should have concluded his brief *Sketch of the Character of Aristotle* with the remark: "He writ upon logic, or the art of reasoning; upon morals and natural philosophy; upon oratory, poetry &c. and seems to be a person of the most comprehensive genius that ever lived."[16] Moreover, it was only four years after the first publication of *A Tale of a Tub,* in which Swift had used Aristotle as a method of ridiculing Catholicism, that he derided the easy cant of those who, like Tindal, "exploded" the schoolmen:

They following Aristotle, who is doubtless the greatest master of arguing in the world: But it hath been a fashion of late years to explode Aristotle, and therefore this man hath fallen into it like others, for that reason, without understanding him. Aristotle's poetry, rhetoric, and politics, are admirable, and therefore, it is likely, so are his logics.[17]

As evidence, finally, that Swift's admiration for Aristotle was no accidental enthusiasm of youth, we find Gulliver in Glubbdubdrib calling up from the grave Homer and Aristotle "at the head of all their commentators," only to find that the poet and the philosopher were "perfect strangers to the rest of the company":

And I had a whisper from a ghost, who shall be nameless, that these commentators always kept in the most distant quarters from their principals in the lower world, through a consciousness of shame and guilt, because they had so horribly misrepresented the meaning of those authors to posterity.[18]

In disparaging the logic taught in the schools, it should be remembered that Swift was familiar with both the technical terminology and the methods employed by it. Accordingly, we find occasional references—usually satiric—to such rhetorical devices as "aposiopesis,"[19] or "epiphonemas"[20] and, more frequently, to purely logical forms; for example, in one place Swift speaks of the "sort of sophistry that the logicians call two mediums, which are never allowed in the same syllogism."[21] In another essay, he posits a question "into the first proposition of an hypothetical syllogism"[22] and denies the possibility of an effective refutation, while in *An Argument against Abolishing Christianity* he establishes the immorality of freethinkers by a "sudden deduction of a long sorites . . ."[23]

Such remarks suggest that not only was Swift acquainted with Aristotle's systematic treatises on logic and rhetoric but he had also absorbed much of the training built on these treatises; and this suggestion is amply borne out by an examination of the rhetorical structure of much of his most telling satire. Nor can Swift's use of the persuasive logic of rhetorical demonstration be interpreted as inconsistent with his contempt either for an overrated system of logical proof or for an unprincipled use of rhetorical persuasion. The apparent dilemma can be reconciled by recalling his assertion in *A Letter to a Young Gentleman* that "reasoning will never make a man correct an ill opinion, which by reasoning he never acquired," and that to deal with such profligate and irrational minds is "almost in a literal sense, to fight with beasts." In the same essay, he urges the young devotee not to arouse passions in a sermon, but, in advising him to read "the two great orators of Greece and Rome, Demosthenes and Cicero," Swift justifies their frequent attempts "to inflame or cool the passions of the audience" by what he calls an "absolute necessity."[24] It is evident that Swift, too, found it an absolute necessity to adopt the rhetorical, rather than the purely reasonable, method of communication when he dealt with "beasts." How far Swift carried this justification may be seen when we note that in the heat of controversy, intent upon demolishing the "spurious logic" of an opponent, he was not above debasing the truth of his means in order to accomplish his ends: in the Drapier letters, for example, he fabricates a quotation from Bacon as an authoritative example of his own point when actually, as Craik has noted, Bacon would not have supported his position.[25] But this sort of thing is not frequent in Swift, and what is truly significant in this aspect of his satiric craftsmanship is the keen-witted and incisive methods he adopted to instill shame in the "beasts" of mankind by pursuing the methods of logic and rhetoric. Swift's own rhetoric, as he said of Demosthenes, appeals by the "strength of his arguments, offered to the understanding and reason"—although in Swift the appeal was often to the understanding *in order to* appeal to the passions of contempt and laughter. It is probable that no critic has more closely noted the source while missing the genius of Swift's eloquent "razor" than did the uninspired writer who, in answer to one of the later Drapier papers, stated of Swift: "In *Rhetorick*, his Figures, and his Tropes,/Denotes [*sic*] his empty Brain, quite out of hopes, &c., &c."[26]

Ridicule as "Eloquence": The Neoclassic Background

"Once kick the world," Swift advised a young poet, perhaps with more honest directness than irony, "and the world and you will live together at a reasonable good understanding."[27] Here lies Swift's justification for his own appeal to the persuasive kick of eloquence. Nor was the appeal startling or strange at a time when ridicule was widely viewed, not as a personal expression of spleen and malice, but as a genuine and desirable branch of rhetoric itself. The connection already established in the minds of Swift's readers and critics between rhetoric and the satire of ridicule not only served, therefore, as a moral justification for a prevalent literary practice, but it also helped to guide and develop the formal methods of satiric writing. In noting the gulf between the effective dexterity of Swift's rhetorical satire and the simple raillery of Philip Wylie a partial explanation may be found in the relative absence, since the mid-eighteenth century, of any formal conception of satire as an important branch of writing with distinctive purposes and methods of its own.

On the other hand, satire, almost inevitably, has never enjoyed universal esteem, even during the period from the Restoration through the eighteenth century. From Otway's poem subtitled "A Satyr against Libells" (1680) in which he attacks satire as "this Dragon *Libel*," and "the Poets Scandall, and the Muses Shame,"[28] to Landor's contention that it has "little to do with Philosophy, less with Rhetorick, and nothing with the Furies,"[29] satire received as many buffets as it gave. Such attacks upon satire were common throughout the century. In spite of them, of course, (or, perhaps, because of the mediocrity of their commonplaces), these attacks remained outside the main stream of criticism. Satire continued to flourish in practice and to acquire in criticism a moral justification.

The writer most responsible for elevating satire through ridicule to a position of moral respectability was, probably, Shaftesbury. His contribution to the theory of satire was simply that ridicule is "a test of truth," a justification which must have gratified many a Grub Street pamphleteer. This thesis reverberated through nearly a hundred years of criticism. The controversy to which this phrase gave rise may be attributed more to its suggestive patness than to its lucidity; Shaftesbury failed to define its meaning with any precision. Believing that Beauty, Truth, and Goodness were one, and that man had a natural "moral sentiment" which directed him towards this unified goal, Shaftesbury urged the Aristotelian view that the perception of deformity is the basis of the ridiculous. If man had a natural sense of beauty, he also had a natural sense of the nonbeautiful—the ugly, the ridiculous. Accordingly, to Shaftesbury "nothing is ridiculous except what is deformed: nor is anything proof against raillery, except what is handsome and just."[30] Thus, any proposition may be freely ridiculed; if it is in truth deformed, the ridicule will make its deformity apparent; if the proposition is true, the ridicule will not injure it but will itself seem absurd. "Whatever humour has got the start, if it be unnatural, it cannot hold: and the ridicule, if ill-placed at first, will certainly fall at last where it deserves."[31] How rigorously Shaftesbury intended this test to be applied is hard to say. But he seems to use the words "good humour," "good breeding," "good manners," as if they were interchangeable with "ridicule" and "raillery,"[32] and he heartily disapproved of the "ridicule" in Swift's *A Tale of a Tub*.

Immediate qualifications took some of the sting and most of the novelty out of Shaftesbury's doctrine.[33] Nonetheless, Shaftesbury's remarks were used to explain and to justify the widespread use of ridicule, especially when applied to the forbidden subject of religion. It is not surprising, therefore, that a few deists turned to Shaftesbury's essay for arguments to support their attacks upon prevailing orthodoxy.[34]

The controversy which arose over Shaftesbury's defense of ridicule as a test of truth degenerated into a widespread quibbling with definitions. But his theory, loosely and vaguely formulated though it was, carried with it certain important implications which fructified in later criticism. He introduced into the eighteenth-century critical vocabulary the "new-fangled Expressions," as Brown called them,[35] of the "Faculty" or "Sense" of ridicule. The instinctive and untutored sense which Shaftesbury posited had a complementary sense of the false and the ugly. If one half of Shaftesbury's doctrine flowered into romanticism, the other nourished the stings and nettles of neoclassic satire and contributed to its acceptance as a legitimate branch of formal rhetoric.

Although Fielding lamented the absence of any "touch-stone"[36] which could distinguish the true from the false, less perceptive critics accepted Shaftesbury's "sense" of ridicule as just such an infallible guide. Shaftesbury did not try systematically to distinguish between the faculties of reason and ridicule as determiners of truth. But one of his disciples, Akenside, undertook it for him. "We have," said Akenside, "a natural sense or feeling of the ridiculous." It is concerned not with speculative problems of metaphysics, nor with abstract propositions or mathematical theorems; these are the province of the "faculty of reason." Reason rejects a proposition as false when it finds that one idea, supposed to be equal to another, is actually unequal. The "faculty of ridicule," on the other hand, judges objects which are presented to the mind for praise and esteem. When there exists an incongruity in any such claim to our approval—when what is presented as being estimable is in fact vicious—then the capacity for ridicule "urges the mind to reject it with laughter and contempt." Accordingly, if reason enables us to arrive at abstract truth, ridicule is better able than "speculative inquiry" to "detect the moral falsehood" of vanity and pretense. In this respect, the "sense of ridicule always judges right."[37] A similar conception of the intuitive character of ridicule was assumed by Francis Hutcheson in his attempt to refute Hobbes's and Mandeville's selfish theory of laughter.

"A sense of the ridiculous," Hutcheson says, "was implanted in human nature."[38] Later, Alexander Gerard, more immediately influenced by Hutcheson than by Shaftesbury, included the "sense or taste of ridicule" among the other "internal or reflex senses." To Gerard, these "subsequent senses" depended initially upon sensory data, but they then gave a finer perception of the object than was possible through the senses alone. Thus, the sense of harmony depends first on hearing the sounds, but is independent of the hearing sense. Similarly, the sense of ridicule depends upon objects being presented clearly to the mind, but its function is to perceive instantly, without recourse to reason, an "incongruity" at which it is "gratified."[39] By the time Lord Kames wrote *The Elements of Criticism* a few years later, he felt justified in "taking it for granted that ridicule is not a subject of reasoning, but of sense or taste," and he insisted that only this sense could judge properly what is or is not ridiculous. "It is not only the true test," Kames said, following Gerard's essay, "but indeed the only test."[40] Originating as an attempt to quiet the objections against satire and to further the war against enthusiasm, Shaftesbury's defense of ridicule had crystallized into a critical principle.

By elevating satire to a position where it was independent of reason, it could be properly applied to any subject, however solemn or grave, even religion. This corollary implication, rather than the concept of ridicule as an instinct, provided a focus for many of Shaftesbury's opponents. Thomas Nowell, in *A Dissertation upon that Species of Writing called Humour, when Applied to Religious Subjects* (1760), expressed a characteristic repugnance for the ridicule of religion, although he insisted, perhaps too much, that it could do no real harm except to "weak minds."[41] Satire and abuse of the deistic defense of ridicule were common throughout the century. John Brown's "Essay on Ridicule" (1751), however, presented the most elaborate and consistent, although belated, attempt to refute Shaftesbury's basic thesis—the contention that ridicule could determine what was truly ridiculous without the intervention of reason. His essay, with its

careful division of the mind into facultative categories each
with a specific and limited function, typifies a theory of psychology which had been generally accepted since the Renaissance. Brown attempted to undermine Shaftesbury's argument by reasserting the classical principle that, in a well-regu-
lated mind, the passions must remain subordinate to reason.
At the same time, Brown's essay reflected the attempts to
strengthen and stimulate the proper use of satire by showing
it to be a branch of rhetoric.

Brown conceived of the mind as divided into the faculties
of sense, imagination, memory, reason, and the passions of
pleasure, pain, and pity and contempt (mixed passions). The
senses, he said, following Locke's rejection of innate ideas,
are the only means of providing data to the memory which
stores these materials; the imagination associates and com-
bines them; the reason then compares, distinguishes and
separates the associations made by the imagination, and it
then determines of these associations "which are *real,* and
which *fictitious."* In other words, the reason must judge
whether or not the associations made by the imagination
present a true concept of the world as it exists outside the
mind. Now, there are three kinds of writing, Brown said,
each of which has a special aim although it may include
some of the aims of the other two: poetry, which primarily
aims to please, is addressed to the imagination and its capacity to associate sensory data into beautiful forms; eloquence
aims to persuade by affecting the passions; argument aims to
instruct by presenting logical truth to the reason.[42] It is,
therefore, the purpose and function of reason, alone, to en-
gage in speculation and novel inquiry, to discover unknown
truth, to inspect conclusions by examining their premises,
and finally, to instruct mankind by unimpassioned logic.
Eloquence, on the contrary, and the branches of poetry which
belong partly to eloquence, aim at arousing pain or pleasure
or both; they are an intensely practical and utilitarian method
of conveying either truth or falsehood; they aim to stimulate
men's actions by exciting their passions. Accordingly, eloquence may stir men to act with or against the dictates of

their reason, just as their passions may or may not be rational. So long as eloquence *"impresses* the Truths which Logic teaches," and stirs men to a passionate conviction in truth, just so long is eloquence a proper and decorous and moral weapon.

Didactic poetry which, Brown says, pleasingly teaches moral truth, is aimed at the reason and convinces because of its logic; but tragic, comic, satiric, and elegiac poetry are species of eloquence because they are addressed to the passions. They operate by presenting the appearance of tragedy or comedy or ridicule or grief; the greater the appearance of truth they present, the more we are moved by them. But reason does not allow them to be represented to us as indeed true; fiction remains fiction, and, as Johnson later said of drama, it is only a "calenture of the brains which makes the stage a field." As a "mode of eloquence," therefore, ridicule, either in prose or poetry, can be one of the most powerful instruments by which falsehood is propagated. Ridicule is equally able to raise contempt in a false as in a good cause; its only function is to present an object in a ridiculous and contemptible appearance. But, concludes Brown, the "sense" of ridicule, which is no more than a sensation of contempt, should not be confused with the "judicial faculty" of reason: reason, alone, "can distinguish Appearances from Realities, and fix the true Nature of Things." [43]

According to Brown, then, ridicule cannot be a test of unknown truth, but it is a powerful and legitimate means of arousing men's active contempt towards known falsehoods. This position appeals today to our common sense; more important in the eighteenth century was its appeal to classical principles. Besides providing criticism with several "new fangled" terms to defend ridicule, Shaftesbury stimulated his opponents to a more limited, but nonetheless strong, defense of satire as a branch of rhetoric. The Renaissance had revived interest in classical rhetoric. As a means of teaching, delighting, and persuading, as Thomas Wilson said, rhetoric consisted of "an artificiall declaration of the mynd, in the handling of any cause, called in contention, that may through reason largely be discussed."[44]

Rhetoric was considered as oratory and as the "Arte of speaking finelie."[45] For this reason, perhaps, earlier rhetoricians, such as Richard Sherry, Dudley Fenner, and Henry Peacham, included the tropes of irony and amplification within their general discussion of rhetorical devices; but satire as a major branch of rhetoric remained unmentioned. Rhetoric, as Thomas Wilson said, must be grounded on logic if it is to be sincerely pursued: proper "invention," accordingly, is "the searching out of things true, or things likely, the which may reasonably set forth a matter and make it appear probable."[46] Rhetoric, then, must be concerned solely with "things true" which could be discussed "through reason." By the beginning of the eighteenth century, satire, or ridicule, became recognized as both the most useful and most dangerous mode of rhetoric. At the same time, the experience of the late seventeenth century had indicated—to those not swayed by Shaftesbury—that reason and truth could not safely be assumed to underlie all ridicule. Not only Brown but many others insisted that there was no necessary connection between satire and moral truth. As one critic said of moral fables, the function of satire was "to convey the Precepts of Philosophy to our Minds,"[47] and John Brightland thought it nonsense even to demand of satire that "it waste itself on Disquisitions on the Nature of Virtue and Vice, which is the proper business of *Moral Philosophy*."[48] The aims of the two, as another writer added, are "absolutely different": the aim of satiric wit is to "strike the imagination; of truth and good reason, to convince the judgment."[49] In spite of this separation between logical truth and the technique of satire, the concept of satire as an aspect of rhetoric remained as the main justification for its proper use. The serious appraisal and acceptance of satire by those opposed to Shaftesbury's thesis is summed up in Arthur Murphy's observation that "Ridicule, by which Comedy works is as much a *Mode of Eloquence*, as the several Arts of Persuasion, and the several Figures, which Rhetoric has reduced into a System for the Excitement of the more serious Passions."[50] It was with this conception of ridicule as a "mode of eloquence," a branch of rhetoric, that Brown could praise Swift's *A Tale of a Tub* for the strength and excellence of its techniques and methods of ridicule, while, at the same time, dismissing the satire as untrue and also dangerous in its appeal to faction and intolerance.[51]

The Example

It was Dr. Johnson who charged that Swift's style was suitable only for the "easy and safe conveyance of meaning," that it was the "best mode" for didactic purposes, but that, making no provision for the reader's "inattention" to known truths, it "instructs, but does not persuade." This judgment is an accurate description of some of Swift's writing, particularly his historical pamphlets; but, as the previous pages have emphasized, one of Swift's principal purposes in his more openly satiric writing *was* persuasion and he often realized this intention with signal success. In Swift's use of the rhetorical "example" and "enthymeme," moreover, we find that instruction and persuasion are not always antithetical or even disparate but may be produced simultaneously. Although Aristotle considered the enthymeme (the rhetorical syllogism) to be more important to rhetoric than the example, and although Swift's style is remarkable for the vigor it sustains with relatively small assistance from simile and metaphor, it is important to note briefly the place that the example held in Swift's satiric practice: for, used as an occasional device in much of Swift's satire, it was one cornerstone of the ridicule in *A Tale of a Tub* and of the allegory in *Gulliver's Travels*.

Swift's first essay on contemporary political problems was *A Discourse of the Contests and Dissensions . . . in Athens and Rome* (1701). Although the pamphlet is not satiric, it is a mature and vigorous piece of rhetorical persuasion, and the method it pursues is that of an extended and detailed historical example. In this brief pamphlet, Swift illustrates the "true meaning of the balance of power" by a careful and closely reasoned interpretation of the causes and consequences of faction in ancient political crises. From these specific and highly particularized historical facts, Swift deduces his general principles, and, in his final chapter, he applies these principles to his own contemporary scene. His approach is summarized tersely in his concluding sentence: "I cannot possibly see, in the common course of things, how the same causes can produce different effects and consequences among us, from what they did in Greece and Rome."[52] Through his use of the historical examples this essay takes on what Aristotle had called an "inductive air": it leads from the concrete to the general and assumes a basic and logical continuity in nature, where like causes must have like effects and where the proof of one implies the proof of the other. Swift's purpose in this pamphlet is to arouse rational conviction, and by appealing to the testimony of historical example to prove the political and social dangers inherent in all dissension. The example here becomes a part of the calm logic of his proof—a logic based upon the line of argument that there is a strict historical continuity between like causes and effects. As a satiric device, however, aimed less at rationally proving a position than at inducing agreement with the author's own evaluation of an idea, the historical example is used somewhat differently by Swift. In *A Discourse on the Contests and Dissensions*, the example provides a *premise* of causal relations from which he deduces analogous conclusions; in his satire, however, Swift's conclusion is already evident and the example becomes a method of rephrasing what is already known, of varying the pattern of diminution.

Aristotle noted that the example was best employed after the enthymeme as "subsequent supplementary evidence." After the enthymeme a large number of examples is unnecessary and indeed a "single one is sufficient." Characteristic of Swift's frequent Aristotelian use of the example in satire is his application of the David and Goliath story to himself and Wood in *The Drapier's Letters*. By the third letter, Swift had amply demonstrated his own antipathy to both Wood himself and Wood's patent for coining money. Having displayed "the most flagrant falsehood and impudence of Wood," Swift explains his own entrance into the problem by comparing himself to David attacking Goliath. Not content, however, with a bare reference to the Biblical story, Swift develops his example in a manner quite typical of his logical and concrete imagination—the example becomes an extended and detailed analogy: "I was in the case of David who could not move in the armour of Saul, and therefore I rather chose to attack this uncircumcised Philistine (Wood I mean) with a sling and a stone." Swift then proceeds to expand this direct diminution—he reduces Wood to the status of Goliath—by pursuing other resemblances between Wood and his historical prototype: "For Goliath had a helmet of brass upon his head, and he was armed with a coat of mail, and the weight of the coat was five thousand shekels of brass, and he had greaves of brass upon his legs, and a target of brass between his shoulders. In short he was like Mr. Wood, all over brass; and he defied the armies of the living God." Having established the analogy between Goliath and Wood, having enforced it by the resemblance between Wood's brass coinage and Goliath's brass armor, Swift then concludes his historical example with an exception which, perhaps, is the most compelling part of the entire conceit:

Goliath's condition [sic] of combat were likewise the same with those of Wood. "If he prevail against us, then shall we be his servants": But if it happens that I prevail over him, I renounce the other part of the condition, he *shall never be a servant of mine,* for I do not think him fit to be trusted in an honest man's shop.[53]

Bad as Goliath was, Wood is worse; for Wood is here made to seem not merely contemptible but *beneath* contempt, without the qualifications necessary for even a domestic servant. The example is used by Swift as a means towards reducing an idea to a simple and concrete illustration, towards diverting to present objects men's hatred of certain traditional objects, towards objectifying his own judgments so that his personal animosity seems to be less private and unique and therefore

more universally valid. In short, as a means towards the primary end of arousing men from their customary and sleepy
"inattention," to repeat Johnson's word, the historical example became for Swift an effective and important weapon.

The *Drapier's Letters* were a direct and undisguised attempt to make ridiculous to the Irish people the person and
patent of Wood. In Swift's more indirect satire, he exploited
the "inductive air" of what may be called the quasi-historical
example. A remarkable amount of Swift's creative energy was
expended on a seeming separation of himself and his own
value-judgments from their direct expression. The quasi-
historical example provided Swift with one ready method of
putting into the mouth of another his own sentiments and
logical conclusions. Frequently, he made a particularly cutting thrust by the simple device of introducing his idea with
a "I once met a man who said . . ." or "It has been determined by a gentleman of my acquaintance that . . ." The
success of this pretended appeal to an actual fact or situation
—in this case for the purpose of direct diminution—can be
seen in an amusing and effective paragraph in *A Letter to
the Bishop of St. Asaph*. Swift ironically commiserates with
Bishop Fleetwood's anger at the suppression of one Daniel
Burgess's meetinghouse for nonconformists. He then proceeds
to recount

an accident that had like to have befallen a poor whore of my
acquaintance about that time, who being big with Whig, was so
alarmed at the rising of the mob, that she had like to have mis-
carried upon it; for *the logical jade* presently concluded (and the
inference was natural enough) that *if they began with pulling
down meeting-houses, it might end in demolishing those houses
of pleasure, where she constantly paid her devotion;* and, indeed,
there seems a close connection between extempore prayer and
extempore love.[54]

Writing in the character of a notorious Whig, Lord Wharton,
Swift was able not only to suggest with graphic concreteness
that the Whigs consorted with whores—his friend was "big
with Whig"—but also to put in the mouth of the Whiggish
and "logical jade" a dramatically conceived analogy between

whoring and nonconformist praying. By embodying this depreciatory analogy in a pretended factual event, Swift converts what might have been a mere acidulous comparison into a "gay contempt" more effective and sustained through the indirectness of the ridicule.

As Aristotle recognized, appropriate historical examples are not easily found, and a rhetorician may extend the range of his analogies while preserving their essential inductive purpose by the use of fables. Swift occasionally adapted the vast store of classical mythology to some present argument, as when he derived a correspondence between Ovid's fable of Pallas and Arachne and England's treatment of Ireland:

> I confess, that from a boy, I always pitied poor Arachne, and *could never heartily love* the goddess on account of so cruel and unjust a sentence; which however is fully executed upon us by England, with further additions of rigour and severity. For the greatest part of our bowels and vitals are extracted, without allowing us the liberty of spinning and weaving them.[55]

The direct application of the fable to England is characteristic of Swift's intention not to use analogy as a means of obscuring his point but rather, by throwing his thoughts into a new combination, to arouse and intensify the emotional reactions of his readers. His "intention," as he said of his *Examiner* papers, and we may extend his remark to all his writing, was that "my hints may be understood, and my quotations and allegories applied."[56] The application is made here with that unequivocal directness which, as we have seen, is viewed in the critical theory of the period as essentially unsatiric, although even in this traditional rhetorical example Swift allows a faint hint of ironic understatement to creep in when he states that he "could never heartily love the goddess." But the fable here is used primarily to indicate a direct parallel between its own internal logic and that of his central theme, England's relation with Ireland. Another form of the "fabulous example," as used occasionally by Swift, is what he himself called the "metaphorical genealogy."[57] This very common and, in the eighteenth century, overworked

staple of literary variety served a common purpose with
other forms of the rhetorical example: it provided a concrete activity for abstractions by materializing ideas into a
story framework. A typical instance of the personified example of this sort appears in the *Examiner* papers in
which he first traces a "poetical genealogy and description of
merit,"[58] and then elaborates and applies a "fable of faction."
More satirical and more effective as a depreciatory example
was the beast fable, which Swift used sparingly but with
devastating effect. Much of the force of the Drapier's "Sea-
sonable Advice to the Grand Jury" may be attributed to the
concluding fable, "ascribed to Demosthenes," which con-
denses and compresses three pages of argument into an example forceful and concrete enough to summarize the entire
preceding argument.[59] Again in keeping with the Aristotelian
rhetorical theory, many of these fables are used as what Aristotle called "supplementary evidence"; that is, they conclude
a series of logical reasonings and have the "effect of witnesses
giving evidence" (1394a). In an anonymous pamphlet, *To
the Gentlemen Freeholders, and Freemen of the City, A Few
Words Concerning the Alderman and Squire,* written somewhat later than the *Drapier's Letters,* we find a characteristic
instance of this piling up of concluding examples. In this
excellent piece of political oratory in which Herbert Davis
detects "the method of the Drapier though the hand is rather
that of Sheridan," the claims for election to Parliament of
one Alderman Stoyte and one Squire Howard are advanced
and compared. The principal argument of the paper is against
the Squire's supposed purchase of votes by dispensing food
and liquor to his constituents, leading his followers, as "Cap-
tain Gulliver drew the ships," with pack threads "fastened
to [their] guts." Having indulged in rather broad ridicule of
the Squire, the writer concludes his attack with "a piece of
history, and after that a fable." The two examples parallel and
complement each other. One example provides an historical
precedent and therefore a logical probability for believing
Squire Howard will prove ungrateful to his bought voters;

while the beast fable of the fox and the lion develops the same idea but with an additional element of bestial diminution.[60]

Swift's skillful use of traditional rhetorical figures is nowhere more evident than in the rigor and precision with which he used the kind of invented example that Aristotle called the "illustrative parallel." This form of argument, which Socrates developed into a fine art, persuades the reader by analogy. In Swift, however, the direction of the argument is usually refutative and, indeed, has often the air of a *reductio ad absurdum*. Our immediate concern is how this figure serves the clear purpose either of explicitly refuting an opponent's *argument* or else of directly reducing to absurdity certain *implications* of his point of view. When Swift excoriated Bishop Burnet's hysterical fear of Popery, he invited "his Lordship to examine a little into the nature of truth" and concludes his own examination with his "desire to put a parallel case":

Suppose his Lordship should take it into his fancy to write and publish a letter to any gentleman of no infamous character for his religion or morals; and there advise him with great earnestness, not to rob or fire churches, ravish his daughter, or murder his father; show him the sin and the danger of these enormities, that if he flattered himself, he could escape in disguise, or bribe his jury, he was grievously mistaken: That he must in all probability forfeit his goods and chattels, die an ignominious death, and be cursed by posterity; Would not such a gentleman justly think himself highly injured, though his Lordship did not affirm that the said gentleman had his pick locks or combustibles ready, that he had attempted his daughter, and drawn his sword against his father in order to stab him? Whereas, in the other case, this writer affirms over and over, that all attempts for introducing Popery and slavery are already made, the whole business concerted, and that little less than a miracle can prevent our ruin.[61]

This illustrative "parallel case" between the abused, innocent gentleman and the Catholic Church is drawn with a bold and sweeping stroke. Whether or not the passage can properly be called satiric is, perhaps, too refined a question to deserve any lengthy discussion. But it is obviously successful rhetoric, and, in its appeal to the logical and rational perception of correspondences, succeeds in diminishing Burnet's fears to absurdity. Although the attack is direct and personal, it avoids the extremities of emotional invective in proportion to its logical persuasiveness. Frequently, Swift heightened the impact and extended the sense of logical detachment in his analogies by multiplying them into several short and pithy illustrations; the result suggests a disciplined restraint in choosing only the most obvious among an infinite number of possibilities. In *A Letter Concerning the Sacramental Test,* Swift wonders at the rhetorical "figure" contained in "that argument used for repealing the Test, that it will unite all Protestants against the common enemy":

Suppose in order to increase the friendship between you and me, a law should pass that I must have half your estate; do you think that would much advance the union between us? Or, suppose I share my fortune equally between my own children, and a stranger whom I take into my protection; will that be a method to unite them? 'Tis an odd way of uniting parties, to deprive a majority of part of their ancient right, by conferring it on a faction who had never any right at all, and therefore cannot be said to suffer any loss or injury if it be refused them.[62]

Again, we find the same kind of superimposed parallels in the *Drapier's Letters* where Swift carefully blended the satiric diminution of ridicule with logical, argumentative rhetoric. In Letter II, for instance, the Drapier attacks the claim, first made in England and then republished in Harding's Newspaper, that Wood's coin had been faithfully assayed and found, "when heated red hot, [to] spread thin under the hammer without cracking," and to be of the "same goodness and value with the copper . . . coined in the King's Mint for England."[63] Swift derides this "proof" of the excellence of Wood's brass in a series of pertinent examples:

Wood takes care to coin a dozen or two halfpence of good metal, sends them to the Tower and they are approved, and these must answer all that he hath already coined or shall coin for the future. It is true indeed, that a gentleman often sends to my shop for a pattern of stuff, I cut it fairly off, and if he likes it, he comes or sends and compares the pattern with the whole piece, and probably we come to a bargain. But if I were to buy an hundred sheep, and the grazier should bring me one single wether fat and well fleeced by way of pattern, and expect the same price round for the whole hundred, without suffering me to see them before he was paid, or giving me good security to restore my money for those that were lean or shorn or scabby, I would be none of his customer. I have heard of a man who had a mind to sell his house, and therefore carried a piece of brick in his pocket, which he shewed as a pattern to encourage purchasers: And this is directly the case in point with Mr. Wood's assay.[64]

There is no effort here to arouse the comic spirit; Swift concentrates entirely upon refuting an argument by revealing its absurdity in the most circumstantial and, to the common people of Ireland, most understandable terms.

The rhetorical efficacy of using such parallel cases for argument and refutation is matched by Swift's use of the illustrative parallel as a means of deriding the logical *implications* of an opponent's position. Swift rarely stopped short after striking down explicit arguments. In fact, he usually devoted even greater care to the development of what actually was, or, at least, could be made to seem, the implicit and necessary logical ramifications of a point of view. We have already noted Swift's use of the beast fable; the traditional symbolic values attached to many lower animals provided him with a ready source for invented parallels. In *A Letter Concerning the Sacramental Test,* for example, Swift assumes that the Protestants who advocate repeal of the Test as a means toward uniting against the "common enemy," Popery, will, when they themselves are in power, deny toleration to the presently existing church. After citing the "perpetual folly" throughout history of "those states who call in foreigners to assist them against the common enemy," until the "allies become at length the masters," Swift concludes his argument with this characteristic example:

'Tis agreed among naturalists that a lion is a larger, a stronger, and more dangerous enemy than a cat; yet if a man were to have his choice, either a lion at his foot, bound fast with three or four chains, his teeth drawn out, and his claws pared to the quick, or an angry cat in full liberty at his throat; he would take no long time to determine.[65]

In Swift's varied repertory of methods of personal invective, the illustrative parallel was indispensable in providing a persuasively detached and logical support for moral judgments. The direct and scathing attack, in *Remarks Upon a Book Intituled "The Rights of the Christian Church, &c.,"* on the deist, Matthew Tindal, is particularly replete with instances in which Swift draws upon a variety of successive illustrations. Thus, in the opening paragraphs, he justifies his intention to describe the character of Tindal. Books "written with ill intentions, to advance dangerous opinions, or destroy foundations" may be confuted by the author's own ill character:

For instance, if any man should write a book against the lawfulness of punishing felony with death; and, upon inquiry, the author should be found in Newgate under condemnation for robbing a house; his arguments would not very unjustly lose much of their force, from the circumstances he lay under. So, when Milton writ his book of divorces, it was presently rejected as an occasional treatise; because every body knew, he had a shrew for his wife. Neither can there be any reason imagined, why he might not, after he was blind, have writ another upon the danger and inconvenience of eyes. But *it is a piece of logic which will hardly pass on the world;* that because one man hath a sore nose, therefore all the town should put plasters upon theirs.[66]

Swift's indignation at the irrationality of man was as deep, honest, and intense as his belief in the innate capacity of reason to extract "sweetness and light" from man's intellectual and moral experience. If one is completely convinced of the potentiality of reason to grasp truth, a confidence in man's immediate reaction against *false* reason would doubtless seem to be a corollary principle. Swift's own practice supports this possibility. Indeed, his practice suggests that he had far more confidence in man's capacity to recognize false logic than, like the Houyhnhnms, to react at once to the dictates of rational insight. At any rate, Swift's literary life may be viewed as a continuing effort to display to mankind one "piece of logic" after another which he hoped, though not without frequent despair, would "hardly pass on the world." The significance of his frequent use of the rhetorical example, then, lies partly in the reflection it gives of Swift's tacit assumption that man is at least partially capable of reasoning: through reason man can detect unreason. In such major works of satire as *A Tale of a Tub* and *Gulliver's Travels,* however, the example has an added significance. For in the former, the rhetorical example is diverted by elaborate indirection to the uses of ridicule; in *Gulliver,* it is imbedded in the very matrix of a half comic and wholly intellectual allegory.

The Enthymeme

Ironic Refutation.   In the satire familiarly known as *An Argument Against Abolishing Christianity*—the full title, though cumbersome, is instinct with the spirit of the whole piece: *An Argument to Prove that the Abolishing of Christianity in England May, as Things now Stand, be Attended with Some Inconveniences, and Perhaps not Produce Those Many Good Effects Proposed Thereby*—Swift has written what is without doubt one of the most logically complex essays in English literature. Both titles are in a sense misleading. For Swift does not offer simply "an argument" to support his thesis. Instead, the essay is a long series of interwoven arguments operating with persistent irony on several levels of satiric intention. But it is unfortunate that the original title should now be often forgotten;[67] for in its opening phrase, *An Argument to Prove,* Swift suggests an emphasis upon the appearance of logical proof which is the informing principle behind his irony.

A characteristic example of Swift's manipulation of "demonstrative" proof occurs near the close. Having furnished ample "proofs" (from the point of view of his *persona,* an unchristian defender of Christianity) of the inconveniences of abolishing Christianity, Swift concludes his essay with a disclosure, developed with spare economy, of what he regards as the true premises beneath rationalistic objections to the Christian religion. His point is that the freethinkers of his time do not argue merely against cruxes in Christian dogma, but that their intention is to subvert all religion in order to free them from the restraints of morality:

For, of what use is freedom of thought, if it will not produce freedom of action, which is the sole end, how remote soever *in appearance,* of all objectors against Christianity? And *therefore,* the freethinkers consider it as a sort of edifice, wherein all the parts have such a mutual dependence on each other, that if you happen to pull out one single nail, the whole fabric must fall to the ground. This was happily expressed by him who had heard of a text brought for proof of the Trinity, which in an ancient manuscript was differently read; he thereupon immediately took the hint, and *by a sudden deduction of a long sorites, most logically concluded;* "Why, if it be as you say, I may safely whore and drink on, and defy the parson." *From which, and many the like instances easy to be produced,* I think nothing can be more manifest, than that the quarrel is not against any particular points of hard digestion in the Christian system, but against religion in general; which, by laying restraints on human nature, is supposed the great enemy to the freedom of thought and action.[68]

This one of "many the like instances easy to be produced" from which he inductively arrives at his conclusion is, of course, an *example;* by means of this instance he seems to demonstrate the prevalence of the logic he is attacking. But the example here has also the secondary purpose of dramatizing what Swift thought to be the true logic of freethinkers, and the form of the "sudden deduction," the logical proof by which the freethinkers arrive at their immoral conclusion, is a sorites expressed as an enthymeme.

Aristotle's soundness as a rhetorical theorist lies in his recognition of the close proximity between logic and rhetoric. Indeed, he takes it for granted that, of the various possible means of persuasion, the "most effective" is ultimately that of demonstration, whether apparent or genuine (1355a). Although, as we have noted, he is aware of the importance of "putting the audience into a certain frame of mind" and of the "personal character of the speaker" and, accordingly, concludes that rhetoric is a branch of ethical study, he stresses them only as subordinate to the orator's actual demonstration. In the demonstration, whoever, as Aristotle said, "effects persuasion through proof, does in fact use either enthymemes or examples there is no other way" (1356b). If the example is a demonstration by a "rhetorical induction," the enthymeme, as defined by Aristotle, is a "rhetorical syllogism": "When we base the proof of a proposition on a number of similar cases, this is induction in dialectic, example in rhetoric; when it is shown that, certain propositions being true, a further and quite distinct proposition must also be true in consequence, whether invariably or usually, this is called syllogism in dialectic, Enthymeme in rhetoric" (1356b). What distinguishes the enthymeme from a syllogism is that it deals with what is contingent and that its syllogistic form is truncated by the omission of one or more premises. It must, as Aristotle added, "consist of few propositions, fewer often than those which make up the normal syllogism. For if any of these propositions is a familiar fact, there is no need even to mention it; the hearer adds it himself" (1357a). Perhaps the most succinct, as well as frivolous, definition of the enthymeme appears in the *Memoirs of Martinus Scriblerus*. In Chapter VII, an hilarious satire upon Aristotelian rhetoric, logic and metaphysics, the extraordinary *Treatise of Syllogisms* by the scholarly punster, Conradus Crambe, is outlined:

He suppos'd that a Philosopher's brain was like a great Forest, where Ideas rang'd like animals of several kinds; that those Ideas copulated and engender'd Conclusions; that when those of different Species copulate, they bring forth monsters or absurdities; that the *Major* is the male, the *Minor* the female, which copulated by the Middle Term, and engender the Conclusion. Hence they are call'd *praemissa*, or Predecessors of the Conclusion; and it is properly said by the Logicians *quod pariunt scientiam, opinionem:* they beget *science*, opinion, &c.

From these principles Crambe deduces "all the rules of Syllogisms"; "But then what is an Enthymem?" Cornelius Scriblerus asks: "Why, an Enthymem (reply'd Crambe) is when the Major is indeed married to the Minor, but the marriage *kept secret.*"[69]

In the passage cited above from *An Argument Against Abolishing Christianity* the marriage is not only "secret" but polygamous. The argument, expanded into an open sorites, might read like this:

A variant textual reading refutes the doctrine in the text;

The refutation of any single doctrine of Christianity refutes the truth of all Christianity;

The refutation of all Christianity refutes the moral precepts contained within Christianity;

The refutation of Christian morality refutes the Parson whose teachings are Christian;

Ergo, A variant textual reading justifies him who says, "I may safely whore and drink on and defy the parson."

By compressing this elaborate sorites into the compact form of an enthymeme, Swift is able to give the passage as a whole a density of meaning and connotation which, as extended syllogistic logic, it would lose. We may recall Swift's general intention to replace the raging of the moralist, which "but stupefies your brain," with the "raillery" which "sets your thoughts upon their mettle." For on close analysis of the passage we see that Swift has exploited three distinct levels of rhetorical "proof" which, as we have seen, in order to be completed demand an agile and active response from the reader himself. On the simplest level, Swift demonstrates, by a direct induction of rhetoric (no logician would accept this appearance of proof) the line of reasoning accepted by freethinkers, and tries to induce the reader to accept this as a fact. On the second level, we have the logic of the enthymeme itself expressed as a conditional argument: *if* the premise is true (*i.e.* a variant textual reading refutes the truth of the doctrine of the Trinity), then the conclusion is true ("I may safely whore and drink on and defy the parson"). Now, Swift's purpose in this paragraph is not to *demonstrate* directly that the rational criticism of one Christian doctrine cannot destroy the truth of Christianity as a whole, but rather to *refute* the opposite contention—the contention that it can. Accordingly, the enthymeme is refutative and its means is a *reductio ad absurdum* of the premise he wishes to deny. But it is the reader and not Swift who completes the argument: Swift has the freethinker assert that the conclusion is true if the premise is true, but he leaves to the reader the completing operation of noting that the conclusion is obviously false, and that therefore the premise leading to the conclusion must be false also. Having attempted to establish what he believed to be the inevitable consequence of the freethinker's premise, Swift concludes his own *direct* argument by concluding that, if the premise results in a vicious absurdity, then the freethinkers have argued backwards from the vicious conclusion to form the premise. That is, if the premise results in vice and is absurd, it is also the consequence of vice. In other words, it is both the product as well as the cause of evil. The two directions of the argument—the one from premise to vicious conclusion, the other from conclusion back to premise—are neatly juxtaposed in the paragraph as two parallel enthymemes. The first includes the opening sentences, in which Swift asserts that the freethinkers want freedom of thought in order to secure freedom of action; and *"therefore,"* they conclude, all the parts of Christianity have such a "mutual dependence on each other" that the destruction of one destroys all. The second enthymeme, which we have just discussed, is simply a reversal of the same logic. The joint result, of course, is that Swift is not only ridiculing freethinking itself but also suggesting a viciousness of motive behind that inquiry. Satire conducted on this complex level of seeming logical precision is rare. As in his use of so many other methods of satire, Swift is unique in sustaining it at a high level throughout the bulk of his satiric writing.

Swift frequently tended, then, to adopt indirect refutation as the most persuasive form of demonstrating the logical absurdity of his opponents. Instead of refuting directly the arguments of an antagonist, Swift's enthymemes were constructed in such a way as to *display* them, if possible, as ridiculous, and in the process of doing so, of course, to imply the affirmation of his own opposed premises. In the instance just examined, Swift attributed the enthymeme to an adversary. It is only a short step from this method of introducing his arguments to that of adopting those arguments as his own— in short, to using *irony* as the vehicle for his refutative enthymeme. The close connection that can exist between indirect refutation and irony has been clearly recognized by an acute logician, Richard Whately, Archbishop of Dublin, who was familiar with Swift's work:

> . . . in the Indirect method the absurdity or falsity of a Proposition (opposed to our own) is proved; and hence is suggested the idea of an *adversary* maintaining that Proposition, and of the Refutation of that adversary being necessarily accomplished in this way . . . In Controversy, the Indirect is often adopted by choice, as it affords an opportunity for holding up an opponent to scorn and ridicule, by *deducing some very absurd conclusion from the principles he maintains, or according to the mode of arguing* he employs.[70]

A substantial part of the irony that Swift said he was "born to introduce" may be best understood by recognizing its basis in this logic of indirect refutation.

Swift's most rigorous and systematic attempt to ridicule an opponent by the ironical use of the refutative enthymeme is the brilliant pamphlet, *Mr. C——ns's Discourse of Freethinking Put into plain English, by way of Abstract, for the Use of the Poor,* written by "a Friend of the Author." Anthony Collins was, perhaps, the best known and certainly among the most vilified of the English deistic writers of the early eighteenth century. His several attacks upon Christian orthodoxy provoked violent opposition from the leading divines of his day. But as Swift perceived, with his characteristic insight into the springs of persuasion, the very violence with which a doctrine is attacked may tend to impart a measure of dignity and respectability to the belief. If an idea is so dangerous that it calls up the deepest emotional and logical responses of eminent men, it is not unlikely (some people will therefore infer) that the idea is worthy of consideration in its own right. Swift, accordingly, took the opposite position, and instead of finding direct arguments to refute Collins's heterodoxy, he restated the arguments in such a way that they would seem to collapse beneath their own absurdity. In an introductory note, Swift ironically justifies his labors in preparing this abstract for the use of the poor and unlearned by suggesting that the logic and learning of Collins might seem too difficult for common understandings:

I considered, that several well-willers to infidelity, might be dis-
couraged *by a show of logic,* and a multiplicity of quotations,
scattered throughout his book, which to understandings of that
size, might carry an *appearance* of something like book-learning,
and consequently fright them from reading for their improvement.[71]

The point of the irony, then, was to represent or dramatize
the reality of nonsense beneath the show and appearance of
valid argument in Collins's original *Discourse.* The lines of
argument he pursues in the series of enthymemes which make
up the essay are diverse, but two of them may be singled out
as most characteristic. On the one hand are the arguments
which ironically pursue Collins's premises to an absurdity,
as in the following delightful paragraph:

How can a man think at all, if he does not think freely? A man
who does not eat and drink freely, does not eat and drink at all.
Why may not I be denied the liberty of free-seeing, as well as freethinking? Yet nobody pretends that the first is unlawful, for a
cat may look on a king; though you be near-sighted, or have weak
or sore eyes, or are blind, you may be a free-seer; you ought to see
for yourself, and not trust to a guide to choose the colour of your
stockings, or save you from falling into a ditch.[72]

The argument is essentially the same as that found in *An
Argument Against Abolishing Christianity;* a position is
defended ironically by a logic so patently false that we are
almost laughed into agreement with Swift. More frequent
than this form of a *reductio ad absurdum,* however, is the
"demonstration" of Collins's absurdity through premises
attributed (ironically) to him which cannot lead to Collins's
conclusion. This line of argument is quite different from that
quoted just above; there the premise was shown to lead to an
absurd conclusion and the enthymeme followed the pattern
of a *reductio ad absurdum.* Most of the arguments in the
Abstract from Collins, however, follow the line of demonstrating the absurdity of the conclusion by the absurdity of
the premises which lead toward that conclusion. Another
paragraph from the *Abstract* may make this direction of
Swift's reasoning clearer:

But besides, the conduct of our priests in many other points, makes freethinking unavoidable; for some of them own, that the doctrines of the Church are contradictory to one another, as well as to reason; which I thus prove: Dr. Sacheverell says in his speech at his trial, That by abandoning passive obedience we must render ourselves the most inconsistent Church in the world: Now 'tis plain, that one inconsistency could not make the most inconsistent Church in the world; *ergo,* there must have been a great many inconsistencies and contradictory doctrines in the Church before. Dr. South describes the incarnation of Christ, as an astonishing mystery, impossible to be conceived by man's reason; *ergo,* it is contradictory to itself, and to reason, and ought to be exploded by all freethinkers.[73]

Instead of arguing forward from Collins's premise to an absurd conclusion, Swift here argues backwards from Collins's conclusion and shows the premises to be absurd.

It is evident that these arguments are refutative and, in their ridicule of Collins's thinking, destructive. What many readers and some critics of Swift tend to overlook, however, is that the logic of a true refutation is similar in character to an affirmative proof. For in traditional logic the refutation of a proposition is an affirmation of the opposite proposition. A half century later, George Campbell, in his *Philosophy of Rhetoric* (1776), noted that the ironic exposure of false logic is analogous to the variety of demonstration "termed by the mathematicians apagogical, as reducing the adversary to what is contradictory or impracticable."[74] In satire, as in mathematics, such a demonstration does more than discomfort the opponent: it serves as an indirect means to assert the contrary idea. If there is any question in the reader's mind about Swift's own affirmative beliefs (it seems hardly credible that such doubt could exist for long), the answer in this essay lies in an inverted method of refutation which reinforces his own affirmative position. After having demonstrated, through an ironic *defense* of deistic principles, the "false logic" by which these principles are *affirmed,* he then proceeds to demonstrate, by an ironic *attack* on orthodox principles, the "false logic" by which his own beliefs are *refuted*. His method is simply to introduce each one of a series of propositions (to

which, of course, he subscribes) by the phrase "it is objected
that . . .," and then to refute these propositions with mere
cavils. These "objections" summarize Swift's own attitudes
towards man and man's need for the order and discipline
of established orthodoxy:

> But to this it may be objected, that the bulk of mankind is as
> well qualified for flying as thinking, and if every man thought
> it his duty to think freely, and trouble his neighbour with
> his thoughts . . . it would make wild work in the world. I
> answer . . .
> It is again objected, that freethinking will produce endless divi-
> sions in opinion, and by consequence disorder society. To
> which I answer . . .

And so on until his final objection, to refute which he devotes
the remainder of the essay:

> It is objected, that freethinkers themselves are the most infamous,
> wicked, and senseless of all mankind . . .[75]

As a body of religious affirmations, these statements are
hardly remarkable for their profundity or insight. Moreover, they suggest that Swift's religious attitude was as
rational, perhaps, as that of the deists he attacked—the chief
difference lying more in the limitations he imposed upon
rational inquiry than in the quality of the experience itself.
As a platform, however, from which to launch the ridicule
of indirect refutation, these affirmations amply serve their
purpose. George Campbell later remarked that the "covert
and oblique" assault of ridicule is based on the axiom: "what
we profess to contemn, we scorn to confute." The ridicule of
an adversary's refutation of one's own beliefs may be seen
as the product of a complementary axiom: what we profess
to believe, we scorn to maintain. If his opponent's principles
are so absurd they deserve no serious and vehement rebuttal,
Swift implies that his own are so self-evident they require no
serious defense. Accordingly, his refutations are a tissue of
incongruities and *non sequiturs*:

> It is objected, that priests ought to be relied on by the people, as
> lawyers and physicians, because it is their faculty. I answer, 'Tis

true, a man who is no lawyer is not suffered to plead for himself; but every man may be his own quack if he pleases, and he only ventures his life; but in the other case the priest tells him he must be damned: *Therefore do not trust the priest*, but think freely for yourself, and if you happen to think there is no hell, there certainly is none, and consequently you cannot be damned; I answer further, that wherever there is no lawyer, physician, or priest, the country is paradise. Besides all priests (except the orthodox, and those are not ours, nor any that I know,) are hired by the public to lead men into mischief; but lawyers and physicians are not, you hire them yourself.[76]

To call this ridicule of the deists "destructive" is to use the word in a technical sense; the obvious purpose of the passage is to destroy only in order to construct. Swift's own affirmation of belief cannot possibly be misconstrued.

The persuasiveness of Swift's ridicule in the many essays which pursue this logic of fallacy is founded upon what Bishop Whately has called "mimic sophistry." The comedy in Swift's logical ridicule is the comedy of imitating the "appearance" of the proud logician confounding himself in the "reality" of absurdity. And yet Swift's method itself is less logical than rhetorical; for in the very process of raising our laughter at the expense of Collins's fallacies Swift is playing upon our credulity by an implicit enthymeme which is as spurious as any in Collins's book. Behind Swift's ironic refutation lies the conditional syllogism: if the premises are true, the conclusion is true; but the premises are false; therefore, the conclusion is false. This reasoning provides the larger framework within which the satire operates, and, as satirical rhetoric, its success is immediate. But, as logic, its demonstration is itself only a seeming and not a reality. We may, for example, agree that Swift was a man. But if we try to prove this conclusion by the argument:

> All men have two eyes;
> Swift had two eyes;
> *Ergo,* Swift was a man,

we have obviously involved ourselves in an absurdity. Our premises lead to the conclusion not only that Swift may have been a man, but that Swift may equally well have been a bat, bear, toad or, for that matter, a potato or a Swiss cheese. And yet the fact that the premises do not lead to the desired conclusion does not in any way invalidate the conclusion; it simply invalidates the method of getting to that conclusion. Similarly, when Swift twists Collins's premises into absurdity, he does not thereby demonstrate logically any necessary refutation of the conclusion, but merely the absurdity of those particular premises leading to that particular conclusion. Accordingly, it is through the "mimic sophistry" of the argument as a whole that the reader leaps to contemn the specific conclusion. We first recognize the absurdity of the stated argument, and then transfer this perception to the stated conclusion. When Swift ridicules a specific proposition in this manner, the success of his spurious enthymeme depends largely on maintaining a delicate balance of distance between the actual premises of an opponent and those which Swift attributes to him. Frequently, his opponent's premises are not self-evidently false and in order to secure the conviction of the reader it is necessary to distort the premises into absurdity. When Swift does not distort them enough, the contempt he seeks may be quite entirely lacking. One such example from the Collins *Abstract* might be the following:

The priests tell me, I am to believe the Bible, but freethinking tells me otherwise in many particulars: The Bible says, the Jews were a nation favoured by God; but I who am a freethinker say, that cannot be, because the Jews lived in a corner of the earth, and freethinking makes it clear, that those who live in corners cannot be favourites of God. The New Testament all along asserts the truth of Christianity, but freethinking denies it; because Christianity was communicated but to a few; and whatever is communicated but to a few, cannot be true; for that is like whispering, and the proverb says, that there is no whispering without lying.[77]

The concluding proverb and its place in the argument gives to the logic its only self-evident sophistry, and the passage as a whole may fail to evoke contempt. With this possible failure of Swift's method, we may compare the following passage from one of the *Examiner* papers in which Swift worries the freethinkers with great satiric success:

First, St. Paul tells us, "there must be heresies in the Church, that the truth may be manifest"; and therefore, by due course of reasoning, the more heresies there are, the more manifest will the truth be made. This being maturely considered by these lovers of the Church, they endeavored to propagate as many heresies as they could, that the light of truth might shine the clearer. Secondly, to shew their zeal for the Church's defence, they took the care of it entirely out of the hands of God Almighty (because that was a foreign jurisdiction) and made it their own creature, depending altogether upon them; and issued out their orders to Tindal, and others, to give public notice of it.[78]

The illogic of this paragraph mimics a sophistry which Swift makes the reader feel might have been a deistic argument. In the process, however, Swift has distorted the deistic premises enough out of line so that the fallacies of thinking which he felt to be implicit in their logic are brought sharply into focus. The fallacy of the first argument lies, of course, in the implied and unexpressed premises of two enthymemes:

> Heresies are necessary in order to manifest truth:
> (*The quantity of truth manifested in the world depends
> on the quantity of heresy*);
> *Ergo*, the more heresies, the more is truth manifest;

> and

> (*The deists want to manifest truth*);
> (*Truth is manifested by propagating heresies*);
> *Ergo*, the deists propagate heresies in order to manifest
> truth.

If we substitute the word "falsehood" for heresy (and it is in this sense of an absolute and fixed dichotomy between "truth" and "falsehood" that Swift is thinking here), we see even more clearly what Swift is about: the deists are made to defend their open and conscious propagation of *falsehood* on the absurd grounds that they thereby manifest the *truth*. The implication is clear that the freethinkers propagate what they know to be false and rationalize their moral obliquity with such logic as this. In the second argument, the fallacy develops from a play on words:

> The Church should be separated from every foreign
>   jurisdiction;
> God is a "foreign jurisdiction";
> *Ergo,* the Church should be separated from God.

The Protestant overtones of the first premise (the Church should be separated from Rome) are extended into absurdity in the second and thence twisted into an atheistic conclusion. Both arguments are self-evidently false and appear so at the first glance. We are amused at the serious, freethinking "author" who uses them and tend to scorn those disbelievers in truth and God. At the same time, of course, the reader must perceive that Swift is not using logic to *refute* even indirectly any specific conclusion of the deists, but is using illogic rhetorically to persuade us by mimicry that the deistic *method* of reasoning is as ridiculous as its conclusions are vicious. Swift's intention of ridiculing the logic as well as the moral purpose of freethinkers is realized only as long as the reader's mind can focus with any delight on the fallacies themselves. Because the intention is serious and, at the same time, depends upon the fallacy's being self-evident, the reader must be struck with an immediate conviction of absurdity without lingering in doubt or pausing for further analysis. The successful satire of the passage we have been discussing depends on making the reader scorn *immediately* the method of argument and encouraging him to transfer this ridicule to specific doctrines; we do not pause to *dispute* with Swift about arguments which may not seem to us to be self-evidently false.

Following, perhaps, the Kantian definition of laughter as based on "the sudden transformation of a strained expectation into nothing," Emerson described the "essence" of comedy as a "well-intended halfness":

> a non-performance of what is pretended to be performed, at the same time that one is giving loud pledges of performance. The balking of the intellect, the frustrated expectation, the break of continuity in the intellect, is comedy; and it announces itself physically, in the pleasant spasms we call laughter.[79]

The description is especially apt when it is applied to false logic. If a reasoner by his serious manner and through customary forms of logical demonstration leads us to expect a convincing argument, his pretension becomes comic when it suddenly collapses into absurdity. Swift, as we have seen, was unusually susceptible to this inherent comedy in false logic. Moreover, his suspicion of everything human which seemed mechanical, and which tended to substitute the artifice of system for the "natural" insight of reason, led him to suspect the systematic methodology of logic as simply one more mechanical operation of the mind. Some of his most comic effects in satire are achieved by his use of logical forms in what often seems to be a parody of logic itself. A brilliant example of this manipulation of spurious syllogisms and enthymemes for the sake of their comic effects is to be found in his pamphlet, *A Vindication of Isaac Bickerstaff Esq.* It may be remembered that Swift, writing under the ironic character of an astrologer, Bickerstaff, had issued his *Predictions for the Year 1708,* the first of which, a mere "trifle," was that a fellow philomath, John Partridge, "will infallibly die upon the 29th of March next, about eleven at night, of a raging fever." Swift pursued this opening gambit in his game against the humbuggery of astrology by announcing, on March 30th, with much circumstantial detail, the "accomplishment" of his first prediction. Other pamphlets by Swift and by fellow wits took up the cause of proving Partridge's death, and they were sufficiently convincing to lead to the maligned man's name being dropped from the register of the Stationer's Hall. When, in the following year, Partridge was dull and heavy enough to insist in print that he was truly alive, it gave Swift a rare opportunity, which he promptly seized: he wrote *A Vindication of Isaac Bickerstaff Esq.,* in which he claims to have "clearly proved, by *invincible demonstration,* that he died, at farthest, within half an hour of the time I foretold." The "demonstration" is a happy *tour de force* of logical nonsense and spurious enthymemes. The first three arguments by which Swift undertakes to "prove that

Mr. Partridge is not alive," are similar in depending on a quotation which Swift applies with an exact literalness:

And my first argument is thus: *above a thousand gentlemen* having bought his almanacks for this year, merely to find what he said against me, at every line they read, they would lift up their eyes, and cry out, *betwixt rage and laughter, "they were sure no man alive* ever writ such damned stuff as this." Neither did I ever hear that opinion disputed; *so that Partridge lies under a dilemma, either of disowning his almanack, or allowing himself to be no man alive.* Secondly, Death is defined by all philosophers, a separation of the soul and body. Now it is certain, that the *poor woman, who has best reason to know,* has gone about for some time to every alley in the neighborhood, and sworn to the gossips, that her husband had neither life nor soul in him. Therefore, if an uninformed carcass walks still about, and is pleased to call itself Partridge, Mr. Bickerstaff does not think himself anyway answerable for that . . . Thirdly, Mr. Partridge pretends to tell fortunes, and recover stolen goods; which *all the parish says,* he must do by conversing with the devil, and other evil spirits: and no wise man will ever allow he could converse personally with either till after he was dead.

The calm acceptance of a statement, proven merely by the *ipse dixit* of testimony, forms the major premise of the first argument and the minor premise of the second and third; it becomes the primary basis for these "invincible" demonstrations. The sense of ridicule, poised on tiptoe "betwixt rage and laughter," is aroused here in the reader not only against Partridge but against Bickerstaff's reasoning process as well: we can laugh at Bickerstaff's *method* while also laughing at its results. Our sense of the comedy of this paragraph is not decreased, moreover, when we recognize that through the false logic of its demonstration Swift has communicated a status of general and universal contempt in which Partridge is held: the *ipse dixit* of the first argument is supported by "above a thousand gentlemen," of the second by Partridge's wife "who has best reason to know," and of the third by "all the parish." Finally, we are amused at the pun on "uninformed" with its double meaning of "ignorant" and of "being without a soul." The fourth and fifth arguments are similar in their effects although slightly different in the particular

kind of fallacy upon which they rest. The fifth is an argument
from the improbability of Bickerstaff's being so "indiscreet,
to begin my predictions with the only falsehood that ever
was pretended to be in them." The fourth, probably the most
brilliantly illogical of them all, is an *argumentum ad homi-
nem* in which Swift deduces his proof from the "sophistry"
in Partridge's own claims to be alive:

Fourthly, I will plainly prove him to be dead, out of his own
almanack for this year . . . He there says, "he is not only now
alive, but was also alive upon that very 29th of March, which I
foretold he should die on:" by this, he declares his opinion, that
a man may be alive now who was not alive a twelvemonth ago.
And, indeed, *there lies the sophistry of his argument*. He dares not
assert he was alive ever since that 29th of March, but that he "is
now alive, and was so on that day:" I grant the latter; for he did
not die till night, as appears by the printed account of his death,
in a letter to a lord; and whether he be since revived, I leave the
world to judge. This indeed is perfect cavilling, and I am ashamed
to dwell any longer upon it.[80]

The "perfect cavilling" in Swift's own "invincible demonstration" serves, as in most of Swift's illogical logic, multiple
purposes. It advances the central joke of affirming the death
of Partridge; it provides a context, a soil for sowing a new
and diversified crop of satiric thistles with which to prick
Partridge; and, finally, it mocks by its own ironic fallacies the
"mode of arguing" adopted by Bickerstaff and his fellow
astrologers.

This last level of satire, the parody of spurious logical
forms, is a persistently recurring aspect of Swift's ridicule.
His contempt for that kind of logical proof, among others,
which depends upon the testimony of authority instead of
the empirical evidence of the senses, is suggested by Bickerstaff's own threefold appeal to the "gentlemen," the wife,
and "all the parish." As it was found in the writings of
philosophers and especially the scholastic churchmen, this
appeal to some authority as a test of particular and immediate experience had been made, at least since Bacon,
a frequent object of satiric attack. "Nothing less than an
ipse dixit," Swift wrote in *A Tritical Essay upon the Faculties*

of the Mind, "and you must pin your faith on their sleeve."[81]
One of the recurrent "proofs" by which Swift, in his several
ironic poses as a freethinker, justifies the conclusions of
deistic thought, was by just such an appeal: "And it is certainly true, (for Bishop Taylor and Mr. Whiston the Socinian
say so) that all churches in prosperity alter their doctrines
every age . . ."[82] The absurdity of this kind of *ipse dixit*
may be expressed, in Swiftian terms, as a "mechanical operation" of the mind: a proof that depends not upon the *reality*
of sensory experience or "rational" interpretation, but upon
a final appeal to a mere opinion accepted as a fact of nature,
results in the systematic errors of a "converting imagination."
A similar error which Swift vituperated directly, ridiculed
through parody, and even, perhaps, succumbed to himself,
was the fallacious use of maxims.

Maxims.   In Aristotelian rhetoric, maxims are defined as
statements "not about a particular fact," but of a "general
kind," which form "the premises or conclusions of Enthymemes, considered apart from the rest of the argument." In
short, a maxim is a statement embodying a general observation about "questions of practical conduct," about what is
generally true in human affairs. As Aristotle notes, many
proverbs are maxims; they embody some conclusion or general observation about human action, and seem to have the
force of a truism developed from the historical experience of
man. The general statement, to use one of Aristotle's examples from the *Medea,*

> Never should any man whose wits are sound
> Have his sons taught more wisdom than their fellows,

is a maxim; "add the reason or explanation," Aristotle continues, "and the whole thing is an Enthymeme; thus—

> It makes them idle; and therewith they earn
> Ill-will and jealousy throughout the city" (1394a, b).

A maxim, then, is a statement of what the author believes
to be a general truth about human action, and no period
was more eager in its search for maxims than was eighteenth-

century England. If Pope's *Essay on Man* characterizes this tendency in philosophical poetry, the most familiar critical pronouncement of the century was to be Imlac's observation in *Rasselas* that the poet's business is to "examine, not the individual, but the species." The poet "does not number the streaks of the tulip"; and the moralist, intent upon finding a representative pattern within which the isolated particular has meaning, concerns himself with the "grandeur of generality."

It is not surprising that Swift, in essays devoted less to satiric diminution than to constructive affirmations, should himself exemplify this tendency. We find a fairly typical instance in one *Examiner* paper, No. 21, in which Swift examines the "art of war," and promises to present "some maxims, relating to it, that will be eternal truths, and which *every reasonable man* will allow." Accordingly, he lists "certain maxims that wise governments have observed," and then proceeds to extend them into enthymemes, proving their truth by historical example. The first maxim is that "no private man should have a commission to be general for life," which he demonstrates by the single instance of Caesar. "Another maxim," Swift continues, "to be observed by a free state engaged in war, is to keep the military power in absolute subjection to the civil . . . ," which he demonstrates by the historical examples of Caesar and "the great rebellion against Charles the First." Finally, because modern armies have, more than formerly, "some degree of humanity," Swift says it is "certainly a good maxim to endeavour preserving this temper among them, without which they would soon degenerate into savages."[83] While Swift presents these maxims as "eternal truths," they have a distinct and sharply directed rhetorical purpose. For these generalities become a standard against which the particular activities of Marlborough and the Whigs are measured. We are reminded of Aristotle's penetrating remark that "one great advantage of maxims to a speaker is due to the want of intelligence in his hearers, who love to hear him succeed in expressing as a universal truth the opinions which they hold themselves about particular cases" (1395b). In logic, of course, these enthymemes of Swift are spurious: one robin does not prove the arrival of spring. But by elevating his own particular political animus to the level of a seemingly general philosophic truth, Swift presents the reader with the choice of either damning Marlborough or admitting himself to be no "reasonable man." This appeal to an axiomatic "eternal truth" as a standard is sometimes supported in Swift's writing by the *ipse dixit* of authority, as, for example, in *The Sentiments of a Church of England Man* when he considers the temporal evil of endangering the "public peace" by religious schism and forwards his argument by the observation: "For this reason Plato lays it down as a maxim, that, 'men ought to worship the gods according to the laws of the country,' and he introduces Socrates in his last discourse utterly disowning the crime laid to his charge, of teaching new divinities or methods of worship."[84] Or, again, Swift occasionally relies upon the authoritative pronouncements of proverbial or Biblical sayings as a basis for further analysis:

The Scripture tells us, that "oppression makes a wise man mad." Therefore, consequently speaking, the reason why some men are not mad, is because they are not wise: However, it were to be wished that oppression would in time teach a little wisdom to fools.[85]

This analytic employment of a maxim as an accepted general standard against which some particular is contrasted is close to the core of the ideal-reality relationship underlying so much of Swift's satire.

But if Swift was aware of the effective use of maxims and used them himself, he was equally conscious of their possible abuse, and much of his most brilliant logical wit derives immediately from this consciousness. Aristotle had insisted that only "experienced" and "elderly men" could properly use maxims in argument: "For a young man to use them is— like telling stories—unbecoming; to use them in handling things in which one has no experience is silly and ill-bred: a fact sufficiently proved by the special fondness of country fellows for striking out maxims, and their readiness to air them" (1395a). For a maxim to be logically valid, in other words, it must be supported by empirical particulars; and to be rhetorically convincing, the speaker (or writer) must 'suggest that the generalization has developed out of particular experience. It was against the absence of solid empirical foundations in Tindal's deistic use of maxims that Swift directed much of his vituperative abuse in his *Remarks Upon a Book Intituled "The Rights of the Christian Church, &c."*. The book is "a bundle of incoherent maxims and assertions," as Swift asserted in his introductory strictures; and in his later detailed marginalia he noted: "See, what danger lies in applying maxims at random"; "this is a maxim deduced from a gradation of false suppositions"; and, "here is another of his maxims closely put without considering what exceptions may be made."[86] To Swift, the generalities of the deists had not grandeur but, at most, grandiloquence; and the absurdity he found in Tindal's reasoning was the same absurdity that Aristotle perceived in the maxims of "country fellows," and that Bacon claimed to underlie the systematic abstractions of scholasticism. Lord Orrery, not often the most acute among Swift's critics, did note this similarity between Swift and Bacon: "Lord Bacon has justly exposed the vain pursuits of ostentatious pedants in the different parts of learning; and their unaccountable temerity in deducing general rules from arbitrary maxims, or few experiments."[87] Swift's own rational contempt for the temeritous and dangerous false logic of either "deducing general rules from arbitrary maxims," or of applying maxims to particulars without discrimination, is well expressed in his essay, *Maxims Controlled in Ireland*.

"There are certain maxims of state," Swift begins, "founded upon long observation and experience," which are true and applicable when applied to the particular kind of state from which they were initially derived. But if some state differs in a real and significant way from the prototype on which the maxim was based, then it is obvious the maxim has lost its truth as a particular statement. "Imagine a legislator," Swift explains, "forming a system for the government of Bedlam, and, proceeding upon the maxim that man is a sociable animal, should draw them out of their cells, and form them into corporations or general assemblies; the consequence might probably be, that they would fall foul on each other, or burn the house over their own heads." To think the maxim, "man is a sociable animal" can be made to correspond to the particular situation of men in an insane asylum is a fundamental failure in good sense. Swift was convinced that upon this failure "are innumerable errors committed by crude and short thinkers, who reason upon general topics, without the least allowance for the most important circumstances, which quite alter the nature of the case."[88] The connection is inescapable between Swift's contempt for this "crude and short" method of recklessly imposing maxims upon particulars and his ridicule of the mechanical imagination "converting" observed reality into a preconceived system. The absurdity he symbolized, as we will see, in the mechanical test of a poem by its rhyme—". . . you are ever to try a good poem as you would a sound pipkin, and if it rings well upon the knuckle, be sure there is no flaw in it"—or in the laboured construction of a sermon by the preacher-mechanic who "wisely moulds, and polishes, and dries, and washes this piece of earthen-ware, and then bakes it with poetic fire, after which it will ring like any pancrock"[89]—the same ridiculousness of these misinterpretations of what is essential in the particular may be discovered equally well in maxims. Of Tindal's writing Swift remarked: "He affecteth to form a few words into the shape and size of a maxim, then trieth it by his ear, and, according as he likes the sound or cadence, pronounceth it true."[90]

The Spurious Enthymeme.   What Swift perceived to be both comic and contemptible in the reasoning process of his opponents he was quick to adapt to his own ironic purposes. If the maxims of mercantile economics or deistic rationalism were absurd when applied to particulars, maxims used as a premise for demonstrating some ironically absurd conclusion had the same potentiality for comedy. "It is an old observation," Swift wrote, in one of his most sparkling though gen-

erally overlooked satires, "that piety is mostly supported by
the female sex; so that whatever is agreeable to them is for
the advantage of religion, and consequently the clergy should
dress in respect to the ladies, *i.e.* for the good of the church."[91]
What gives this demonstrative enthymeme its uniquely Swiftian air, is the gravity and high seriousness with which the
logical fallacy is self-consciously developed from what is taken
as an axiomatic truth. In this case, the fallacy—if we admit
as true the rather dubious maxim—turns, of course, upon the
direct synonymy assumed to exist between what is agreeable
and what is advantageous. A more frequent fallacy, though
not entirely unrelated to this one, into which Swift could fit
a maxim is that of *ambiguous terms*. This form of logical
error is mentioned by Aristotle as one of the "spurious enthymemes" which may seem logical but is not; he defined it
simply as the "use of similar words for different purposes,"
an example of which would be the proof "that speech is a
very excellent thing, since good men are not said to be worth
money but to be worthy of esteem—the phrase 'worthy of
esteem' also having the meaning of 'worth speech' " (1401a).
The fallacy actually depends on nothing more than a play on
words, a pun, and Swift resorted to it often as a means of
parodying logical demonstration. A characteristic example
of Swift's application of this fallacy to a proof through a
maxim appears in his elaborate justification for reading indexes of books as "an admirable expedient for being very
learned with little or no reading." After observing that
authors are to be treated like lobsters—whose best meat is
in their tails—he proves his point with a philosophical
maxim: "Lastly, you are taught thus much in the very elements of philosophy, for one of the first rules in logic is,
Finis est primis in intentione."[92] When this enthymeme is
stated as a syllogism, the ambiguous term "finis" becomes
quite evident:

> The end should be one's primary consideration;
> The index is the "end" of a book;
> *Ergo*, the index should be one's primary consideration.

The play on the word "end" arises in taking it in its figurative sense in the major premise, and then interpreting it literally in the minor premise. Or, stated differently, the "end" in the major premise has an abstract and conceptual meaning whereas the "end" in the minor has a concrete and localized meaning. This literal and false application of a general rule, a maxim, to a particular is precisely the fault of those who, like Tindal and the rest, used maxims "at random." The enthymeme in this case is self-satirizing; it is a parody.

Swift frequently condemned what he thought to be the arbitrary and artificial conversion of what is literally true (e.g., a Dublin tavern sign) into something figurative fraught with deep and hidden mystery (e.g., the same literal signpost interpreted as a symbol of Jacobitism). The converse of this imposition of one's own imaginings upon external reality is the arbitrary assumption that figurative expressions can be applied as literal maxims to prove or support an argument. Swift's essay ridiculing the dispute over the "Right of Precedence" between physicians and other professions supplies us with an extensive illustration of his use of this satiric device. Several pages of the essay are devoted to an elaborate proof that the stomach is the seat of honour and of "all the properties of the mind." The chief characteristic of the ridicule is the reduction of man's reason to physical mechanism; the principal means by which Swift accomplishes this satiric diminution is to prove its truth by the literal interpretation of figurative expressions. "Don't we use to say," Swift asks, "a man of honour stomachs an indignity?" He reserves for another treatise his intention of "chemico-mechanically" resolving men's honour, wit and genius "into their feeding," but, he adds,

this I will say, that a writer's stomach, appetite, and victuals, may be judged from his method, style and subject, as certainly as if you were his mess-fellow, and sat at table with him. Hence we call a subject dry, a writer insipid, notions crude and indigested, a pamphlet empty and hungry, a style *jejeune;* and many such-like expressions, plainly alluding to the diet of an author; and

I make no manner of doubt, but Tully grounded that saying of "*helluo librorum*" upon the same observation.

The logic of this fantastic and comic nonsense obviously derives from the fallacy of ambiguous terms. We may take any element in the list of expressions, for example "the notions [are] crude and indigested," and reduce it to a syllogism in which the fallacy glitters like fool's gold: the notions are crude and indigested; only food may be "crude and indigested"; *ergo,* the notions are a food which is taken into the stomach. The meaning of these phrases is thus taken literally in one premise and figuratively in another, so that the conclusion is an arrant absurdity. A splendid instance of this fallacy of ambiguous terms appears in the same essay. The enthymeme here could be rendered into a syllogism as follows: The prefix, Sir, denotes a title of knighthood; "sirloin" has the prefix, Sir; *ergo,* sirloin denotes a knight. The crowning touch to this logical nonsense is the complex and brilliantly characteristic irony of the phrase with which Swift concludes his argument: "and I have often chosen it." He not only pretends to operate on the principle he describes, but, in reality, he does it, too, for the reason, however, that he would rather eat sirloin than sit next to a squire.

. . . it will be granted, that to sit even at the foot of the table next a sir-loin, which is a dish of dignity, and of old hereditary knighthood, is in strictness of heraldry, more honourable than a place next the biggest plain country squire at the upper end; *and I have often chosen it.*

This playing upon the appearance of logic against the reality of nonsense is, in the same essay, employed to prove, finally, that the right of precedence actually belongs to physicians. As Swift's satire is aimed at the absurd irrationality of the whole dispute, it is not surprising to find him ironically utilizing a logic which is patently absurd. Accordingly, Swift presents his proof:

The nicest logicians will allow it a fair way of arguing in all cases, to refer to things what is true as to persons; and therefore I conclude, if physic be a faculty more ancient than that of civil law, then it literally *goes before* it, *i.e.* takes place of it.[93]

Swift then proceeds to prove that "physic" is the oldest profession because the "first distemper," which was "epidemical," was the "falling sickness." In these two carefully contrived fallacies we have, again, the fallacy of ambiguous terms. In the first, the syllogism turns upon the ambiguous identification of "going before" (in time) with "taking place" or precedence (in space). In the second, we may set up the implied syllogism to read something like this: the Fall of the Angels was a "falling sickness"; the "falling sickness" is a medical phenomenon; *ergo,* the Fall of the Angels was a medical phenomenon. The cream of this jest is, of course, the detachment and gravity with which the fallacies are permitted to stand alone.

The ironic humour of false logic is nowhere in Swift's writing more successfully or diversely employed than in *A Tale of a Tub.* "Good God!" Swift is said to have cried out loud many years after its publication, "What a genius I had when I wrote that book!" This praise has withstood the test of time, even though the particularity of the *Tale's* topical satire has, no doubt, for many readers, dulled the edge of much of its pristine wit. It would be futile, as well as erroneous, to attempt to discover any single comic device or technique which could be said to dominate this intricate *tour de force.* The *Tale* itself is an elaborate piece of ironic posing (the "author" is a Grub Street hack who, happily well-deceived, is an encomiast for everything modern), but within this flexible framework appear an extraordinary variety of satiric methods. We may, however, note in its technical virtuosity one salient aspect which has not been sufficiently stressed, namely, Swift's skillful and sustained parody of a general intellectual failure. The satire directed against Aristotelian logical categories, particularly in the "sartorist" description of man as clothes, has been well elucidated by Miriam Starkman in her book, *Swift's Satire on Learning in A Tale of a Tub* (1950). But Swift was not primarily concerned with demolishing the false repute and application of a particular logical system. Relevant to Swift is Nietzsche's remark upon his own writing, that he used particulars chiefly in order to "render visible a general but creeping calamity which it is otherwise hard to get hold of."[94] Swift's avowed intention in the *Tale*—to satirize *"the numerous and gross Corruptions in Religion and Learning"*[95]—was realized by attacking the rational perversity in *all* religious and scholarly zealots. Accordingly, in his attempt to demonstrate by parody the rational absurdities of fools, their defective "reasoning," Swift consistently employs illogic as a source of his comic satire. In addition, we should also recognize that to Swift one general abuse of reason—an abuse of which the *Tale* itself is ironically a preëminent example—is empty, splenetic and high-flown rhetorical argument. As a symbol of modernity, the spider in *The Battle of the Books* represented to Swift "the true Spirit of Controversy" because of his resolve to be "heartily scurrilous and angry, to urge *on* his own Reasons, without the least Regard to the Answers or Objections of his Opposite; and fully predetermined in his Mind against all Conviction" (pp. 230-231). The *Tale* is written ironically in the same spirit, and the jest lies in our perception of the diverse ways in which this appearance of logical demonstration succeeds only in unveiling real absurdity, ignorance, and error.

The pompous illogic which gives the *Tale* its uniquely intellectual wit often derives from the fallacy of "ambiguous terms"—that kind of error we have already discussed which interprets one term of a syllogism in two different ways. An example of the conscious and satirically effective use of this fallacy is Swift's discovery of the "Cause" of his "accurate Deduction" about the scheme for gaining public attention. The "deepest Account," Swift says (and we may recall the connotations of useless difficulty which Swift attributed to the idea of depth), of this phenomenon is found in the "System of *Epicurus*":

. . . Air being a heavy Body, and therefore . . . continually descending, must needs be more so, when loaden and press'd down by Words; which are also Bodies of much Weight and Gravity, as it is manifest from those deep *Impressions* they make and leave upon us; and therefore must be delivered from a due Altitude, or else they will neither carry a good Aim, nor fall down with a sufficient Force (p. 60).

In order to display this sidling jab at Epicurean metaphysics in its logical fallaciousness, we may break it down into a syllogism: words have weight and gravity and impress us; all things which have weight and gravity and leave *"Impressions"* are solid objects which tend to fall downwards; *ergo,* words are solid objects which tend to fall downwards. The ambiguity which suports this straight-faced logical nonsense lies in the *double-entendre* of the three words *weight* (figuratively profound, literally possessing heaviness), *gravity* (figuratively serious, literally a law of physics), and *impression* (figuratively a mental impression, literally a physical impression). These three words comprise the "ambiguous term" in the syllogism; in the minor premise they are interpreted in their figurative sense, and in the major they are interpreted in their literal sense. It is evident, also, that this passage does more than ridicule the logic of Epicurus; the technique of logical fallacy is united with Swift's reduction of the mind to mechanism and matter. Similar to the logical fallacy by which Swift deduced his "Physico-logical Scheme of Oratorial Receptacles or Machines" (p. 61) is the fallacy which he assigns to the Aeolists as a "Maxim" of "much Weight." This maxim is itself dependent upon another syllogism which Swift proves in the opening paragraph: *anima* (and *Spiritus, etc.)* means wind; *anima* means soul; *ergo,* the soul is wind.[96] The obvious fallacy here is the notion that because two things have the same name they are, therefore, the same thing. The synonymity of being, as well as meaning, which is thus assigned to wind and soul is then incorporated by Swift into a syllogism with *anima* as the ambiguous middle term: The most excellent being is that which has the most wind; Man alone has "three distinct *Anima's* or *Winds*" (plus a fourth added by the Aeolists); *ergo,* man is the most excellent being.

Much of the preceding illustration of the fallacy of ambiguous terms depends for its initial impetus upon some well-established maxim, proverb, or common figure of speech. In

A Tale of a Tub this literal interpretation of a figure of speech or common saying is similarly imbedded in the matrix of his illogical deductions. To the absurd syllogism which Swift instances as one proof of the Aeolists' conception of learning as wind (*"Words are but Wind; and Learning is nothing but* Words; Ergo, *Learning is nothing but Wind."*), he adds a second: ". . . it is generally affirmed, or confess'd that Learning *puffeth Men up*" (p. 153). The fallacy implicit in this literal application of the Biblical phrase is that of ambiguous terms: learning "puffeth men up"; only wind can "puff" anything up; *ergo,* learning is wind. The alternate use of a literal and a figurative meaning in the two premises performs the same function here as it was to do in the essay on *The Right of Precedence.* Not only does the deduction further the process of mechanizing the satiric object, but in itself it parodies false logic. A similar effect is occasioned in Swift's compressed multiple satire on the vanity of fashionable dress and the vainness of metaphysical speculations about the origin of the soul. Swift presents several professors, who belong to the sect of tailor-worshipers, as maintaining that the "outward" soul was a dress "of daily Creation and Circumfusion. This last they proved by *Scripture,* because, *in Them we Live, and Move, and have our Being:* As likewise by Philosophy, because they are *All in All, and All in every Part*" (pp. 79-80).

This technique of the fallacious logical use of ambiguous terms is applied also by Swift as a means of ridiculing the misdirection of learned pedantry and the absurdity he found in the Puritan belief in a subjective and inward light. His playing upon the ambiguity of "end" in both its literal and figurative senses became in Swift almost a stock device for ridiculing the misdirected learning from indices and abstracts. We will recall that in *A Letter of Advice to a Young Poet,* he proves the validity of his method by the authority of logical rules: "Lastly, you are taught thus much in the very elements of philosophy, for one of the first rules in logic is, *Finis est primus in intentione.*"[97] In *The Mechanical Operation of the Spirit* Swift ridicules those modern authors ". . .

who have too *literal* an Understanding: and, because Antiquity is to be traced *backwards,* do therefore, like *Jews,* begin their Books at the wrong End, as if Learning were a sort of *Conjuring.*"[98] And in *A Tale of a Tub* this logical fallacy underlies the series of analogies to the artificial methods of learning which Swift develops as the canon of modern scholarship: "For, the Arts are all in a *flying* March, and therefore more easily subdued by attacking them in the Rear . . . Thus Human Life is best understood by the wise man's Rule of *Regarding the End"* (p. 145).

If Swift's reasoning in the *Tale* is intended partly to evoke the comedy implicit in logical fallacy, it also serves another purpose, namely, of permitting him to penetrate his ironic pose and communicate more explicitly his own affirmative beliefs. We have seen how Swift, writing in the guise of a freethinker paraphrasing *Mr. Collins's Discourse,* interjected his own convictions by failing (with vigorous self-confidence) to refute the objections brought against deism. This kind of ironic objection and attempted refutation is brilliantly handled in *A Tale of a Tub,* and within the compass of this device Swift manages to attain remarkable variety. He occasionally steps out of his assumed character of a modern author and incorporates his own beliefs in a refutation. For instance, Swift apprehends "some curious *Wit* may object against me" for not "declaiming, according to the Custom, against the Multitude of Writers . . ." In making his "Defence, against this Objection," Swift points out that "I do not well understand the Justice of this Proceeding, because I observe many of these polite Prefaces, to be not only from the same Hand, but from those who are most voluminous in their several Productions" (pp. 45, 40). Except for the litotes of "I do not well understand," this passage contains little irony, and the reader is aware of Swift's own direct contempt for such illogical affectations. But argumentation is more frequently employed by Swift to introduce indirectly his own real opinions and, by inference, to prove them valid by the evident absurdity of the "author's" refutation. Characteristic of this device is the "author's" attempt, in "The Epistle Dedicatory," to disprove Time's assertion that the age is illiterate. The "author" promises to prove the contrary by "uncontroulable Demonstration" (that is, irrefutable proof), supported by an "undisputed Argument," but his proof evaporates like a cloud and he is reduced to the *ipse dixit* of admitting that ". . . I can only avow in general to *Your Highness,* that we do abound in Learning and Wit; but to fix upon Particulars, is a Task too slippery for my slender Abilities" (pp. 34, 35).

This impotent failure to disprove logically the truth of the original objection results in the unconscious self-criticism implicit in all parody. Swift often enforced this element of ignorant self-destruction by making the attempted refutation include additional levels of satiric content. Accordingly, to the criticism implied in the initial objection a new level of criticsm is suggested by the attempt to refute it. The "secret Detractors," for example, of the True Critics reported that "a *True Critick* is a sort of Mechanick, set up with a Stock and Tools for his Trade, at as little Expense as a *Taylor*." It is indubitable that we should include Swift, himself, among these detractors. But Swift then includes a new level of his own judgment in the "author's" refutation of this charge on the grounds that to become a True Critic requires infinite expense and, indeed, "will cost a man all the good Qualities of his Mind" (pp. 101, 102). Similarly, the refutation of the "morose, detracting, ill-bred People," who despise the excessive use of digressions, includes the additional idea that "the Society of Writers would quickly be reduced to a very inconsiderable Number" if men were forced to keep to the point (pp. 143, 144). A final illustration of this device, repeated so often throughout the *Tale,* may be drawn from Swift's elaborate sorites to "refute the objections" of those who insist upon the modernity of the True Critics. Swift constructs a careful syllogism which may be paraphrased as follows: the objectors admit that if True Critics existed among the ancients, they would have been mentioned; but Swift proves that the ancients did mention the True Critics under the hieroglyphic of "ASS"; *ergo,* the True Critic existed among the ancients. Through the complex detachment of this device, therefore, Swift is able not only to suggest that the True Critic in human form is solely a modern phenomenon, but also to insist that he is an "ASS" (pp. 98-100). And throughout the entire passage, it is the hypothetical "author" and not Swift who makes the charges; the reader is not overcome by an invective inducing strong emotion but is able to laugh while he condemns.

The use of logical processes of thought thus illustrates with even more refined precision both the object and the methods of Swift's satire. For the logical fallacies of human thinking are not only an ultimate object of attack. With an eminent adaptation of means to the end, of method to the object, they also serve as the tool or device with which to secure a powerful satiric effect. We must also recognize, moreover, that to Swift illogic was something more basic than a simple error in syllogistic reasoning. From one point of view, Swift's satiric intensity is directed above everything else to the misguided imagining, to the converting and distorting zeal, which either hastily or systematically mistakes the means for the end, the trivial or the unessential for the basic and fundamental: to *any* misuse, in other words, of the mental process —a misuse which Swift found analogous to a mechanical, impervious, and therefore blind and ultimately disastrous procedure. From a somewhat different point of view, much of Swift's greatness as a comic artist derives from his capacity to perceive in this intellectual deformity a universally valid source of comic diminution. The rational basis of Swift's satire, the connection between his intellectual principles and his literary craftsmanship, is nowhere better established than in his treatment of *mechanism* in life.

IV

The Mechanical Operation
of the Spirit

The Subjective Element in Mechanism

Few satirists have found such a plethora of objects for their contempt as did Swift. He incorporated into his human comedy the foibles of poets and clergymen; politicians, economists, and philanthropists; scholars, lawyers, physicians, kings, courtiers, nobles, philosophers, and scientists. Although he tells us that the foundation of his misanthropy was his hatred for "all nations, professions, and communities," and although we have concrete evidence as well as his own statement that all his love was "towards individuals," he singled out for individual abuse an imposing number of Whartons, Wottons, Walpoles, and Whistons. It is this encompassing breadth, as well as the violence, of Swift's satire that has misled so many readers to conclude that it must have been Swift who was out of step and not the world. But, on closer study, what is even more remarkable than the breadth of Swift's onslaught is the consistency of the premises upon which it is based and of the devices he used to embody these assumptions. If the pervading preoccupation of Swift was with the distinction between appearance and reality, the technique he most frequently employed to exhibit that dichotomy has its own · unique homogeneity. When Swift ridicules the criers of doom who read evidence of popery into every signpost; when he describes lawmakers, who have "reduced politics into a science," by the analogy of taking a turnip, tying a string to it, and then turning away all the servants who refuse to call it a watch; when he "chemico-mechanically" resolves "all the properties of the mind" into men's "feeding"; when he gravely depicts a self-righteous philanthropist presenting his horrific, though modest, proposal; when he demonstrates that the Bible is only useful as "a piece of necessary furniture for a wit and a poet"; when he finds the same pedantry in social manners and in polite conversation as in the arts and sciences—in every case, Swift is striking at the affectation of those who, by formula and artifice, impose some rigid subjective perception upon the world and then pay honour to this graven image as truth and to themselves as its discoverers. The folly of man's refusal to see things as they really are is thus consistently translated by Swift into symbolic representations of man as a *mechanism*. Inflexible, blinded to external truth by his own conceit, contentious in his assumption of the infallibility of his subjective responses, man becomes a puppet in life's Punch-and-Judy show of artifice, system, and self-delusion.

It is often maintained by historians of philosophy that England has had only one school of philosophy, or rather, that it has had none at all, "for its philosophy is a perpetual protest against Scholasticism."[1] A faith in experimental science, based upon the empirical evidence of the senses, and a complementary distrust of scholastic and rationalistic *a priori* speculation, may be said to form the cornerstone of the English philosophical tradition. Although Swift developed no systematic philosophy—this absence, too, seems to be characteristic of the tentative and experimental English mind—a peculiarly English and to some degree Lockeian nexus of assumptions underlies one major area of his satiric techniques. This area may be called, on the basis of Swift's own vocabulary, "the mechanical operation of the mind."

Locke's distinctive position in the history of English philosophy rests, of course, upon his thoroughgoing rejection of innate ideas and his thesis that the senses are the sole, initial source of all men's knowledge. He dismissed the *a priori* assumptions of scholastic rationalism; he was equally disdainful of the Neoplatonic insistence upon innate truths, and of the Cartesian attempt to build a rationalistic system upon geometric abstractions, rather than upon the evidence supplied directly from the external world. The tendency of Locke's philosophy was to force men's eyes outwards and to undermine their faith in the inherent powers of abstraction. One effect of Locke's basic assumption was to force men to inspect the objects of the external world and to avoid the metaphysical error of confusing words with things. That is, such concepts as species, genera, universality, are not, Locke believed, inherent in any object in itself, but they are abstractions of the mind having no objective counterpart in the world outside the mind. According to this view, the abstractions of Aristotelian, Platonic, and, Swift would add, Epicurean metaphysics are so many verbal tricks which merely conceal our ignorance of the real matter underneath. Words, therefore, often become mere appearance which hide the reality of the objects they describe.

Locke's refusal to accept conclusions of logic, which are based upon abstract principles and not upon concrete and empirical data, has a close counterpart in Swift's rejection of "mechanical" thinking. Although Swift disagreed strongly with many of Locke's beliefs,[2] and although he thought Locke had advanced some "dangerous tenets" (the deists' own dependence upon Locke may, from Swift's point of view, have proved his point), he also believed that "people are likely to improve their understanding much with Locke."[3] For Swift's persistent concern with the ironic incongruity between appearance and reality was based, in large part, upon the idea that man blinded himself to the accurate and total observation and evaluation of external objects. Some men, he thought, tended to confuse words with the objects they describe; some converted the objective facts of nature to fit a system or scheme of philosophy, religion, or learning without observing that the facts themselves failed to conform to these artificial abstractions; others confounded the accidental and secondary qualities of an object with the truth of the whole object; still others, finally, were content to observe only the external and first appearances of objects without further empirical examination of the truth beneath the surface. In all these kinds of intellectual fallacy, the mind may be said to delude itself through its mechanical operation. This "mechanical operation" of the mind occurs, then, ". . . when a Man's Fancy gets *astride* on his Reason, when Imagination is at Cuffs with the Senses, and common Understanding, as well as common Sense, is Kickt out of Doors."[4] Under the influence of such delusions, facts lose their inherent meaning and truth retires before the systematizing artifice of the brain. The machinery of the mind grinds out syllogisms, interpretations, and schemes, without sensory proof (or, at best, with only the sensory evidence from the surface of things). The two most frequent departures, then, from an ideal rationality may be summarized as (1) man's refusal or inability to "inspect beyond the surface and the rind of things"—that is, man's tendency to confuse the external appearance of a thing with its internal meaning and value; (2) man's rejection of all sensory evidence in favor of some subjectively conceived system or interpretation into which all things are fitted, if necessary by force and always after dispute and argument. The former is manifested by confusing, say, the external robes and mantles of a judge with the existence of an internal sense of justice in the wearer; Swift found evidence for the latter in, for example, the Catholic dogma of transubstantiation (the conversion of wine into blood by means of a systematic faith). Both extremes—the one a complete withdrawal from matter, the other an incompleted acceptance of matter—result, Swift believed, in common perversions of truth. And in man's consequent refusal to adapt his ideas to the discoverable truths of life, man ceases to be truly human and begins to resemble a mechanism operating in isolation from the normal world.

The converse of this mechanistic thinking may be called common or good sense. Instead of molding superficial impressions to fit some *a priori* fancy of the brain, or creating non-existent "facts" through a diseased imagination, common sense forms its concepts upon materials based on experience. Reason, Swift affirmed in one ironic denial, must depend upon the "memory" of things which have had a real existence and which have been supplied by the senses.[5] When the mind depends upon fanciful and therefore fictional associations for the facts upon which the reason must operate, the mind loses the flexibility of common sense and operates with an inhuman rigidity. Common sense, then, sees things as they really are; it is deluded neither by the mere sensory perception of externals (a perception which, Swift says, "never examine[s] farther than the Colour, the Shape, the Size, and whatever other Qualities dwell, or are drawn by Art upon the Outward of Bodies"),[6] nor by some inflexible system imposed mechanically upon the external objects. The function of the reason is, first, to perceive through the senses what exists, and then, by distinction and judgment, to determine the total truth of the object. Enthusiasts in religion, politics, or learning were, to Swift, the prime illustrations of the mechanical operation of the mind in conflict with the pliable adjustment of the mind to truth.

But the common sense, or Reason, that Swift postulated as the mean between the extremes of system and sensory delusion is not the discursive reason of the logician. W. B. C. Watkins, in a suggestive essay on Swift, has shown that the dilemma of a man who was both an antirationalist and a worshiper of Reason can only be reconciled by recalling Gulliver's definition of the ideal Reason of the Houyhnhnms:

Neither is reason among them a point problematical as with us, where men can argue with plausibility on both sides of the question; but *strikes you with immediate conviction;* as it must needs do where it is not mingled, obscured, or discoloured by passion and interest.[7]

Watkins has pointed out that this "highest, purest aspect of Reason is really intuition; it is above and distinct from what we should ordinarily regard as intellectual processes."[8] Because "intuition" may suggest a purely subjective and private response, it may not be a very useful synonym. The Reason of the Houyhnhnms is intuitive only to the extent that it is *immediate*, without long and intricate circumlocution. But it is not intuitive in another sense: it does not draw its materials from inside. The spider, Swift's symbol of the latter kind of intuition, builds his cobweb from *inside* himself; the bee, symbolizing ideal reason, fetches honey from *without*. In the absence of a better word, perhaps "intuitional" reason will do to describe a position between elaborate logical debate (ordinary reason) and completely subjective impulse (the neoclassic view of intuition). In a sense, the "protest on behalf of an organic view of nature" that Whitehead has so aptly attributed to the romantic movement finds a thoughtful though limited expression in Swift. For if the *values* perceived by Swift's Reason are characteristically neoclassical in their static simplicity and not "emergent," to use Whitehead's phrase, the reasoning *process* is nonetheless conceived as being essentially dynamic. It is this intuitional kind of reason, depending upon the senses for its information but then proceeding at once without dispute to a true evaluation of that sensory experience, which is Swift's "rational" ideal. And we must bear this ideal clearly in mind when, for example, we read Swift describing himself as one

> Sunk over head and ears in matter,
> Nor can of metaphysics smatter;
> Am more diverted with a quibble
> Than dreams of worlds intelligible;
> And think all notions too abstracted
> Are like the ravings of a crackt head.[9]

The "ravings of a crackt head" were, to Swift, the necessary consequence of a subjectivism which sought for truth in the resources of one's own "original" nature. In discussing the relation of Dr. Johnson's thinking to the neoclassic concept of "general nature," W. J. Bate presents a lucid analysis of the meaning of that vague but popular term. In emphasizing the classical concern of Johnson with the discovery through reason of stable and universal moral values in nature, Bate reminds us that Johnson would have regarded the complete "original" as being rather remote from the ideal nature of man, and would have sanctioned Goethe's remark that we get little from our own entirely native feelings but stupidity and awkwardness. "The mental disease of the present generation," Johnson stated, "is impatience of study, contempt of the great masters of ancient wisdom, and a disposition to rely wholly upon unassisted genius and natural sagacity."[10]

Swift's point of view was similar to Johnson's in his contempt for the claims of an unbridled subjectivism. The connection that Swift was to make all his life between extreme subjectivity and the mechanical operation of the mind is clearly expressed in *The Battle of the Books* by the admirable Restoration comedy scene between the spider and the bee. The bee, symbolizing Swift's ideal rational man, looks to objective experience as the initial source and ultimate test of his subjective awareness; and he claims with the whole weight of the classical heritage behind him that it is only through this process that man can find "honey and wax" and can produce "the two noblest of things which are sweetness and light." The spider, on the other hand, is shown to employ only the materials of his own being and then, by art and mechanical methods, to shape those materials into a system. The source of his materials is subjective; the product is artificial. The bee's comment is conclusive:

Now, for you and your Skill in Architecture, and other Mathematics, I have little to say: in that Building of yours, there might, for ought I know, have been *Labor* and *Method* enough, but by woful Experience for us both, 'tis too plain, the Materials are nought, and I hope, you will henceforth take Warning, and *consider Duration and matter, as well as method and Art.*[11]

The distinction drawn here by the bee between "labor and method" and "duration and matter" provided Swift with a frequently reiterated premise of satirical judgment. When, for example, in *A Letter of Advice to a Young Poet,* he satirizes modern poets as verbal mechanics who depend, he feels, upon method and "originality" instead of rational insight, he ironically states the modern position as his own:

For, to speak my private opinion, I am for every man's working upon his own materials, and producing only what he can find within himself, which is commonly a better stock than the owner knows it to be. I think flowers of wit ought to spring, as those in a garden do, from their own root and stem, without foreign assistance. I would have a man's wit rather like a fountain, that feeds itself invisibly, than a river, that is supplied by several streams from abroad.[12]

Upon this premise of a confident subjectivism, Swift then proceeds to consider the poet's methods by which he can achieve the "modern" ideal, expressed in *A Tale of a Tub,* of being deep-learned and shallow-read. His satiric purpose was to expose the false artifice of method as the reality beneath the pretensions of a poetry that had lost its contact with humane learning and moral values.

This fundamental premise—that mere "labor and method" can produce neither sweetness nor light and that they delude mankind through false appearances—is very clearly stated in Swift's poem, "The Progress of Beauty." The real point behind Swift's so-called "unprintable" poems is not, as Aldous Huxley and others would have us believe, that they reflect only the disease of a mind incapable of adjusting to physical reality. Maurice Johnson has reminded us recently in *The Sin of Wit,* that these poems were directed against both a specific literary convention of romanticizing women's physical beauty and a more general failure of confusing physical attraction with moral excellence. What Pope more delicately satirized in Belinda's adoration of "cosmetic powers" has often been a subject for the moralist. Swift's treatment of it simply extends beyond a usual decorum the gap between the artifice of cosmetic deceits and the physical reality of the woman beneath these appearances. Swift, who was "ignorant of any one quality that is amiable in a man, which is not equally so in a woman," certainly had no intention to make us misogynists because women are animals and subject to the unlovely and physical activities of all beasts; his concern was to shock mankind from the practice of admiring what is bestial as if it were, somehow, something quite different. And that his criticism was not simply *destructive* (one of the more annoying clichés that still lingers

in the minds of some of Swift's critics) is specifically illustrated by the conclusion of "Strephon and Chloe." But the
point here is that because physical beauty, unlike moral
virtue, is fleeting and impermanent and its progress necessarily is a withering and a decaying, Swift ridiculed the
attempts to conceal the reality of this declension beneath the
mechanical "workmanship" of "pencil, paint and brush":

> But, Art no longer can prevayl
> When the Materialls all are gone,
> The best Mechanick hand must fayl
> Where Nothing's left to work upon.
>
> Matter, as wise Logicians say,
> Cannot without a Form subsist,
> And Form, say I, as well as They,
> Must fayl if Matter brings no Grist.[13]

Swift's satire is pointed here not against the decay of beauty,
an inevitable fact of life, but at a defect which, he well knew,
"all mortals may correct": the attempt or desire to substitute
artifice for nature and then to admire the delusion as if it
were real and not merely a mechanism.

It is evident that in these matters Swift was neither very
original nor rigorously thorough; his contempt for abstractions which were divorced from any empirical examination
was held in common with many other skeptical and more
disciplined thinkers of his day; and his concern for the
discovery of stable and permanent values beneath the flux
of appearance was at least as old as Parmenides. What lends
a unique importance to these attitudes is the manner in
which they were translated into satire. For Swift not only
despised the common intellectual fallacies of mankind, he
also discerned an inherent comedy in them—a comedy deriving from the absurdity of a human being behaving like a
machine. This comic perception has always been one basis
for satiric humour: Aristophanes pilloried Socrates with
a mechanical analogy and, to cite a satirist whose influence
on Swift was more recent and probably more direct, Samuel
Butler's *Hudibras* draws much of its satiric impetus from its
mechanical symbols. When, for example, Butler ridicules

the artifice of achieving salvation through means other than
spiritual, he writes of priests,

> Supplied with spiritual provision,
> And magazines of ammunition;
> With crosses, relics, crucifixes,
> Beads, pictures, rosaries, and pixes;
> The tools of working out salvation
> By mere mechanic operation (Part III, Canto 1).

The comedy Butler found in a "mere mechanic operation"
became for Swift an important aspect of the "ridiculous
tragedy" of human delusion; and Swift exploited this insight
with an unprecedented brilliance and consistency.

The Comedy of Mechanism

Swift was more concerned with the immediate problems
of his literary production than with reflecting critically upon
his own techniques. However, a modern French philosopher,
Henri Bergson, whose total dynamic conception of life has
little in common with Swift's Christian empiricism, has
advanced a theory of comedy that may be applied without
distortion to Swift's comic practice. Bergson's central thesis
is that most comedy derives from "something mechanical
encrusted on the living."[14] A review of some of Bergson's
basic tenets may throw considerable light upon this major
aspect of Swift's satiric craftsmanship and his perennial appeal
even to readers who are unfamiliar with the topical subjects
of his attack.

Bergson starts from the position that "common sense," the
expected and necessary attribute of a human being, is the
norm, and departures from that standard make comedy
possible:

common sense represents the endeavour of a mind continually
adapting itself anew and changing ideas when it changes objects.
It is the mobility of the intelligence conforming exactly to the
mobility of things. It is the moving continuity of our attention to
life.

This conception of common sense is not far removed from
Swift's own. The emphasis of both men was upon the neces-

sity of the mind perceiving things as they are and not imposing upon them some biased abstraction. To Bergson, "tension" and "elasticity" are complementary forces which are
necessary to social adjustment; the mind must be elastic
enough to form its conceptions upon the alert awareness
of the evidence of the senses, and it must have tension enough
to mold these impressions into thought. When, for example,
the easy "automatism of acquired habits," or some "absent-
mindedness," operates in a person with "mechanical inelasticity," we laugh; "rigidity is the comic, and laughter is its
social corrective." Whenever the "mobility of life" gives
place to rigidity there is comedy. Surprise, incongruity, and
contrast were defined by the ancients as causes of humour;
Kant argued that the sudden disappointment of expectation
is the principal cause of laughter. According to Bergson,
however, these are not primary causes of laughter but serve
merely to illustrate a rigidity which is comic in itself. Life
depends upon continual adjustment to present facts. When
an official performs his duties like a machine, or when we
see "an administrative regulation working with inexorable
fatality, and setting itself up for a law of nature," or whenever artifice is substituted for the natural, there is comedy.
Similarly, laughter may arise whenever the physical in a
person takes precedence over his moral nature. This comedy
arises when we see

the body taking precedence of the soul . . . the manner seeking
to outdo the matter, the letter aiming at ousting the spirit . . .
the means substituted for the end . . . no longer is it the profession that is made for the public, but rather the public for the
profession.

When a person behaves like a "thing," when the institutions
of men lose their original purpose and become Frankensteins
no longer controlled by reason, but by their own internal
machinery devoid of thought; whenever, in short, there is
"the illusion of life and the distinct impression of a mechanical arrangement"—in all these, Bergson saw the operation of
comedy.

No theory of comedy is more clearly applicable to Swift

than Bergson's. We need not subscribe to his theory as a total explanation of all laughter, nor as a total explanation even of the laughter arising from mechanism, in order to perceive its relation not only to Swift's "Mechanical Operation of the Spirit" and *A Tale of a Tub*, but also to *Gulliver's Travels* and to much of the satire in his other works. The present discussion is concerned with the techniques Swift employs to convey his impression of men's mechanical thinking. At the same time, it is well to note that the techniques themselves often fuse into the object of the criticism. That is, when Swift describes a man or institution operating with the immobile rigidity of a mechanical engine we should also remember that this description both arouses our laughter and, at the same time, represents directly what Swift himself is condemning. The technique is successful as comedy because the content, the mechanical thinking of the object, is laughable in its own right.

The "Converting Imagination"

When Swift promises, in *A Tale of a Tub*, to describe the artful conceptions of Jack's fevered imagination, he adds that

. . . they will furnish Plenty of noble Matter for such, whose converting Imaginations dispose them to reduce all Things into *Types;* who can make *Shadows,* no thanks to the Sun; and then mold them into Substances, no thanks to Philosophy; whose peculiar Talent lies in fixing Tropes and Allegories to the *Letter,* and refining what is Literal into Figure and Mystery (p. 190).

This is the imagination which led Don Quixote to convert wineskins and windmills into giants and to see an army in a flock of sheep. The inability or frank refusal to inspect external objects and to see them as they are in their physical concreteness is the common point of departure for Swift's satire against the abuses of learning and of religion. In both, the "virtuosi" of religious zeal and pedantic enthusiasm "converted" external objects by artifice into conformity with an *a priori* conception of the mind. To Swift,

. . . the *Senses* in Men are so many Avenues to the Fort of *Reason,* which in this Operation is wholly block'd up. All Endeavors must be therefore used, either to divert, bind up, stupify, fluster, and amuse the *Senses,* or else to justle them out of their Stations.

By this "operation," Swift is referring not to natural or supernatural enthusiasm, but to the mechanical and artificial ". . . *lifting up of the Soul or its Faculties above Matter.*"[15] Swift conceived the natural operation of the mind to be the use of reason working upon the materials supplied by the senses. When the mind refuses to accept sensory impressions, when writers have "spiritualized and refined" their works from the "Dross and Grossness of *Sense* and *Human Reason,*"[16] then the mind seemed to Swift to become an artificial machine working in a vacuum. The artificial attempt to spiritualize matter, to convert sensory impressions into abstract fictions, or, on the other hand, to ". . . put Men upon *Visions* in Things *Invisible,*"[17] were to Swift the inevitable result of excessive contemplation divorced from the senses. The point of that excellent fragment, *A Discourse Concerning the Mechanical Operation of the Spirit* is summarized at its conclusion:

Too intense a Contemplation is not the Business of Flesh and Blood; it must by the necessary Course of Things, in a little Time, let go its Hold, and fall into *Matter.*[18]

Accordingly, Swift goes on, the Platonic lovers who seem to cast their eyes on the immaterial beauties of their ladies prove the moral of the philosopher "who, while his thoughts and eyes were fixed upon the constellations, found himself seduced by his lower parts into a ditch." This mechanical contemplation of ideas separated from any acceptance of matter as matter was allegorized a few years later by Swift in a *Tatler* paper. "Charles Sturdy" writes to the paper that he has fallen in love with a "Platonne" who "would contract herself into mere spirit," and he asks: "Why should she wish to be a cherubim, when it is flesh and blood that makes her adorable?" Swift ridicules the impossibility of so perverting nature by answering the letter with a tale of several ladies who formed a college to preserve their chastity: most of them concluded the experiment by their pregnancy.[19] What prompted this fair Platonne to wish her body converted into spirit was her talent "in fixing tropes and allegories to the letter." The sturdy empiricist writing the letter complained that he was tormented by her talk of the Neoplatonic "intellectual triflers": ". . . to a lover who understands metaphors, all this pretty prattle of ideas gives very fine views of pleasure, which only the dear declaimer prevents by understanding them literally." Swift believed that to the intelligent mind operating with common sense, what was written metaphorically should be read as it was intended. To convert an allegory or metaphor into a literal interpretation was to act mechanically without reason. In religion, particularly, was this tendency of the converting imagination apparent, and Swift in his *Thoughts on Religion* lamented the literal application of Biblical parables and metaphors: "I have been often offended to find St. Paul's allegories, and other figures of Grecian eloquence, converted by divines into articles of faith."[20]

Swift satirized this conversion of the figurative into the literal in *Gulliver's Travels* when the Lilliputians list the objects found in Gulliver's pockets. Having discovered his watch, they conjectured that it was the god he worshiped because he told them that he ". . . seldom did anything without consulting it," and called it his "oracle."[21] The Lilliputians, being ignorant of watches, converted his figurative expressions into a sense meaning a literal God.

Complementing this abuse of thought is the conversion of what is literally explicit and open into a mystery or allegory. The mind which is not content with what is presented to it through the senses and interpreted through common sense, will twist the simplest external facts into something rich and strange. This conversion of fact into fiction reflects the mechanical operation of imposing upon facts an interpretation which one has first established in the mind. Instead of observing facts and then basing one's conclusions upon them, the mind finds the conclusion and interprets the facts to fit the conclusion. This conversion, Swift thought, was the basis of much of the political and religious fanaticism which, for example, found evidence of popery in the most unlikely places. He satirizes this corruption of the senses in *An Examination of Certain Abuses . . . in the City of Dublin* by interpreting the street-cries, tavern-signs and other things common in a large city, as being code words of sedition. For example, Swift, writing as a Whig, insists that the Tories had hired men with baskets on their shoulders

. . . to call aloud at every house, "Dirt to carry out;" giving that denomination to our whole party, as if they would signify, that the kingdom could never be cleansed, till we were swept from the earth like rubbish.[22]

It is characteristic that Swift here joins with the main object of satire (the converting imagination) an implicit shaft at the Whigs themselves; their very self-consciousness implies a sense of guilt. Swift finds similar evidence of popery in the cries of "Flounders" (meaning, he says, Flanders), "Turnip" (meaning "turnups"—which, he insists, has no lewd insinuation but is certainly a rallying cry for Catholics) and the like. He also finds ciphers in signposts, so that the spread eagle on one tavern sign "exhibits to us the perfect figure of a cross which is a badge of popery." Swift's ridicule is directed in this essay against that rigidity of mind and judgment which marks the thinking of all violent partisans, whether in politics or religion or learning. To the man whose mind operates with mechanical inelasticity, even the most commonplace things may be converted to fit into the fixed and preconceived grooves of his expectations.

The mechanical pursuit of one's own conceptions and the imposition upon external facts of one's own *a priori* conclusions is likewise satirized on the political level in *Gulliver's Travels*. In the trial of Atterbury, Bishop of Rochester, for high treason in 1723, the evidence was derived largely from deciphered letters; Swift thought Atterbury was innocent, and that the Walpole ministry had predetermined his guilt and then converted his correspondence into ciphers to prove it. Swift considered this methodized construction of intrigue

to be the "workmanship of those persons who desire to raise
their characters of profound politicians . . ." Swift then proceeds to describe the mechanical workings of this conversion
of fact into fiction:

It is first agreed and settled among them, what suspected persons
shall be accused of a plot; then, effectual care is taken to secure
all their letters and papers, and put the criminals in chains. These
letters are delivered to a set of artists, very dexterous in finding
out the mysterious meanings of words, syllables, and letters. For
instance, they can discover a close-stool to signify a privy-council;
a flock of geese, a senate; a lame dog, an invader . . . ; a broken
reed, a court of justice; an empty tun, a general; a running sore,
the administration.

In addition, Gulliver notes the acrostic and, finally, the
"anagrammatic method" of discovering plots and intrigues.[23]
Throughout this passage Swift's use of such words as "instrument," "workmanship," "artists," "dexterous," and the
like emphasizes the mechanical artifice of the trial. We may
also note that, incidental to this principal satire, there is the
overtone created by the correspondence between the ciphers
and their counterparts; Swift not only strikes at the artifice
of political methods, but the ciphers themselves are a series
of similes reflecting Swift's general contempt for the government (to Swift, the administration is *like* a running sore, a
court of justice is *like* a broken reed, and so forth).

The mechanical ingenuity, which Swift satirized in the
factional thinking of the politicians, is closely paralleled by
the same converting imagination in religious and scholarly
"artists." *A Tale of a Tub, the Battle of the Books,* and *A
Discourse Concerning the Mechanical Operation of the Spirit*
are all based upon that fallacy of mental rigidity which artificially imposes false and delusive interpretations upon external facts. "Section II" of *A Tale of a Tub* contains much
the same technique of ridiculing the artificial conversion of
literal truths into allegory as do the works discussed above.
For example, the brothers determine that the will of their
father must give them authority to wear silver fringe. On
this preconception, they examine the will which, they find,

explicitly denies them that luxury. Accordingly, Peter, the brother most skilled in the mechanics of dialectic and criticism,

> . . . found in a certain Author, which he said should be nameless, that the same Word which in the Will is called *Fringe,* does also signifie a *Broom-stick;* and doubtless ought to have the same Interpretation in this Paragraph. This, another of the Brothers disliked, because of that Epithet, *Silver,* which could not, he humbly conceived, in Propriety of Speech, be reasonably applied to a *Broom-stick;* but it was replied upon him, that this Epithet was understood in a *Mythological,* and *Allegorical* Sense. However, he objected again, why their Father should forbid them to wear a *Broom-stick* on their Coats, a Caution that seemed unnatural and impertinent; upon which he was taken up short, as one that spoke irreverently of a *Mystery,* which doubtless was very useful and significant . . . (p. 88).

To common sense, of course, "fringe" meant "fringe," and only the inflexible converting imagination of the religious enthusiast would interpret this literal word into allegory.

A somewhat different technique of ridiculing the same type of thinking is found in Swift's conversion of ancient natural philosophy into allegories of critics. The brilliance of this section of "A Digression Concerning Critics" lies in the double-edged intention of the satire. On the primary level, of course, is his intention to equate critics with asses. But the whole technique of this equation is an elaborate parody of the artificial method of reading mystery into what is literal and explicit. As a consequence, Swift here very nimbly uses the methods of critics to satirize both the critics and their methods. Swift argues that the ancients had, through "mythology and hieroglyphic," described the "True Criticks," and that ". . . these *Antient Writers* in treating Enigmatically upon the Subject, have generally fixed upon the very same *Hieroglyph,* varying only the Story according to their Affections or their Wit." The ensuing illustrations are drawn from classical references to asses and applied by Swift as undoubted references to critics. Swift then concludes that this hieroglyph of the ass was abandoned ". . . as too nearly approaching the *Prototype*," and that, thereafter, ancient authors concealed their meaning under accounts of weeds and serpents (pp. 98-100). The whole passage is intended mainly, as I said, to diminish the critics by equating them with beasts and other things which connote disgust or contempt. But the second level of parody represents the mechanical operation of a mind intent only upon proving a thesis and indifferent to the validity of the external evidence.

Swift's *personae* regularly exhibit this imaginative conversion of literal truth into allegory and mystery. The "author" of *A Tale of a Tub,* for example, comments repeatedly upon the profundity of his work—a depth and significance he deduces from its obscurity. He avails himself of those "common Privileges of a Writer" which enable him to assume that ". . . where I am not understood, it shall be concluded, that something very useful and profound is coucht underneath" (pp. 46-47). Swift's ridicule is again directed here both against those writers who pretend that their own works are deep when they are merely obscure, and the readers who pretend to find abstruse meanings in such works. The converting imagination which leads a political enthusiast to find popery symbolized in a common signpost, or which prompts a religious zealot to find his own fanatic conclusions mythologized in the Bible, operates also among learned commentators who convert mere obscurity into profundity of meaning. It is in the guise of being one of the modern "mysterious writers" that Swift challenges "every Prince in Christendom" to take seven of the "deepest scholars," shut them up for seven years in seven chambers and, he concludes, after they have commented on *A Tale of a Tub,* ". . . whatever Differences may be found in their several Conjectures, they will be all . . . manifestly deduceable from the Text" (p. 185). Swift continues this satire upon scholarly grubbing for nonexistent meanings by a parody of the Rosicrucian and Cabalistic mystical writings. He states that he has "couched a very profound Mystery in the Number of O's multiply'd by *Seven,* and divided by *Nine*"; he urges his readers to find the "Opus Magnum" which he has concealed in certain syllables and letters which must be rearranged to uncover his meaning, with other equally absurd pretensions to mystery (p. 187). Swift adds that the "judicious World is resolved to list me" among the *"Profound Writers,"* because the *Tale,* itself, will appear obscure to them. He then translates this abstract fallacy of logic into a characteristic physical image that "it is with *Writers,* as with *Wells"* which shall pass for "wondrous *Deep,* upon no wiser a Reason than because it is wondrous *Dark"* (pp. 207-208). The artificial conversion of obscurity or darkness into depth and profundity exhibits the incapacity of the mind to see things as they are.

The signpost which is *really* a signpost is converted by these dexterous artists into the *appearance* of a signpost concealing reality beneath an elaborate symbolism. This absurdity of converting shadows into substances is also expressed by Swift with an entirely different relation between appearance and reality. The imagination which interprets words as exact and accurate descriptions of things, suffers, too, from mechanical inelasticity. To Swift, words are shadows which men frequently convert into substances; they are the appearance which may conceal, but can certainly never change, the reality they pretend to describe. Swift, of course, accepted the philosophical view that external reality had a real existence, independent of man's perception of it. Accordingly, the words men use are merely artificial and arbitrary labels or symbols constructed to represent this objective reality, and words have in themselves no necessary connection with the facts they describe. One frequent fallacy of the converting imagination, then, is to expect, by tagging a name to a thing, to influence the essential nature of the thing itself. In his *Remarks upon a Book,* Swift develops a distinction between what the supreme legal authority in the real world can and cannot do; Swift's conception of the relationship between the appearance of words and the reality of things is well illustrated in this attack upon Tindal. For, he argues, in England the absolute power of the government may decree anything it wishes and its wish becomes the law; "their decrees may be against equity, truth, reason and religion, but they are not against law." Nevertheless, Swift continues, these edicts cannot in themselves "alter the nature of things":

So, if a king and parliament should please to enact, that a woman who hath been a month married, is *virgo intacta,* would that actually restore her to her primitive state? If the supreme power should resolve a corporal of dragoons to be a doctor of divinity, law, or physic, few, I believe, would trust their souls, fortunes, or bodies to his direction.

He then instances the hypothetical case of a man who is required by parliament to walk a slack rope as a necessary qualification for his becoming a bishop. Such a man might then sit in the House of Lords and perform the actions of a bishop. But, Swift concludes, in a passage which serves as a commentary upon the Lilliputian test of political excellence, few would believe "this tumbler to be one whit more a bishop than he was before; because the law of God hath otherwise decreed; which law, although a nation may refuse to receive it, cannot alter in its own nature." The purpose of the reason was, to Swift, the discovery of things in their own nature; the false coverings and artificial lights, which delude the senses and deceive men into converting the appearance of things into reality, include the misapplication of words. In this same essay, Swift exhibits this absurdity of conversion by a characteristic analogy with a low object. The mechanical rigidity of the refusal to see things as they are becomes at once apparent:

They may make laws, indeed, and call them canon and ecclesiastical laws, and oblige all men to observe them under pain of high treason. And so may I, who love as well as any man to have in my own family the power in the last resort, take a turnip, then tie a string to it, and call it a watch, and turn away all my servants, if they refuse to call it so too.[24]

The arbitrary assignment of words to things, in order to convert the things into something else was, at least partially, behind Swift's contempt for the legal profession in the abstract. The jargon of all professions seemed to him to represent the constant attempt to cover reality by the appearance of learned words. In "A Voyage to the Houyhnhnms," Swift castigates the legal profession as composed of men "bred up from their youth in the art of proving by words multiplied for the purpose, that white is black, and black is white." This society, he tells us, "hath a peculiar cant and jargon of their own . . . whereby they have wholly confounded the very essence of truth and falsehood, of right and wrong."[25] The incongruity between the jargon of lawyers and the facts which this jargon succeeds in hiding leads Swift to include lawyers in his proposed hospital for incurables:

How many lawyers, attorneys, solicitors, under-sheriffs, intriguing chambermaids, and counter-officers, are continually guilty of extortion, bribery, oppression, and many other profitable knaveries, to drain the purses of those with whom they are any way concerned! And yet, all these different expedients to raise a fortune, pass generally under the milder names of fees, perquisites, vails, presents, gratuities, and such like; although, in strictness of speech, they should be called robbery, and consequently be rewarded with a gibbet.[26]

Through the medium of the mixed catalogue (lawyers are lumped together with chambermaids, the fees to one equated with gifts to the other) Swift is striking out against the disparity between the true nature of a thing and its false verbal appearance. The verbal machinery which helps lawyers disguise their real criminal practices is analogous to the artificial creation of a wit. The mechanical method of being witty with no further natural qualification than the testimony of friends exhibits a similar incongruity between the appearance created by words and the reality existing in nature. This incongruity underlies Swift's proposal that only wits be admitted as members to his projected academy: "No Person to be admitted Member into any of these Schools, without an Attestation under two sufficient Persons Hands, certifying him to be a *Wit*."[27]

The mechanical method of converting a turnip into a watch by tying a string to it and calling it a watch is precisely the same fallacy of the rigid converting mind as changing a fool into a wit by certificate. If this artificial substitution of a name for the true nature of the thing fails to create a wit

from a natural fool, how much greater a failure is the religious attempt to convert commonplace objects into mysterious religious tokens. Swift, therefore, in *A Tale of a Tub*,
ridicules the Catholic practice of attributing universal properties to such an ordinary thing as bread. Thus, Swift interprets
the only difference between ordinary bread and the universal
bread of the church as being in the words given to the latter
by Peter (pp. 116-119). The gaiety of this satiric passage
derives from the vivid dramatic representation of Peter's inflexible mind imposing its verbal artifice by force of will upon
the incredulous Martin and Jack. In its fundamental antithesis between the acceptance of sensory evidence and the
rigid rejection of the senses in favor of the converting imagination, this scene resembles Quixote's arguments with Sancho
Panza. Throughout the several pages in which Swift develops
this antithesis he emphasizes the inelastic aggressiveness of
Peter's mind; the success of the passage seems to consist
largely of the fusion of Swift's contempt for the kind of thinking practiced by Peter and his ability to portray it in its
mechanical rigidity.

In addition to the several kinds of converting imagination
already discussed—the conversion of the literal into the
figurative, the figurative into the literal, and words into
things—Swift, finally, ridiculed that kind of conversion which
disposed men to "reduce all things into types." One ludicrous
error of the scientific mind, whether operating in religion,
politics, or scholarship, was, in Swift's opinion, the fallacy
of making all experience conform to systems pretending to
be universal. Here, too, the mechanical and artificial operation of the mind is evident and Swift made frequent use of
its laughable potentiality. For the multifariousness of life
and the necessity of continuous adjustment to the perpetually
shifting facts of experience make it impossible to impose any
all-inclusive system upon nature—at least any *new* system
pretending to replace the standards of Christian orthodoxy.
Moreover, Swift shared with Locke and other contemporary
thinkers the belief that man is incapable of understanding
many cosmic mysteries which were, he argued, "above" and

therefore not "contrary" to reason. The attempt, therefore, to draw the universe into novel systems conforming to various sets of rational abstractions not only contained impossibilities in the practice, but also evidenced the extreme vanity of a libertine rationalism.

The quasi-scientific attempts by Descartes and others to explain the complex human being in physical terms of mechanical impulses served to reduce the variety of human nature to a systematic machine. This mechanical conversion of the multiplicity of human reason and emotions (not to mention the soul) into the rigid framework of an abstract principle is often ridiculed by Swift. In one essay, which has been mentioned before for its logical ambiguities, Swift assumes the ironic character of a physician reviewing the results of a debate concerning the precedence between professors of law and physic, and he determines for the latter. The main object of this satire is the effeminacy of any such factional dispute; his principal technique is to arouse "gay contempt" at the argument by reducing the contention to a mechanical and therefore laughable premise. The cornerstone of this satiric structure, however, is the "author's" insistence upon the stomach as the "seat not of honour only, but of most great qualities of the mind." Accordingly, Swift says:

I think I can reduce to this one principle, all the properties of the mind . . . I could here chemico-mechanically resolve men's parts into their feeding, and shew what sort of humours and genius must necessarily proceed from particular sorts of meats, and explain a great deal of the heathen mythology by it; but this I reserve for a treatise by itself.[28]

The chemico-mechanical reduction of human psychology to the physical operation of feeding may be extended to include the larger abstract systems which reduce all mysteries of the universe to one inclusive system. The virtuosi who create these elaborate schemes to comprehend the universe simply project upon the world some subjective scheme concocted by artifice in their own brain without any correspondence with objective reality. Such a virtuoso, for example, was the man who wrote "a small tract about worms, proved them to be in more places than was generally observed, and made some discoveries by glasses." What began with him as a minor tract was then converted by his imagination into a major system of universal explanation:

This having met with some reception, presently the poor man's head was full of nothing but worms; all we eat and drink, all the whole consistence of human bodies . . . in short, all nature throughout was nothing but worms; And, by that system, he solved all difficulties, and from thence all causes in philosophy.[29]

This reduction of philosophy is made humorous by Swift's own description of it in mechanical and physical terms. A less laughable reference to precisely the same kind of contemptible conversion of facts into systematic science is made by Gulliver after his account to the Houyhnhnm king of the use of gunpowder. Swift ironically contemns the "narrow principles and short views" which, he says, must account for the king's remarkable dislike for European warfare; he excuses the king's defective judgment because it must "have risen from their ignorance, they not having hitherto reduced politics into a science, as the more acute wits of Europe have done."[30]

Swift's contempt for the systematic and scientific reduction of life into principles which have no relation to morality, common sense, or the real, physical world, finds its most persistent expression in *A Tale of a Tub*. His contempt for those "great Introducers of new Schemes in Philosophy" who take it into their heads "to advance new Systems with such an eager Zeal, in things agreed on all hands impossible to be known," is developed in some detail in "A Digression on Madness." These scientific philosophers who disdained the "vulgar Dictates of *unrefined* Reason," and whose converting imaginations reduced all nature to some abstract system of their own, must have been insane: "For, what Man in the natural State, or Course of Thinking, did ever conceive it in his Power, to reduce the Notions of all Mankind, exactly to the same Length, and Breadth, and Heighth of his own?"

(p. 166). Yet, Swift goes on, Epicurus and Descartes hoped to see all men concur in their universal explanations of nature. Swift's conception of the "natural state" of man's reason may not have been well-defined, even in his own mind. Or if his view of the natural state of man is reflected in the tameness and uniformity in the social structure of the Houyhnhnms, it is hard to see how it differs from the rigidity of mind which he is attacking here. On the other hand, despite Swift's own affirmative ideals, it is apparent that he negated the scientific uniformity which pretended to explain the deepest mysteries of nature in terms of a single rational but nonempirical system. The absurdity of converting facts into a mathematical system is also included by Swift as one of the "abuses of learning" especially singled out for ridicule. Just as Descartes and Epicurus tried to reduce all philosophy to their own systems, so some philosophers were wont to convert the facts of nature into a system which accorded with some mystical number. Accordingly, Swift, writing as the modern author *par excellence,* insists that he has prepared a dissertation for the press which will prove the number three to be the most mystical of all numbers; to this number he has "not only reduced the *Senses* and the *Elements* under its Banner, but brought over several Deserters from its two great Rivals *SEVEN* and *NINE.*" The basis of this attempt is Swift's ironic intention to imitate the "prudent method" of modern philosophers who

. . . grow fond of some proper mystical Number, which their Imaginations have rendered Sacred, to a Degree, that they force common Reason to find room for it in every part of Nature; reducing, including, and adjusting every *Genus* and *Species* within that Compass, by coupling some against their Wills, and banishing others at any Rate (pp. 57, 58).

The converting imagination molds facts to fit its own concepts. The scientific "reducing, including, and adjusting" of external reality to fit an artificially contrived subjective system may well be likened to the operation of a machine. The procedure lacks the elasticity of mind which characterizes "natural reason"; it operates with a relentless automatism, resembling human thought but differing from it in its rejection of facts which it cannot include within its systematic construction. To employ one's reason with the inflexible automatism of a robot, to couple all possible facts into one's own system and banish or ignore the rest, is to mechanize the mind and, as Swift perceived, is to render it laughable as well as contemptible.

The essential characteristic of this mechanized thought is that by concentrating upon the fabrications of one's own brain instead of looking at nature, one never sees things as they are. According to this kind of thought artifice is substituted for nature, the means for the end, the manner for the matter, the nonessential for the essential. In a sense, the prevailing characteristic of the converting imagination is what we may properly call "misdirection," or an elaborate and artificial missing of the point. Swift concentrates so frequently upon this aspect of the mind's inability to see truth, and often with such gaiety in his contempt, that it may be well to consider it separately.

Misdirection

"Pedantry," Swift once observed, "is properly the overrating any kind of knowledge we pretend to. And if that kind of knowledge be a trifle in itself, the pedantry is the greater; For which reason I look upon fiddlers, dancing masters, heralds, masters of the ceremony, &c. to be greater pedants than Lipsius, or the elder Scaliger."[31] No human knowledge or skill is great or profound enough, Swift reasserts here, to justify man's pride in its possession; man has no adequate method of his own by which he can unlock the secrets of the universe. The absurd incongruity implicit in being vain over trifles, therefore, when the deepest mysteries are still unsolved, contains an essential ingredient of the ridiculous: the chasm between the proud appearance of knowledge and the ignoble reality of being ignorant of what is essential. In addition, Swift perceived that this kind of overrating of trifles was in itself a source of the ridiculous from a somewhat different point of view. For the knowledge which men most value is often composed of the trifling secondary and accidental properties of true knowledge. What roused Swift's resentment, for instance, against professional men more than anything else, it seems, was their tendency to consider the order and procedures of their professions as ends in themselves. In this kind of pedantry, the end for which the profession was established as a means has, by the misdirected energies of its members, been supplanted by the means itself. The satiric and contemptuous gaiety which Swift evokes from this substitution of the means for the end is founded upon the mechanical and laughable automatism of the professional man.

We have seen Swift's distaste for the professional jargon of the law which, he thought, converted criminal practices into the appearance of virtue. Moreover, the law is eminently liable to the ridiculous automatism of misdirection. The comedy attached to the inflexible operation of a law independent of the exigencies of real life has been described by Bergson. In illustrating his thesis that comedy arises from *"something mechanical encrusted on the living,"* and that "any form or formula is a ready-made frame into which the comic element may be fitted," Bergson cites the law as a source of comic automatism:

. . . complete automatism is only reached in the official, for instance, who performs his duty like a mere machine, or again in the unconsciousness that marks an administrative regulation working with inexorable fatality, and setting itself up for a law of nature.[32]

When a judge, as Fielding pointed out much earlier,[33] rejects the spirit of law and dispenses justice according to the lifeless letter of a codified legal system, mistaking "mere form for substance," his automatism becomes ridiculous and the proper subject of satire. To Swift's generalized misanthropy, this misdirection of attention from the real purpose of human law was more than a source of occasional satire. It was his conviction that most, if not all, lawyers were little concerned with the merits of the cause they pleaded: their zeal was transferred to the operation of the law itself. Swift's

constant technique of ridiculing the legal profession consists
in emphasizing this disregard of the proper judicial end. It
is not surprising, therefore, that he thought the finest satire
on lawyers to be one which illustrated the indifference of the
law to justice:

I never heard a finer piece of satire against lawyers, than that of
astrologers, when they pretend, by rules of art, to tell when a suit
will end, and whether to the advantage of the plaintiff or de-
fendant; thus making the matter depend entirely upon the influence of the stars, without the least regards to the merits of the
cause.[34]

Swift's contempt for lawyers is stated with equal directness
in "A Voyage to the Houyhnhnms." In his direct satire
against the legal profession, Swift employs several devices for
which the mechanical indirection of the law serves as the
basis. He reduces his intellectual idea of legal injustice to a
concrete illustration of a neighbor who goes to the law to get
one of Swift's cows; he inverts the assumption of the law's
concern with justice and pursues the logic of the premise
that only injustice can win a trial. But the essential technique
in this passage is Swift's portrayal of the law as existing for
itself and the perpetuation of its own system to the total
neglect of the immediate issues at stake. He thus depicts the
lawyer on the side of justice as being "quite out of his element," and in an awkward position with his colleagues, "as
one that would lessen the practice of the law." The physician
who would keep his patients ill in order to continue the
cure is no different from the lawyer who is more concerned
with the continuity of his profession than with the cause he
is espousing. Instead of inspecting the true issues, the lawyer
bases his judgment upon precedents: "It is a maxim among
these lawyers, that whatever hath been done before, may
legally be done again: and therefore they take special care
to record all the decisions formerly made against common
justice, and the general reason of mankind." The concern
with a system of precedents is one more illustration of legal
misdirection in which an artificial system supplants present

observation. Swift likewise attacks the pleadings of the law, in which, he says,

> . . . they studiously avoid entering into the merits of the cause; but are loud, violent, and tedious in dwelling upon all circumstances which are not to the purpose. For instance, in the case already mentioned: they never desire to know what claim or title my adversary hath to my cow; but whether the said cow were red or black . . . (etc.).[35]

In effect, this satire against the legal profession is, like much of the satire in the final voyage of Gulliver, a direct and unequivocal statement of Swift's own conclusions upon life. Accordingly, the laughter which Bergson indicated could arise from the mechanical operation of legality is here overpowered by the direct intensity of Swift's feelings. In other words, the element of "gaiety" has been overwhelmed by "contempt." A more ironic, detached and, perhaps for that reason, more successful satire upon the automatism of following the letter of a legal code appears in "A Voyage to Lilliput." The Lilliputian queen's aversion to Gulliver's prompt, effective, but illegal action in putting out the palace fire has been converted by some commentators into an allegory of Queen Anne's reception of *A Tale of a Tub*. Whether this or some other ingenious explanation is the proper interpretation is, it seems to me, rather difficult to determine. Moreover, a detailed and particularized allegorical explanation is hardly necessary for our understanding of the central purpose of Swift's satire; whatever precise and specific satire (if any) was intended by Swift, the implications of the general satire are clear enough. Swift has Gulliver describe in meticulous detail the situation leading up to his extinction of the fire with his urine. All other methods had failed; Gulliver had neglected to bring his coat with which he could have extinguished the fire; "the case seemed," he said, "wholly desperate and deplorable; and this magnificent palace would have infallibly burnt down to the ground," if he had not acted immediately. According to the logic of the law, however, Gulliver was judged a traitor and the first article of impeachment against him was on the grounds of his fire-fighting methods. In this first article Swift ridicules the misdirection of a legal code which operates without relation to any larger concern with justice:

Whereas, by a statute made in the reign of his Imperial Majesty Calin Deffar Plune, it is enacted, that whoever shall make water within the precincts of the royal palace, shall be liable to the pains and penalties of high treason; notwithstanding, the said Quinbus Flestrin, in open Breach of the said law, under colour of extinguishing the fire kindled in the apartment of his Majesty's most dear Imperial Consort, did maliciously, traitorously, and devilishly, by discharge of his urine, put out the said fire kindled in the said apartment, lying and being within the precincts of the said royal palace, against the statute in that case provided, *etc.* against the duty, *etc.*[36]

The service of extinguishing the present fire is reduced to insignificance beside the grievous offense against a law enacted in the reign of Emperor Plune.

The inability of the Lilliputians to see the point, their energetic and proud misdirection, has a parallel abuse in men's study of the Bible. Swift persistently satirized many of the prevailing religious beliefs and practices of his day by pointing out that Christianity was no longer accepted in its true and original sense, but that men retained merely the outward forms of worship without grasping the inward purposes for which the forms were established. The *Argument Against Abolishing Christianity* is founded upon this device of assuming that the real purpose of Christianity had been supplanted by new and secondary ones. Accordingly, Swift remarks with fine irony, "I hope no reader imagines me so weak to stand up in the defence of real Christianity, such as used in primitive times (if we may believe the authors of those ages) to have an influence upon men's belief and actions." Instead, Swift points out and defends all the wrong reasons why Christianity should be preserved: it provides men with a God to revile and denounce, and, like *A Tale of a Tub*, thus diverts men's attention from the state; it is useful to keep children quiet, its clergy increase the population, and other equally ironic reasons for its preservation.[37] In this conception of Christianity, religion becomes a mechanical instrument; it loses its relation to the immediacies of life and its proper purposes are subverted by the operation of secondary characteristics. The same blindness which obscures from men the true purpose of the Christian religion makes them approach the Bible from every angle except that of Christian belief. One of Swift's many points of departure against the freethinkers was his belief that their pride in their own knowledge led them to misdirect their attention from the central purpose of the Bible to the mechanics of their own hyperrationalism. Writing in the ironic pose of a freethinker and apologist for Anthony Collins, Swift argues that the Bible

> . . . is the most difficult book in the world to be understood; it requires a thorough knowledge in natural, civil, ecclesiastical, history, law, husbandry, sailing, physic, pharmacy, mathematics, metaphysics, ethics, and everything else that can be named.

The central satiric technique in this passage is, obviously, the satiric catalogue; but the informing logic of this ironic attack upon freethinking is misdirection. The freethinking bishop who "allows the Scriptures to be so difficult, that God has left them rather as a trial of our industry than a repository of our faith,"[38] uses the Bible as an exercise book for his own faculties. The comic element resides in an overevaluation of one's own knowledge so complete that all sense of original purpose is lost in a morass of trivia. The insistence that the Bible should be read for every reason other than piety and as a source of religious authority finds an ironic expression in Swift's *Letter of Advice to a Young Poet*. He recommends that the young man read the Scriptures, but, he adds,

> I intend nothing less than imposing upon you a task of piety. Far be it from me to desire you to believe them, or lay any great stress upon their authority . . . but to read them as a piece of necessary furniture for a wit and a poet; which is a very different view from that of a Christian.

Here the Bible is ironically equated with a mechanical object, furniture: the lessons of Christianity are no longer valid means to fulfill their real purpose of reforming or guiding action and morals. Instead, they have been converted into an artificial system which supplies wit to the courtier and allusions to the poet. Without this mechanical aid to poetry, Swift says, modern poetry would expire, and the poets, therefore, "abound" as much with the phrases of the Bible as do the divines: "They have read them historically, critically, musically, comically, poetically, and every other way except religiously, and have found their account in doing so."[39]

From the relatively simple irony of these attacks upon misdirection to the more complicated allegory of *A Tale of a Tub* is but a short distance. Swift's ironic negation of the idea that Christianity should "have an influence upon men's beliefs and actions" affirmed his anger with the freethinkers who misdirected their attention to the Bible for other reasons. Swift was equally contemptuous of the religious enthusiasts who sought to find in the Bible a systematic explanation and guide for every aspect of human conduct. Under the allegory of the will, Swift asserts his basic premise that "it consisted wholly in certain plain, easy Directions about the management and wearing of their Coats, with Legacies and Penalties, in case of Obedience or Neglect." But the "converting imagination" of Peter sought to find deeper meanings in these simple and explicit rules. The lawyer who transfers his concern from the purpose of law to the law itself and considers the legal code to be a law of nature has been said to mechanize the legal profession; in the same way, the Dissenters who have a "superstitious veneration for the Bible" and attempt to bring all nature and every event in their own lives within its compass may, also, be said to mechanize religion. Good sense gives way to the rigidity of mind which no longer perceives distinctions; the Bible as a means to guide one's conduct becomes an end in itself, a final statement of all law. With this conception of the mechanical application of the Bible to "the most necessary, as well as the most paltry Occasions of Life" Swift proceeds to consider the Bible as a *thing,* useful for a nightcap, umbrella, for the relief of sore toes and other physical properties.[40]

The conversion of the judicial purposes of the law results in an artificial contrivance operating, so to speak, under its own steam for the sake of filling its own boilers: the "mechanizing" of the Bible converts it into a vehicle for extraneous purposes instead of its proper employment as a guide to conduct. In other scholarship and learning, too, Swift found ample evidence of the misdirection of the converting imagination. Insight into Swift's views of the proper ethical approach to learning is given without satire in *A Letter to a Young Gentleman:*

If a rational man reads an excellent author with just application, he shall find himself extremely improved, and perhaps insensibly led to imitate that author's perfections, although in a little time he should not remember one word in the book, nor even the subject it handled: for books give the same turn to our thoughts and way of reasoning, that good and ill company do to our behavior and conversation; without either loading our memories, or making us even sensible of the change.[41]

This is a good statement of the classical emphasis upon the "formative" power of knowledge. Like religion, all secular knowledge is useful and admirable only in proportion to its capacity to influence and control the thinking and reactions of its possessor. Knowledge, then, is a means to the furthering of moral action. When the accumulation of facts or the wise sayings of others becomes an end in itself without direct relevance to one's own thinking and behaviour, erudition is lifeless and learning turns into the machinery of artifice:

Whoever only reads in order to transcribe wise and shining remarks, without entering into the genius and spirit of the author, as it is probable he will make no very judicious extract, so he will be apt to trust to that collection in all his compositions, and be misled out of the regular way of thinking, in order to introduce those materials, which he has been at the pains to gather.[42]

When one's reason is "advanced, indeed, but not overlaid by commerce with books," the mind is free to act with the mobility which good sense requires; the mere transcription of the learned matter of knowledge is a mechanical process rigid in its operation and fruitless in its results.

In *A Tale of a Tub,* Swift ridicules modern learning by illustrating that the modern's knowledge derived from being "plentifully instructed, by a long Course of useful Study in *Prefaces* and *Prologues.*"[43] Not at all concerned with the "genius and spirit of the author," such a reader carries away only the appearance of learning. The misdirection of the mind away from the body of the book and into the preface was carried, Swift says, to its logical extreme by Dryden, whose reputation rests not upon his works but his prefaces:

Our Great *Dryden* has long carried it as far as it would go, and with incredible Success. He has often said to me in Confidence, that the World would have never suspected him to be so great a Poet, if he had not assured them so frequently in his Prefaces, that it was impossible they could either doubt or forget it.[44]

There is a double satire here; on the one hand the implicit vanity of Dryden's assurance and on the other the mechanical judgment of the world which bases its critical pronouncements upon the insistence of the author rather than upon the true merit of his worth.

A different technique used by Swift to ridicule the exaggerated emphasis upon accidental properties of books was to insist upon their bulk and size in contrast to their quality and merit. Swift suggests that he should describe in his own preface a domestic misfortune which "would also be of great Assistance towards extending this Preface into the Size now in Vogue, which by Rule ought to be *large* in proportion as the subsequent Volume is *small.*" Swift's contempt for the inclusion of domestic misfortune in a preface to a work purporting to increase knowledge is as great, perhaps, as his disdain for the bulk. The misdirection which Swift employs to ridicule the size of prefaces is sometimes transferred to the book itself. Thus, Swift challenges his *"Rivals"* to a comparison of their several productions in *"Weight* and *Number,"* and quotes his bookseller who, when "he had manifestly considered the two Principal Things, which were the *Bulk,* and the *Subject,*" said the book would probably never *"take"* that year.[45] Underlying this whole technique of misdirection is a use of false logic which Swift is illustrating by concrete example. The natural reason inspects a production on its merits and concludes it to be good or bad; the mechanical and rigid mind inspects the preface, or the bulk of the preface or book, to determine the worth of the whole book. In other words, this mechanical logic runs something like this: great books are usually long and bulky; this book is long and bulky; *ergo*, this is a great book. Or, again: only a great book deserves a lengthy preface; this book has a very lengthy preface; *ergo*, this is a very great book.[46]

The humorous automatism of this kind of mental rigidity may be illustrated, finally, by a short passage from the *Memoirs of Martinus Scriblerus*, which, from the humour of its misdirection, suggests the influence if not the actual writing of Swift. The determination of the quality of a book by the preface or the quantity of pages is mirrored in the logic of assuming accidental qualities of genius to be fundamental and primary. So we see Cornelius, the proud father of Martin Scriblerus,

infinitely pleas'd to find, that the Child had the Wart of Cicero, the wry Neck of Alexander, knots upon his legs like Marius, and one of them shorter than the other like Agesilaus. The good Cornelius also hoped he would come to stammer like Demosthenes, in order to be as eloquent; and in time arrive at many other Defects of famous men.[47]

The causal connection of writing in bulk "in order to" produce a great book is exactly the same as stammering "in order to" be as eloquent as Demosthenes. In both cases, the mind is turned from a precise and honest examination of the external subject matter to the secondary properties.

V

The Triumph of Artifice

Art versus Nature

Of the many ways in which men's awareness is misdirected from what is essential to what is nonessential, the false emphasis upon the artifice of methods and schemes is, in Swift's satire, among the most prominent. Both directly and obliquely through parody, logic, and allegory, Swift reduces the substitution of art for nature to the ridiculous and contemptible. The inflexibility and blind precipitance of method and artifice when separated from the natural ends to which they should work may be readily seen to resemble the mechanical efficiency and unawareness of a machine. It is not surprising, therefore, to find that Bergson defined the "very quintessence of pedantry" as "nothing else than art pretending to outdo nature."[1] A similar distinction between natural process and the artificial creation of man's brain is made by Swift as the basic premise in *The Mechanical Operation of the Spirit* for ridiculing the enthusiasm of fanatic preachers:

. . . I desire the curious Reader to distinguish, First between an Effect grown from *Art* into *Nature,* and one that is natural from its Beginning; Secondly, between an Effect wholly natural, and one which has only a natural Foundation, but where the Superstructure is entirely Artificial. For, the first and last of these, I understand to come within the Districts of my Subject.[2]

The trenchancy and humour of this satire derives largely from Swift's remarkable talent for reducing an intellectual

concept to a physical and mechanical operation. Instead of
criticizing directly the beliefs and practices of the Puritans,
Swift concentrates upon the physical artificiality of their
enthusiasm. Thus, he distinguishes the *"Enthusiasm"* which
transports the soul above matter as being either *"Possession"*
(from the devil), *"Inspiration"* (from God), "natural" (from
the excess of violent emotion), and, fourthly, "the Method
of *Religious Enthusiasm,* or launching out of the Soul, as . . .
an Effect of Artifice and *Mechanick Operation."* This last
kind of enthusiasm, which is not "an Effect of Nature" but
"wholly an Effect of Art" created by *"British Workmen"*
(pp. 268-269), is then ridiculed for its methodology and artifice. This same technique informs many of Swift's other
satires with the combined gaiety and contempt which we
have seen to be a neoclassic satiric ideal. The distinction
which Swift makes here between art and nature, his perception of the ridiculous incongruity of the former's mechanical
precedence over the latter, and his embodiment of this incongruity in his satire is certainly one of his unique contributions
to the art of gay contempt.

"There is a pedantry in manners, as in all arts and
sciences," Swift wrote in *A Treatise on Good Manners and
Good Breeding,* and his depiction of the pedantry of artificial ceremony is a clear account of the distinction between
art and nature upon which *The Mechanical Operation of
the Spirit* is founded. The essay is a direct attack upon the
"bigotry of forms" which leads men to substitute the "artificial good sense" of ceremonies for the purpose which they
were intended to serve. "Good manners is," Swift says, "the
art of making those people easy with whom we converse,"
and "good sense is the principal foundation of good manners."
For those without good sense, it is necessary to fix certain
rules of behaviour which will guide their conduct, but when
these artificial ceremonies are multiplied for their own sake
good manners degenerate into "ridiculous accidents."

I have seen a duchess fairly knocked down, by the precipitancy
of an officious coxcomb running to save her the trouble of opening a door. I remember, upon a birthday at court, a great lady

was utterly desperate by a dish of sauce let fall by a page directly upon her head-dress and brocade, while she gave a sudden turn to her elbow upon some point of ceremony with the person who sat next her.[3]

The absurdity of an artificial method taking precedence over the purpose for which the method was initially designed is as ridiculous in the pedantry of learning as in that of manners. The simple misdirection which makes men judge books by their bulk or their prefaces becomes even more absurd and laughable when it is converted into a method of learning; similarly, the usefulness of indices and abstracts intended as an aid in reading degenerates quickly into the ridiculous when they are converted into a systematic substitute for learning. In *A Tale of a Tub,* one of Swift's most persistent techniques of satirizing Bentley and "modern" writers in general was to emphasize the extent to which artificial methods of learning had supplanted the natural. Accordingly, Swift promises a work called *"My New Help of Smatterers* or the *Art of being Deep-learned, and Shallow-read"* (p. 130), and Swift praises his own prudent methodology in contrast to the "natural" learning of the ancients:

. . . we of this Age have discovered a shorter, and more prudent Method, to become *Scholars* and *Wits,* without the fatigue of *Reading* or of *Thinking.* The most accomplisht Way of using Books at present, is twofold: Either first, to serve them as some Men do *Lords,* learn their *Titles* exactly, and then brag of their Acquaintance. Or Secondly, which is indeed the choicer, the profounder, and politer Method, to get a thorough Insight into the *Index* by which the whole Book is governed and turned, like *Fishes* by the *Tail.*

Swift then concludes that the numbers of writers must have increased greatly, "Now the Method of growing Wise, Learned, and *Sublime,* having become so regular an Affair, and so established in all its Forms" (pp. 144-145, 146).

Similarly, in *A Letter of Advice to a Young Poet* Swift ridicules modern learning by concentrating upon its artful methodology which supplants the natural purposes of study. In this essay he tells the young poet that it is not "a very severe task, to arrive at a competent knowledge" of the ancients, although, he adds,

. . . it would be really so, but for the short and easy method lately found out of abstracts, abridgements, summaries, &c. which are admirable expedients for being very learned with little or no reading . . . And to this is nearly related that other modern device of consulting indexes . . .

In the same essay Swift translates this glorification of method into a comparison between the physical methods of poets and those of tradesmen. The comparison is invidious not only because of the generally accepted prejudice against commercial persons, but especially because of its concrete assertion of the mechanics of poor poetry. In comparing the "business of a poet" with that of a shoemaker, Swift shows that the poet's "stock of similes," like the shoemaker's lasts, should be "sized, and ranged, and hung up in order in his shop, ready for all customers, and shaped to the feet of all sorts of verse."[4] This depreciation of modern poets by equating them with tradesmen vending physical wares is also employed in *A Tale of a Tub*. Thus Swift ridicules the True Critic as "a sort of Mechanick, set up with a Stock and Tools for his Trade" (p. 101), and, in *The Mechanical Operation of the Spirit,* he suggests the connection of religious enthusiasm with mechanical artifice:

Therefore, I am resolved immediately, to weed this Error out of Mankind, by making it clear, that this Mystery, of vending spiritual Gifts is nothing but a *Trade,* acquired by as much Instruction, and mastered by equal Practice and Application as others are.[5]

The device of ridiculing modern scholarship by pointing out the mechanics of its methodology is carried by Swift into other fields. A good illustration appears in his "Introduction" to a *Compleat Collection of Genteel and Ingenious Conversation* in which he continually emphasizes the mechanical "art of conversation" for which the treatise was intended as a manual. By furnishing wits with a scientifically prepared treasury of "at least a thousand shining questions, answers, repartees, replies, and rejoinders, fitted to adorn every kind of discourse," Swift assures every aspiring wit that if he learns them by rote he will never be "once at a loss in applying the right answers, questions, repartees, and the like, immediately, and without study or hesitation." This introduction is as penetrating a satire upon "polite" conversation as the treatise itself, and its principal satiric force and humour arises from its reiterated assumption that polite talk is a "science" governed by "essential rules" and that the successful practitioner of this art needs only a strong memory and a grasp of the methods of talk to shine in company.[6] By reducing polite conversation to the art of being deeply witty and shallow read Swift reduces the proper fluidity of social conversation into a rigid, mechanical pattern. The gaiety of Swift's contempt for the unthinking clichés and frigid wit of polite company is conveyed principally by his depiction of its mechanical operation.

To remove such examples from their context for the purpose of description and analysis is not, of course, to imply that the relevant devices operate singly or exclusively. In fact, few of Swift's devices of ridicule (if we except such a broadly inclusive category as irony) can properly be considered by themselves. But we should note the extent to which Swift's concern with the flexible operation of the "natural" reason tended to express itself in the ridicule of all mechanical thought and behaviour. Affectation, whether in manners, learning, wit or anything else, is, in its rigid refusal to see and abide by things as they are, essentially artificial and mechanical; and Swift employed many devices to make this machinery of the mind both ridiculous and self-evident. A corollary device to his satire upon methodized wit and learning is his complete separation of the method from its intended purpose. Abstracts and compendiums as well as clichés have some direct relevance to the subject they mimic. They create gaiety by showing men methodically missing the point. Swift sometimes reduces the artifice of method to an even greater absurdity by supposing methods which have no conceivable relation to their purpose. The appearance of mechanism which makes misdirected learning ridiculous in itself is here translated literally into a physical or mechanical device of learning. The Academy of Lagado furnishes us with several examples of this technique. The "first professors" seen by Gulliver in that school were "employed in a project for improving speculative knowledge by practical and mechanical operations":

Every one knew how laborious the usual method is of attaining to arts and sciences; whereas, by his contrivance, the most ignorant person at a reasonable charge, and with a *little bodily labour,* may write books in philosophy, poetry, politics, law, mathematics, and theology, without the least assistance from genius or study.[7]

Gulliver then describes this "wonderful machine" and "engine" of learning in all the intricacies of its mechanical operation. The reduction of an intellectual problem into a "little bodily labour" is ridicule at its most effective. Swift's contempt for intellectual short cuts is here masked under the detached gaiety of his technique of expressing it: we contemn the satiric object but we laugh at the mechanical artifice of the projector. Other projects with a similar intent and founded upon the same satiric device are the elaborate mechanical method of "artificial converse" and the artificial method of learning mathematics:

The proposition and demonstration were fairly written on a thin wafer, with ink composed of a cephalic tincture. This the student was to swallow upon a fasting stomach . . . As the wafer digested, the tincture mounted to his brain, bearing the proposition along with it.[8]

Evidence of Swift's hand in the *Memoirs of Martinus Scriblerus* is suggested by a similar scheme of Cornelius for teaching his young prodigy Greek:

But what most conduced to his easy attainment of this Language was his love of Ginger-bread; which his Father observing, caused it to be stampt with the Letters of the Greek Alphabet; and the child the very first day eat as far as Iota.[9]

Unlike the young Scriblerus, however, the Laputans were unable to hold the wafer in their stomachs, and the project came to no fortunate conclusion.

Swift shared with many of his contemporaries an abiding distrust of all "projectors"—those "men of vision" who elaborated schemes for the "universal benefit of mankind." And one of Swift's characteristic methods of demonstrating the vacuity and impertinence of panacean "bubbles" was to focus upon the ironic contradiction between the appearance of free will and what he pretends to be the reality of a merely physical determinism. If schemes are absurd because of their artifice, schemers are equally ridiculous because of the "unnatural" and mechanical springs of their action. The tragic irony of Sophocles develops out of the disparity between the appearance of man's freedom to act and the reality of man's subjection to cosmic forces which have determined his situation. Swift's comic irony sets up a similar incongruity between appearance and reality; but instead of positing the cosmic forces of fate Swift reduces man's determining factor to some mechanical operation within the mind itself. "Comedy," as James Feibleman has said, "becomes the avoidance of the terrible outcome of the events which were threatened in tragedy . . . The difference between them relies merely on an exposure of the fact that power is not what at first it was supposed to be."[10] Swift deprives the event of having "power" not, however, by changing the "terrible outcome" so much as by shifting his focus to the causes. Instead of diminishing what Plato called the "hateful" and "detestable" quality of dangerous effects, Swift frequently ridicules effects by demonstrating the ludicrousness of the determining causes. How early in his writing career he recognized the satiric possibilities of diminishing important political events to a level of concealed machinery is suggested by his "Ode to Sir William Temple," written possibly as early as 1689:

> The wily Shafts of State, those Juggler's Tricks
> Which we call deep Design and Politicks
> (As in a Theatre the Ignorant Fry,
> Because the Cords escape their Eye

> Wonder to see the Motions fly)
> Methinks, when you expose the Scene,
> Down the ill-organ'd Engines fall;
> Off fly the Vizards and discovers all,
> How plain I see thro' the Deceit!
> How shallow! and how gross the Cheat!
> Look when the pully's ty'd above!
> Great God! (said I) what have I seen!
> On what poor Engines move
> The Thoughts of Monarchs, and Designs of States!
> What petty Motives rule their Fates![11]

The poetry is, perhaps, not distinguished but the passage is significant as an early statement of the idea that by the exposure of mechanism beneath the deceit of appearances the object is made contemptible.

In *A Tale of a Tub,* this device is the pivot around which Swift develops his satire on the French king, Henry IV. In "A Digression on Madness," after describing the ranging conquests of a "certain Great Prince" Swift concludes that they were all caused by a rush of vapours to the head. He then asks:

What secret Wheel, what hidden Spring could put into Motion so wonderful an Engine? It was afterwards discovered, that the Movement of this whole Machine had been directed by an absent *Female,* whose Eyes had raised a Protuberancy, and before Emission, she was removed into an Enemy's Country (pp. 163-164).

Swift arouses the comic and satiric spirit not by diminishing the terrible effects of warfare but by disgracing the cause which motivated the conqueror. The prince is conceived of as a machine operated by physical vapours which, if they proceeded to his head, might make him a conqueror, but which also, if they proceeded downward, might cause him to leave the world in peace. Mechanistic determinism, thus allied with the associations of sexual frustration, strips all nobility from the act of conquest and, in the process, arouses laughter as well as contempt.

This careful and panegyrical investigation into the mechanical causes of conquest, new religions, and new schemes of philosophy is an example, developed in detail, of what

Swift called in the "Introduction" a "Physico-logical Scheme." Swift applies the phrase to the three kinds of "Oratorial Machines" which he deduces were erected in order to give men their desired "Eminency":

Now this Physico-logical Scheme of Oratorial Receptacles or Machines, contains a great Mystery, being a Type, a Sign, an Emblem, a Shadow, a Symbol, bearing Analogy to the spacious Commonwealth of Writers, and to those Methods by which they must exalt themselves to a certain Eminency above the inferiour World (p. 61).

The multiple levels of satiric objective which exist simultaneously in many passages of *A Tale of a Tub* also complicate this scheme. In the passage just quoted, the catalogue of similes for "analogy" indicate that Swift's development of the "Oratorial Machines" and his subsequent identification of their allegorical meaning is a satiric parody on all excessive mystification. Moreover, the progress of the logical proof—as well as the "hiatus" in the manuscript with its accompanying footnote—support the conclusion that Swift is using an elaborate method to satirize all elaborate methods. A similar hiatus appears in the midst of Swift's intricate logical deduction of vapours as a cause of madness and is prefaced by exaggerated praise for his dialectical skill:

The present Argument is the most abstracted that ever I engaged in, it strains my Faculties to their highest Stretch; and I desire the Reader to attend with the utmost Perpensity; for, I now proceed to unravel this knotty Point.

The hiatus which follows is footnoted so that the satire against "metaphysical cobweb problems" is given a direct and immediate application (p. 170). It is evident that Swift's description of rhetorical machines serves a triple purpose: by parody it satirizes any exaggerated emphasis upon allegory and symbolism, and the absurdity of its own logic parodies all other overrefined and difficult reasoning; but the scheme is also a distinct method of ridiculing by mechanical analogy. In his scheme of "Oratorial Machines" the primary focus of Swift's attention is shifted from the mental mechanism of the orators to the physical mechanism of the pulpit, the ladder, and the stage. He first defines the physical nature of the three machines and then, by analogy, associates them with divines, poets, and comic writers. The pulpit, for instance, is described as being of Scotch wood and the better for being rotten and therefore resonant; the pulpit is then used by Swift as a symbol for fanatic preachers who, like their pulpits, are often Scotch, rotten (therefore give light) and worm-eaten. The mechanism of the machines is thus transferred to the orators. As a technique of "disgust educing pleasure," this physico-logical scheme of mechanical explanation is eminently successful. For it enables Swift both to reduce his satiric objects to a dependency upon mechanism, and at the same time, by disgracing the machine itself, to ridicule the object. The identity between poetry and the hangman's ladder not only makes the poet dependent upon the machine for his fame but also equates all poets with thieves and other confounders of *meum* and *teum* who deserve hanging.

The correspondence between the "oratorial machines" and the orators themselves is, in this physico-logical scheme, deduced by analogy. A complete and unsymbolic identification of the mechanical with the human is made by Swift in his occasional satire upon fashions in dress. According to the system of the "Grand Monde" the tailor "did daily create Men, by a kind of Manufactory Operation" (p. 76), and Swift confounds the distinction between appearance and reality: clothes are no longer "artificial charms," as Scriblerus said, which conceal beneath them "a forked stradling Animal, with bandy legs, a short neck, a dun hide, and a pot belly."[12] Instead, clothes have become the total reality: artifice does not conceal nature but, like the artificial inception of fanaticism described in *The Mechanical Operation of the Spirit*, what began as artifice has turned into nature. Appearance has become reality and the dignity of man is reduced to a manufactory operation of a tailor:

'Tis true indeed, that these Animals, which are vulgarly called *Suits of Cloaths,* or *Dresses,* do according to certain Compositions

receive different Appellations. If one of them be trimm'd up with
a Gold Chain, and a red Gown, and a white Rod, and a great
Horse, it is called a *Lord Mayor;* If certain Ermins and Furs be
placed in a certain Position, we stile them a *Judge,* and so, an
apt Conjunction of Lawn and black Sattin, we entitle a *Bishop*
(p. 79).

Swift's varied means of diminishing the vain dignity of man
—and this diminution lies at the heart of the satiric muse—
included no method more effective than his reduction of
nature to mechanical artifice. The schemes, projects, and
systems which he ascribed to others or deduced for himself
not only succeeded as vehicles for the objective impersonality
of "situational satire"; they also were basic devices by which
he could elicit laughter as well as contempt by depriving
man of his humanity and reducing him to the inelasticity of
machinery.

An incidental device by which Swift elicits laughter
through the suggestion of man's physical mechanism is found
in his reiterated comparison of the body and mind to a
"vessel" filled with the "furniture" of ideas. In *A Tale of a
Tub,* for example, Swift plays upon "vessel" by means of a
pun, in one instance, which implies a correspondence between
the pulpit of decayed and Scotch wood and the heads of
the congregation; the pulpit, Swifts remarks parenthetically,
"ought to be the only uncovered *Vessel* in every Assembly
where it is rightfully used" (p. 58). The obvious suggestion
is that the *other* vessels, that is, the heads, should be covered.
A similar reference is found in Swift's physical derivation
of the word as it appears in the Biblical phrases, ". . . he is
a chosen vessel unto me," and ". . . God . . . endured with
much long-suffering the vessels of wrath fitted to destruction."[13] Swift deflates this metaphor by explaining its origin
in the extreme methods pursued by the Aeolists to blow "up
each other to the Shape and Size of a *Tun*" (p. 153). The
same scatological diminution of man to a vessel filled with
excrement is repeated a few pages later (p. 156), and the
analogy appears twice more in *The Mechanical Operation
of the Spirit* (pp. 283, 288). A like suggestion is conveyed

early in *A Tale of a Tub* when Swift mythologizes the parable of the whale and the "empty tub": the latter, of which Swift's whole satire is an elaborate parody, is said to represent schemes "whereof a great many are hollow, and dry, and empty, and noisy, and wooden, and given to Rotation" (p. 40). The effect of this reiterated correspondence is to add one more subtle level of physical and mechanical diminution; the connotations of a vessel or tub correspond to Swift's own view of modern learning, and the vessel becomes a concrete symbol of all the noisy vacuity of modern religious and intellectual productions.

A similar indirect suggestion of man as a machine occurs in Swift's almost symbolic use of "furniture" to imply stock methods of thought and general mental rigidity. The whole distinction so carefully preserved in Swift's mind between the natural reason and artificial reason operating mechanically by art and method seems to have been symbolized by this word. The connotations of clutter, triviality, bric-a-brac, fixity, and the like which attend the word "furniture" are transferred to the artificial methodology of the irrational man. It is characteristic of Swift, therefore, that the poem which begins:

> A Set of Phrases learn't by Rote;
> A Passion for a Scarlet-Coat,

should be entitled: "The Furniture of a Woman's Mind."[14] The associations of "furniture" with an immobile irrationality are expanded in *A Letter of Advice to a Young Poet* to a simile between a trading pedlar and the work of a "painful and judicious editor of the classics":

Every author by his management, sweats under himself, being overloaded with his own index, and carries, like a north-country pedlar, all his substance and furniture upon his back, and with as great a variety of trifles.[15]

In addition to the effects of Swift's elaborate method of physical diminution by "physico-logical" schemes in *A Tale of a Tub*, there is also a strong impression of human mechanism created by his frequent and incidental references to the mind as a thing of brute matter. To these allusions Swift's metaphorical use of "furniture" is closely allied. Not only does Swift equate the mind with a "vessel," but he also imbrutes the mind in such references as to the *"Impedimenta Literarum"* (p. 19) of Wotton's wit; he deplores his own imagination which made a tour of his invention and returned empty because the latter was "wholly drained by the following Treatise" (p. 42); he refers to Peter's brain which violently *"shook* itself, and began to turn round for a little Ease" (p. 114), to Jack as "a Person whose Intellectuals were overturned, and his Brain shaken out of its Natural Position" (p. 162), and to Wotton whose "Brain hath undergone an unlucky Shake" (p. 169). The persistence and repetition of this technique of materializing the mind results in depriving the objects of his satire of all natural humanity; it is a principal method of arousing that "anaesthesia of the heart" which permits us to laugh *at* a person so long as we do not sympathize *with* him. So we find Swift asking, when Jack is annoyed at being mistaken for Peter, "How could it avoid having terrible Effects upon a Head and Heart so furnished as his?" (p. 199). Here, the word "furnished" is, in its context, an admirable instance of a proper word in a proper place. For it returns the reader at once to Swift's central idea of the inflexible and mechanical inelasticity of mind which accompanies all frenzied religious fanaticism. Elsewhere in the satire, Swift fuses the immobile connotations of "furniture" with the ignoble connotations of lower animals; thus, for instance Swift ridicules the production of "second parts" as being "the *Furniture of an Ass,* in the Shape of a *Second Part*" (p. 184; cf. p. 16). This incidental device of dwelling upon the mind and its productions by allusions to vessels, furniture, and similar material props is a minor part of Swift's larger technique of satirizing the mechanical operation of the mind.

The Puppet Symbol

Pope's contemptuous dismissal of Hervey as speaking with "florid impotence" has been mentioned as a characteristic example of diminution. The conclusion of the couplet—"and as the prompter breathes, the puppet squeaks"—is a compact instance of another technique that Swift used as frequently as did Pope. The dehumanizing of an idea or human situation to a level of a physically determined mechanism finds its parallel in this device. There is potential comedy in any personal description which so exaggerates a posture, or gesture, or other physical attributes that one's sense of the natural mobility of man is supplanted by a distinct impression of his physical artificiality. Bergson's thesis is again directly applicable to Swift:

The attitudes, gestures and movements of the human body are laughable in exact proportion as that body reminds us of a mere machine . . . [a portrait] is comic in proportion to the clearness, as well as the subtleness, with which it enables us to see a man as a jointed puppet.[16]

In "The Puppet Show," a poem included by Faulkner in Swift's *Works* published in 1762, is a sustained example of this kind of ridicule:

> The Life of Man to represent
> And turn it all to Ridicule,
> Wit did a *Puppet-Show* invent,
> Where the Chief-Actor is a fool.
>
> . . . .
>
> Some draw our Eyes by being Great,
> False Pomp conceals mere Wood within,
> And Legislators rang'd in State
> Are oft but Wisdom in Machine.
>
> A Stock may chance to wear a Crown,
> And Timber as a Lord take Place,
> A Statue may put on a Frown
> And cheat us with a thinking Face.
>
> Others are blindly led away,
> And made to act for Ends unknown,
> By the mere Spring of Wires they play
> And speak in Language not their own.[17]

Harold Williams cites evidence to demonstrate the doubtful authenticity of the poem; but the extended puppet conceit,

as well as other internal evidence, suggests strongly that if
Swift did not write the poem himself he at least had a hand
in its composition. Regardless of this particular poem's
validity in the canon of Swift, we find ample illustrations
of similar reductions of man to a "jointed puppet" elsewhere
in his works. In his *Preface to the B——P of S——M's Introduction,* Swift draws a neat and telling analogy between
Bishop Burnet's introduction in relation to the promised
main work and the conduct of a puppet show:

> I have seen the same sort of management at a puppet-show. Some
> puppets of little or no consequence appeared several times at the
> window to allure the boys and the rabble: The trumpeter sounded
> often, and the doorkeeper cried a hundred times till he was
> hoarse, that they were just going to begin; yet after all, we were
> forced sometimes to wait an hour before Punch himself in person
> made his entry.[18]

The passage marks the conclusion of a brilliant series of
diminishing comparisons and allusions, and it fulfills its
function of ridicule with a vivid concreteness. But Swift's
use of the mechanical connotations of the puppet is at its
most effective when applied directly to persons. We have
already seen how his reaction to the false appearance given to
women by cosmetics and other devices led him to attack the
mechanical artifice of such deceits: the appearance is all art
that conceals the ugly reality of human physical imperfection.
In "Strephon and Chloe" Swift varies this approach by presenting the analogy of a puppet master concealing the
machinery of his dolls beneath the beauty of their robes:

> Why is a handsome Wife ador'd
> By ev'ry Coxcomb, but her Lord?
> From yonder Puppet-Man inquire,
> Who wisely hides his Wood and Wire;
> Shews *Sheba's* Queen completely drest,
> And *Solomon* in Royal Vest;
> But, view them littered on the Floor,
> Or strung on Pegs behind the Door;
> *Punch* is exactly of a Piece
> With *Lorraine's* Duke, and Prince of *Greece.*[19]

The spirited but on the whole coolly detached comedy of wit created in *A Tale of a Tub* by the mechanical schemes is supported and encouraged by Swift's concentration upon physical posturing. In fact, the puppetlike postures and the schemes often coalesce. So, for example, Swift presents a purely physical scheme by which his readers can understand his book:

Whatever Reader desires to have a thorow Comprehension of an Author's Thoughts, cannot take a better Method, than by putting himself into the Circumstances and Postures of Life, that the Writer was in, upon every important Passage as it flow'd from his Pen; For this will introduce a Parity and strict Correspondence of Idea's between the Reader and the Author (p. 44).

Swift then explains that to imitate his own posture, the reader must himself retire to a garret, sharpen his invention with hunger, and take a "long course of Physic." Similarly, Peter's project for remedying worms consists not of a mechanical or chemical contrivance, but a series of absurd postures:

The patient was to eat nothing after Supper for three Nights: as soon as he went to Bed, he was carefully to lye on one Side, and when he grew weary, to turn upon the other: He must also duly confine his two Eyes to the same Object; and by no means break Wind at both Ends together, without manifest Occasion. These Prescriptions diligently observed, the *Worms* would void insensibly by Perspiration, ascending thro' the *Brain* (p. 107).

In addition to the logical absurdity inherent in advising the patient to behave normally and the mechanized conception of the brain, the laughter of this passage arises from the visual image of the patient's physical positions.

Witty support is given to Swift's physico-logical scheme of "oratorial" machines by his description of the posture of the assemblies gathered to hear the orators. Swift conjectures that because words are weighty and have gravity and must, therefore, fall, a *"superiour Position of Place"* is necessary for the orator. He supports this deduction from his own personal observation that the hearers always stand

. . . with their Mouths open, and erected parallel to the Horizon, so as they may be intersected by a perpendicular Line from the

Zenith to the Center of the Earth. In which Position, if the Audience be well compact, every one carries home a Share, and little or nothing is lost (pp. 60-61).

To the physical immobility conveyed by this description may be contrasted the violent and extreme distortions of face and body which Swift frequently emphasizes in describing zealots in learning and religion. Swift reduces the "great Characteristick" of the Aeolists to "a certain Position of Countenance" caused by the sour belches of vapour which "distorted the Mouth, bloated the Cheeks, and gave the Eyes a terrible kind of *Relievo*" (p. 154). He describes their preaching by a scatological description of their "Posture" which the preacher assumes ("you behold him swell immediately to the Shape and Size of his *Vessel*") before he "disembogues whole Tempests upon his Auditory."

And the *Wind* in breaking forth, deals with his Face, as it does with that of the Sea; first *blackning*, then *wrinkling*, and at last, *bursting it into a Foam*. It is in this Guise, the Sacred *Aeolist* delivers his oracular *Belches* to his panting Disciples (p. 156).

The description of a preacher swelling to the size and shape of the vessel of his pulpit is used as a device to describe the absurd posturing of the spider in *The Battle of the Books*. Swift introduces the spider as being "swollen up to the first Magnitude, by the Destruction of infinite Numbers of *Flies*"; after the bee's accidental assault upon the cobweb, the spider "stormed and swore like a Mad-man, and swelled till he was ready to burst"; and, finally, the spider "having swelled himself into the Size and Posture of a Disputant, began his Argument . . ." (pp. 229, 230). Swift's description of the absurd postures of the spider and the often scatological positions of the Aeolists is closely paralleled by his account of *The Mechanical Operation of the Spirit*. The *"Phenomenon of Spiritual Mechanism"* is described by Swift as an artificially produced series of gestures and movements of the body. The "Method" by which the assembly arouses the *"Spirit"* in them is reiterated by Swift so frequently in three pages that the physical posture of the audience is indelibly

impressed upon the reader's visual imagination: the hearers'
eyes must be "in the Posture of one, who endeavors to keep
himself awake"; when the eyes have been "disposed according
to Art" the body makes a "perpetual Motion of *See-Saw*"
while the "loud Hum" of the preacher is promptly returned
by the assembly (pp. 273, 274, 275). Thereupon, Swift turns
to the artifice of the preacher whose rhetoric is produced not
by sense but by the music of letters and syllables—a "single
Vowel" can "draw Sighs from a Multitude," and a whole
"Assembly of Saints" will "sob to the Musick of one solitary
Liquid" (p. 281)—and the melodies of *"Snuffling"* through
a nose broken by syphilis (p. 282). In short, when Swift
invites the reader to "Observe, but the Gesture, the Motion,
and the Countenance, of some choice Professors" of *"artificial
Enthusiasm"* (p. 284) he is directing our attention to one of
his own basic techniques.

In the service of an unparticularized satire, this device of
transferring attention from the matter of the sermon to the
manner of the preacher is an effective means of giving general contempt a local and specific application. As a device of
personal satire it succeeds in making a person's intellectual
pretensions ridiculous by concentrating upon his grotesque
physical gestures. In *A Tale of a Tub* Swift equates Wotton's
deformity of mind with that of his body and argues that

Surely, no Man ever advanced into the Publick, with fitter Qualifications of Body and Mind, for the Propagation of a new
Religion. Oh, had those happy Talents misapplied to vain Philosophy, been turned into their proper Channels of *Dreams* and
Visions, where *Distortion* of Mind and Countenance, are of such
Sovereign Use; the base detracting World would not then have
dared to report, that something is amiss, that his Brain hath
undergone an unlucky Shake . . . (p. 169).

A similar phraseology with a similar satiric result is applied
by Swift to Wotton in *The Battle of the Books.* Swift
describes Wotton after the Goddess of Criticism threw one
of her monsters in his mouth, "which flying strait up into his
Head, squeez'd out his Eye-balls, gave him a distorted Look,
and half over-turned his Brain" (p. 243). The pictorial image

of Wotton's facial distortion, as well as the assumption of
brute matter (which can be shaken and overturned) com-
posing his brain, not only reduces Wotton to a caricature
but tend to caricature his thinking as well.

Much of the scarifying satire in *A Tale of a Tub*, *The
Battle of the Books* and *The Mechanical Operation of the
Spirit* results from this technique of vulgarizing caricature.
The same technique of eliciting laughter by portraying man
as a nexus of physical attributes without natural humanity
appears with somewhat less savage and caustic intensity in
many of Swift's other satires. The subtle humour of the following passage, for instance, develops from the same reduction of man to an ugly or posturing puppet, but here the
reduction is implicit rather than an explicitly defined series
of external gestures:

Being with some other students over a pot of ale, one of the company said so many pleasant things, that the rest were much diverted, only Corusodes was silent and unmoved. When they
parted, he called this merry companion aside, and said, "Sir, I
perceive by your often speaking, and your friends laughing, that
you spoke many jests; and you could not but observe my silence:
But sir, this is my humour, I never make a jest myself, nor ever
laugh at another man's.[20]

Corusodes' humour, expressed with a solemn oblivion to its
own absurdity, becomes comic through the inflexibility of
mind and lack of mobile awareness which perceives a joke by
the gestures of others. By casting this satire into the form of an
anecdote, Swift further removes himself from a direct commentary upon the situation; Corusodes' ignorance of his own
absurdity enables him to satirize himself. A more direct
technique and, for that reason, one more closely related to
Swift's practice in *A Tale of a Tub,* is sustained throughout
the "Introduction" to a *Compleat Collection of Genteel and
Ingenious Conversation*. To accompany the rote memorization of his system of artificial wit, Swift urges his readers to
cultivate the appropriate "postures" of witty converse. He
ironically argues that the "very manner of introducing the
several points of wit and humour" is more entertaining and

instructive than the "matter" in which, he adds, "I can
pretend to little merit." Accordingly, Swift presents the
"doctrine and discipline" of the "military management of
the fan, the contortions of every muscular motion in the
face, . . ." and the like. The mechanical operation of being
witty in polite society is said, in this satire, to depend upon
two things: the rote memorization of the collected witticisms
and the appropriate "twistings, and movements, and different
postures of the body."[21] By this combined emphasis Swift,
in his role as a *cognoscente* of politeness, establishes an inti-
mate correspondence between the intellectual rigidity of
pursuing artificial methods and the physical automatism of
a puppet, activated by artifice into curious postures. The
resulting impression upon the reader is the equation between
a learned mental gesture and a learned physical gesture. Both
become equally absurd. The "Introduction" is an elabo-
ration and embodiment of the ideas in an early stanza quoted
already:

> Matter, as wise Logicians say,
> Cannot without a Form subsist,
> And Form, say I as well as they,
> Must fayl if Matter brings no Grist.

The use of the mechanical symbol also characterizes the
more good-natured satire in *Gulliver's Travels*. Particularly is
this true in the first two voyages. In "A Voyage to Lilliput" the
very diminutiveness of the Lilliputians in relation to Gulliver
creates the sense of their being tiny, mechanical toys, imitating the gestures of men but without, so to speak, man's soul.
Certainly this suggestion of automatism has contributed to
the perennial popularity among children of the *Travels;* it
probably is also a cause, among adult and more critical
readers, of the feeling that the Lilliputians are better vehicles
for comic satire than for *directly* expressing moral ideals. At
least, chapter six, which details the noble and "original institutions" before the "degenerate nature of man" had produced
"scandalous corruptions,"[22] comes upon us with less of a fine
suddenness than do the chapters with a critical and satiric
intent. With the exception of that chapter, much of the satire

of the voyage arises largely from the disparity between the Lilliputians' vain affectation of human grandeur and the reality of their littleness. And Swift dramatizes the externality of their imitations of humanity by continual reference to their physical gestures and movements. For example, he describes the Lilliputian king standing before the figure of Gulliver: "He held his sword drawn in his hand, to defend himself, if I should happen to break loose; it was almost three inches long, the hilt and the scabbard were gold enriched with diamonds."[23]

We may well recall on reading this and similar passages Plato's distinction between powerful and impotent affectation. The king's gesture is, obviously, a hollow and ineffectual motion when directed against the giant Gulliver; and, as his posture is neither "hateful" nor "detestable," but a diminutive physical imitation of a dangerous gesture, we laugh and contemn without terror or bitterness. The king who thinks himself the "delight and terror of the universe . . . whose feet press down to the centre, and whose head strikes against the sun . . ." is ridiculous in proportion to his mechanical imitation of the external forms of humanity without possessing the real power and dangerousness of men. Another illustration may profitably be included here because of its technical similarity to Swift's diminution of the spider in *The Battle of the Books*. While Gulliver remained on the beach in the bonds of his tiny captors he is addressed by a man of rank who "seemed to be somewhat longer than my middle finger": "He acted every part of an orator, and I could observe many periods of threatenings, and others of promises, pity and kindness."[24] The oratorical posturing of the spider rendered him no more absurd than this physical motioning of the Lilliputian. When, in addition, we recall that Gulliver at that time had no command of the language and must have determined the oratorical purpose of the Lilliputian entirely by his movements of face and hands, the technique of ridicule is seen to come close to that of the man who understood that jests were being spoken because of his companion's laughing and often speaking. But here the object

of the satire is the orator rather than Gulliver. The stand-
ardized positioning of an official who is mechanically pursuing the fixed and established forms of behaviour is ludicrous in the same way that the postures assumed in artifical
wit are ludicrous. The comedy in Swift's satire against vanity
arises from a perception more acute than the simple juxtaposition of big men and little men. The diminutive size of
the Lilliputians is used by Swift as a concrete visual aid
towards exciting in the reader a strong sense of the comedy
of mechanism.

Needless to say, the satiric objective of Swift in Gulliver's
first voyage is to force men to equate themselves with Lilliputians—to make them aware of their own puppetlike
appearance of power in contrast to the reality of their
weakness. The device of dramatizing the physical gesture
as a means to suggest men's intellectual automatism is
clearly seen in Swift's satire upon religious schism and
political climbing. In the two scenes in which Swift describes
the Lilliputian method of gaining court preferment and their
dissensions over the High Heels and Low Heels, Swift
employs the kind of allegorical technique peculiar to himself. He establishes a correspondence between his own intellectual, pejorative judgment of an idea or situation and a
mechanical or physical gesture. Thus, Swift's contempt for
the misdirected methods of gaining court favour (by flattery,
verbal dexterity, and the like, instead of moral integrity or
political acumen) is translated into a series of physical methods (cutting capers on a tight rope and leaping over a stick).
Swift enforces the pictorial clarity of this courtly puppet-
show by describing an incident, with a possibly particular
allegorical application, in which Flimnap is preserved from
a nearly fatal accident by the lucky interposition of a pillow
(p. 39). This description differs from a "physico-logical
scheme" in that there is nothing explicitly vulgar in the
described situation; it resembles the scheme in its appeal to
our visual sense of the mechanism of puppet man. Similarly,
Swift's description of the squabbling between religious and
political factions as consisting of the difference between High

Heels and Low Heels, and the breaking of an egg at the proper end, also reduces Swift's conception of the absurdity of faction to a concrete level of mechanism. The extent to which this technique is successful in reducing intellectual activity to the level of physical automatism is apparent in Swift's brilliant description of the heir to the throne: "We apprehend his Imperial Highness, the Heir to the Crown, to have some tendency towards the High-Heels; at least we can plainly discover one of his heels higher than the other, which gives him a hobble in his gait" (p. 49).

The "gay contempt" toward the Lilliputians which Swift arouses by stressing the automatism of their personal movements and gestures is closely paralleled by a similar reduction of Gulliver himself to the likeness of a mechanical toy in *A Voyage to Brobdingnag*. The absurd posture of defense assumed by the Lilliputian king, for example, finds almost a carbon copy in Gulliver's own pretentious manner in the company of his gigantic master: "I drew out my hanger, and flourished with it after the manner of fencers in England. My nurse gave me part of a straw, which I exercised as a pike, having learned the art in my youth" (p. 100). This emphasis upon the empty physical gesture is also the motivating force behind Gulliver's laughter at the thought of the posturing vanity of the English nobility:

. . . if I had then beheld a company of English lords and ladies in their finery and birth-day clothes, acting their several parts in the most courtly manner, of strutting, and bowing, and prating; to say the truth, I should have been strongly tempted to laugh as much at them as the King and his grandees did at me (p. 110).

In emphasizing Swift's technique of representing first the Lilliputians and then Gulliver as tiny mechanisms which imitate the external gesture and movements of men, I by no means intend to suggest that this technique alone "explains" either the criticism or the comedy in the first two books of *Gulliver's Travels*. On the contrary, this technique is only one of many which fuse into a totality of comic satire. The comic potential, however, summarized in the Brobdingnagian king's thought of Gulliver as being a "piece of clock-work . . . contrived by some ingenious artist" (p. 105), has been generally overlooked by Swift's commentators. The seriousness of this critical omission is, it seems to me, augmented by two considerations. In the first place, it is clear that the perception of man as a mechanism is one fundamental source of comedy; by incorporating this comic perception into the framework of criticism, therefore, Swift's satire, although often particular in intent, succeeds in its appeal to a general and universal cause of laughter. In the second place, this technique is not confined merely to *Gulliver's Travels* as an occasional device for creating verisimilitude, but it appears in the various ways I have indicated throughout the long course of Swift's satiric writings. In Swift's first published work, "Ode to the Athenian Society," he noted that

> . . . when the animating Mind is fled,
> (Which Nature never can retain,
> Nor e'er call back again)
> The Body, tho' Gigantick, lyes all *Cold and Dead*.[25]

Swift realized the comic and satiric potentiality of this observation through the *process of devitalizing his opponents* by proving their animation to be the product of artifice alone. In short, we may conclude that one of Swift's most basic and characteristic techniques of satire is this method of arousing gay contempt by depicting artifice triumphing over nature.

Recurrent Symbols of Height and Depth

Swift's remarkable talent for ridiculing persons and ideas by a grave and scientific depiction of their physical and mechanical operation was not an artificial technique imposed *ab extra* upon his satiric objects. Instead, it seems evident that it was as natural as indignation for Swift to conceive ideas in a spatial and visual sense. The extent to which Swift's imagination tended to grasp and express intellectual concepts in a physical image is suggested by the recurrence, through many different works, of particular images or patterns of imagery representing the same ideas. Psychological critics of Swift's imagery, more interested, perhaps, in proving Swift a psychopath than clarifying his literary productions, have had a field day with Swift's reiterated use of sexual and scatological allusions. One such critic, for example, has even found a dark, sinister, and presumably maniacal meaning behind Swift's use of the word "coffee" in his letters to Vanessa, and he views all references to "coffee drinking as the cloak or symbol of stain or dalliance . . ."[26] The path through Swift's recurrent imagery to his insanity has been so thoroughly beaten by such critics that it seems unnecessary for me to re-tread it now or even to consider in detail the usefulness or propriety to literary criticism of such psychiatric analysis. More important to the study of Swift's satire as a genre of literature is the recurrence of certain images which reflect his persistent translation of intellectual ideas into satirically effective physical metaphors. I have already mentioned Swift's frequent use of "vessel" and "furniture"; Swift's disgust with mechanical thinking and methods found a natural expression in these concrete similes. An even more complex and frequent instance of his use of a recurrent image pattern consists of the embodiment of his contempt for intellectual extremism into images of height and depth.

In the section devoted to the Aeolists in *A Tale of a Tub* Swift affirms his own belief in moderation in religious thinking by describing in a physical and spatial metaphor the meeting of extremes:

AND, whereas the mind of Man, when he gives the Spur and Bridle to his Thoughts, doth never stop, but naturally sallies out into both extreams of High and Low, of Good and Evil; His first Flight of Fancy, commonly transports Him to Idea's of what is most Perfect, finished, and exalted; till having soared out of his own Reach and Sight, not well perceiving how near the Frontiers of Height and Depth, border upon each other; With the same Course and Wing, he falls down plum into the lowest Bottom of Things . . . Fancy, flying up to the imagination of what is Highest and Best becomes over-short, and spent, and weary, and suddenly falls like a dead Bird of Paradise to the Ground.[27]

Swift's object in this satiric passage is to ridicule man's extreme rationalism which posits impossible or unknowable attributes to God and the Devil. Formed in his own mind in spatial terms of height and depth, rising and falling, the same image is used in *The Mechanical Operation of the Spirit* to show that man has "most horribly confounded the frontiers of both" good and evil:

. . . Men have lifted up the Throne of their Divinity to the *Caelum Empyraeum,* adorned with all such Qualities and Accomplishments, as themselves seem most to value and possess; . . . they have sunk their *Principle* of *Evil* to the lowest Center, bound him with Chains . . . (p. 277).

As a technique of satire this perception of the bordering frontiers of height and depth provided Swift with a ready visual framework in which abstract ideas or emotional reactions could be fleshed with concrete imagery. As satire depends for its effect upon arousing an emotional persuasion based on the laughter of contempt, so the satirist often tends to oversimplify the complexity of truth into a kind of shorthand. Swift's use of the antipodal relations of height and depth is just such a hieroglyphic. To the visual idea of height Swift added the concrete connotations of many things which, through common association, are thought to rise; thus, air rises, and fire and scum and oil. Similarly, the connotations of depth are associated with heavy things which sink or fall, with excessive materiality, with dullness, stupidity, and thickheadedness. By resort to the shorthand of these connotations Swift was able to elicit immediate and emotional contempt without demanding extended intellectual pursuit. Before illustrating the extent to which this conception of height and depth was useful to Swift in *A Tale of a Tub,* some examples drawn from other works may help to show how widespread was this device in his satire.

As the two quotations above indicate, Swift generally ascribed equal contempt to the idea of rising and falling. Occasionally, however, he set the volatility of true intellectual wit in opposition to stupidity, equating extraordinary brilliance with the idea of rising. In *An Essay on the Fates of Clergymen*, for example, Swift laments the evil fortune which attends men of unusual wit and concludes that when "a great genius appears in the world, the dunces are all in confederacy against him." Accordingly, he decides that

. . . fortune generally acts directly contrary to nature; for in nature we find, that bodies full of life and spirits mount easily, and are hard to fall, whereas heavy bodies are hard to rise, and come down with greater velocity, in proportion to their weight; but we find fortune every day acting just the reverse of this.

This opposition between the natural law of physics and the unnatural law of worldly success is sustained throughout the essay. On the plane of fortune, Swift describes the talent of discretion as being the most "useful towards rising in the world," as the cause of one prelate's ascending "so high," and of Corusodes' "full career of success, mounting fast toward the top of the Ladder Ecclesiastical"; in antithesis to the rising fortunes of the men of discretion, Swift places the declining fortunes of the talented man who meets "universal opposition when he is mounting the ladder, and every hand ready to turn him off when he is at the top," and whose spirits, finally, like his fortunes, are "quite sunk" by the world's neglect. On the level of natural law, this progress is reversed: the "life and spirits" and "marks of levity" in men of wit and learning are contrasted to the sober qualifications of the discreet man who is weighty as "ballast" and possessed with "heavy intellectuals."[28]

In at least one instance, Swift uses the image of weight with a favorable meaning, in contrast to lightness: "While dignity sinks with its own weight, the scum of mankind will naturally rise above it."[29] The pattern of this imagery resembles one part of the preceding illustration in its analogy between rising in the world and rising as a natural phenomenon in physics. It differs in the favorable suggestions of the "weight." But this is an exception to Swift's usual attribution of equal contempt to images of height and depth with their attendant connotations of rising and falling. As in the passages already quoted from *A Tale of a Tub* and *The Mechanical Operation of the Spirit,* Swift frequently brings together in one passage the pejorative implications of both height and depth as a means to demonstrate how near are the "frontiers" of each. Typical of this double-barreled satiric device is Swift's linking together of the catastrophic South Sea Bubble and the projected scheme for a National Bank in Ireland:

The ambitious citizens, who from being plunged deep in the wealthy whirlpool of the South-Sea, are in hopes of rising to such seats of fortune and dignity, as would best suit with their mounting and aspiring hopes, may imagine that this new fund, in the sister nation, may prove a rival to theirs.[30]

Here Swift, while presenting his own scheme of a Swearers' Bank, suggests that the "mounting and aspiring hopes" in the projected national bank will probably fall at last into another and similar whirlpool. The framework of its pattern of visual imagery bears a close resemblance to that of the enthusiasts who try to fly up to the secrets of the universe and succeed only in falling to "the bottom of things."

In *A Proposal . . . for Preventing the Further Growth of Popery* which appeared in the *Tatler* (No. 220, Sept. 4, 1710) and which early editors ascribed to Addison, there is strong presumptive evidence of Swift's hand. For the proposal is a mechanized version of the image pattern I am describing. The author of this piece, which Temple Scott includes in an appendix to his edition of Swift's works, wants to propagate the religious doctrine that "we should be careful not to over-shoot ourselves in the pursuits even of virtue. Whether zeal or moderation be the point we aim at, let us keep fire out of the one, and frost out of the other."[31]

To this end he describes his invention of a thermometer containing a new fluid which is "a compound of two different liquors": one is drawn from wine and is apt to "ferment" and "burst the vessel that holds it, and fly up in a fume and smoke"; the other is a kind of "rock-water," very cold and crystalline, which, unless mingled with the first,

tends to "sink almost through everything it is put into."
The thermometer is marked as follows:

> Ignorance
> Persecution
> Wrath
> Zeal
> CHURCH
> Moderation
> Lukewarmness
> Infidelity
> Ignorance

The Church, Swift, then explains,

is placed in the middle point of the glass between Zeal and
Moderation, the situation in which she always flourishes . . .
However, when it mounts to Zeal, it is not amiss; and when it
sinks to Moderation, it is still in admirable temper. The worst
of it is, that when once it begins to rise, it has still an inclination
to ascend . . . which often ends in Ignorance, and very often proceeds from it. In the same manner it frequently takes its progress
through the lower half of the glass; and, when it has a tendency
to fall, will gradually descend, . . . which very often terminates
in Ignorance, and always proceeds from it.[32]

The terminal points away from the center are the same,
and this invention expresses an identical philosophy, although
by means of a more elaborate mechanical contrivance, to
Swift's statement in *A Tale of a Tub* of the bordering
frontiers of height and depth.

Swift also fits into this image pattern his contempt for
the two opposing abuses of learning: those arising from dullness and the weight of pedantry as opposed to those which
spring from any superficiality and especially that of excessive
speculation, unballasted by sensory evidence. This pattern
reappears in Swift's contemptuous rejection of Tindal's
Rights of the Christian Church by implying that the preface
was superficial and the body of the work dull and obscure:
"But, before I plunge into the depths of the book itself, I
must be forced to wade through the shallows of a long
preface."[33] A more expanded variation of the same pattern
occurs in *The Battle of the Books* in which Swift compresses

into the antipodal relationship of height and depth the opposing abuses of dull pedantry and excessive speculation. The
result is the compression into a single visual image of the two
directions of contempt. Swift describes Bentley's failure in
attempting to climb Parnassus and "knock down two of the
Antient Chiefs" who guarded a pass at the summit:

endeavoring to climb up, [Bentley] was cruelly obstructed by his
own unhappy Weight, and tendency towards his Center; a
Quality, to which, those of the *Modern* Party, are extreme subject; For, being lightheaded, they have in Speculation, a wonderful Agility, and conceive nothing too high for them to mount;
but in reducing to Practice, discover a mighty Pressure about their
Posteriors and their Heels.[34]

As a satiric technique this visual image is successful in eliciting contempt. By reducing his judgment of the initial
attempts and final results of modern scholars to a description of Bentley's climbing hopes and heavy falling practice,
Swift provides a highly concrete and physical object at which
we laugh far more quickly than at some detailed intellectual
reasoning. Moreover, by devitalizing Bentley's learning and
converting it into a physical opposition between his light
head and heavy posterior, Swift introduces the element of
mechanism, of something mechanical encrusted upon the
living: the "animating mind is fled," and Bentley appears
to us as a gross, puppetlike contrivance.

   To the spatial and material image of climbing Swift sometimes added a secondary level of base connotation by associ-
ating it with an object having some contemptible or disgusting connotations of its own. Thus, Swift writes of Bishop
Fleetwood:

I know your lordship had rather live in a blaze, than lie buried
in obscurity; and would, at any rate, purchase immortality,
though it be in flames. Fire, being a mounting element, is a
proper emblem of your lordship's aspiring genius.[35]

Although there is nothing intrinsically contemptible about
fire, Swift is using it here in reference to the order from the
House of Commons that the Bishop's preface be burned. Fire,

therefore, is not only an emblem of mounting aspiration, but of political heresy as well, and the two meanings are compressed into one image. A more immediate use of the image pattern under discussion as a vehicle for introducing depreciatory allusions is found in Swift's frequent equation of rising with scum, froth, oil, and the like. In his satire upon the dispute which arose over the question of "precedence" between physicians and civilians, Swift describes how some men tend to *mount* in company:

some have a strange oiliness of spirit which carries them upwards, and mounts them to the top of all company, (company being often like bottled liquors, where the light and windy parts hurry to the head, and fix in froth) . . . [36]

The description of the clergymen rising on the Ecclesiastical Ladder and this frothy rise in company reflect the same technique of translating the figurative sense of the word "rise" into a literally physical and visual sense. The same pattern of imagery is used by Swift to establish the analogy between men's rise in company and scum: ". . . the scum of mankind will naturally rise. . . ." This same association of rising with froth and scum gives to the author's preface of *The Battle of the Books* its satiric visual impact:

THERE is a Brain *that will endure but one* Scumming . . . *Wit, without knowledge, being a Sort of* Cream, *which gathers in a Night to the Top, and by a skilful Hand, may be soon* whipt *into* froth; *but once scumm'd away, what appears underneath will be fit for nothing, but to be thrown to the Hogs.*[37]

In *A Tale of a Tub* Swift repeatedly uses what to him were often the equally unpleasant and vilifying connotations of height and depth, lightness and weight, rising and falling. The double-barreled image in which Swift demonstrates the proximity of the frontiers of this physically realized dichotomy appears in several forms. As a method of compressing two satiric ideas into one image, Swift uses the device in ridiculing modern learning which he demonstrates to be both trifling and so dull that it sinks to oblivion; in his

"Dedication to Prince Posterity," Swift asks what Time has done to these writings:

Who has mislaid them? Are they sunk in the Abyss of Things? 'Tis certain, that in their own Nature they were *light* enough to swim upon the Surface for all Eternity. Therefore the Fault is in Him, who tied Weights so heavy to their Heels, as to depress them to the Center (p. 32).

The same contrast between weighty dullness and airy frivolity is incorporated into Swift's "Physico-logical Scheme of Oratorial Receptacles." Swift deduces from the architecture of modern theaters that the pit is "sunk below the stage" so that "whatever *weighty* matter shall be delivered thence (whether it be *Lead* or *Gold*) may fall" into the critics' mouths; the "whining Passions, and little starved Conceits, are gently wafted up by their own extreme Levity, to the middle Region . . ."; and, finally, "Bombastry and Buffoonery, by Nature lofty and light, soar highest of all . . ." (p. 61). Corresponding to this physical explanation of the theater is Swift's physical explanation of man's desire for conquest or peace, deduced from the rising or falling of vapours in the body (pp. 165-166). Not only does this pattern appear in these rather elaborate physical deductions, but it also occurs in such passing observations as the author's remark that his work has "included and exhausted all that Human Imagination can *Rise* or *Fall* to" (p. 129), and the comment that because, in dispute, the "*Gravity* of one Side advances the *Lightness* of the Other . . . the *Weight* of *Martin's* Argument exalted *Jack's Levity,* and made him fly out and spurn against his Brother's Moderation" (p. 140).

Closely associated with the recurrence of this dual pattern is the even more frequent repetition of either one or the other element in it. Swift attached to the word "height" and to corollary words which suggest rising and climbing his whole contempt for speculative refinements. In *A Tale of a Tub,* he quotes the "famous *Troglodyte* Philosopher" who concluded that "it is with Human Faculties as with Liquors, the lightest will be ever at the Top"; in "an Apology" Swift remarks that *"under the Notion of Prejudices, he knew to what dangerous Heights some Men have proceeded."* A less direct and more ironical contempt is expressed by Swift's use of height in seeming praise for intellectual skillfulness, his own or that of others. Accordingly, he praises Peter whose projects "discovered him to be Master of a high Reach, and profound Invention"; he applauds Peter's Bulls which "had *Fishes Tails,* yet upon Occasion, could *out-fly* any Bird in the Air"; he promises to describe Jack's mysterious and difficult conceptions as "far as Notions of that Height and Latitude can be brought within the Compass of a Pen"; and referring to the Horatian formula of *utile et dulce* Swift congratulates himself for "carrying the Point in all its Heights." [38] Similarly, Swift charges the word "weight" and its corollary suggestions of falling and dullness, as well as its figurative connotation of profundity, with a contempt which is often concealed beneath a layer of irony. Swift introduces his account of the sect of tailors by the bland assurance that he must have "recourse to some Points of Weight, which the Authors of that Age have not sufficiently illustrated." Moreover, the Aeolists are described as deducing the maxim "of much Weight" that man is the best animal because he contains the most wind. Therefore, "Upon these Reasons and others of equal Weight," the Aeolists affirm belching to be man's noblest act. Or again, Swift derides the moderns as *"heavy, illiterate Scriblers,"* and he alludes to Mr. Sharp, who showed the *Tale* to the queen, as one of the "weightiest *Men in the* weightiest *Stations."* [39]

Taken singly, this pattern of imagery is an effective technique of suggesting contempt by indirection and irony and by the embodiment of an idea in a physical and graphic dichotomy. Taken in its accumulative effect, the persistent recurrences of these images of height and depth, rising and falling, scum and weights, are a significant contribution to the texture of brilliant intellectuality which distinguishes *A Tale of a Tub.* The elaborate construction of engines, machines, and projects, manufactory operations, physiological schemes, embellished coats, and the phenomenon of vapours, in addition to the subtle but constant repetition of this imbruted imagery, all tend to objectify Swift's satiric objects on a plane of brute matter and natural laws; our contempt is directed at the object by way of Swift's dehumanizing technique, instead of immediately and, so to speak, face to face. Powerful emotions of hate and fear are not aroused, therefore, and *A Tale of a Tub* attains, to a degree probably unparalleled by any other work, one necessary quality of great satire: "gay contempt."

From a technical point of view, Swift achieves the compelling sincerity and pervasive comedy of his satire by his ability to dramatize and, through the action of concrete symbols, to objectify his own intellectual and moral judgments. But a detailed study of Swift's satiric techniques can only suggest some levels of complexity in his writing; no technical analysis can "explain" Swift's writing as a whole. Professor Sherburn has advised that readers of Swift listen to his "tone of voice"; this tone is a complex of reverberant notes which escape precise definition and description. We may listen, for example, to such a statement as this: "Last Week I saw a Woman *flay'd*, and you will hardly believe, how much it altered her Person for the worse," or to a sentence describing the plight of the Irish people: "But I am not in the least pain upon that matter, because it is very well known, that they are every day dying, and rotting, by cold, and famine, and filth, and vermin, *as fast as can be reasonably expected*." The force of these observations cannot be confined within the narrow compass of such a description as the ironical device of "understatement." There is here a quality that transcends technical virtuosity: it is the pressure of an outraged conviction subdued and controlled by a sustained artistic intention. This pressure is everywhere apparent in Swift's satire, but it releases itself in a multiplicity of ways which give it form and purpose. If Swift's anatomy of life demonstrated to him that "Defects encrease upon us in Number and Bulk" as we proceed from the outside appearances to the inside reality, and if this disparity moved him to anger and despair, he was nonetheless able, and indeed, found it necessary, to control his intensity of emotion and to objectify his vision of life as a "ridiculous tragedy." Moreover, Swift seems never to have completely lost—not even, perhaps, in the concluding pages of *Gulliver's Travels*—a faith and hope in man's capacity to mend himself, to approach more closely the ideal of man as *animal rationale*. This hope, combined with the controlled intensity of his feelings, expressed itself in the exploitation of satiric techniques so diverse and penetrating that he stands apart from all other writers of satire. But in achieving that distinction and universality, he nevertheless represents the satiric aims and techniques of his age—the attempt at dispassionate analysis, at detached evaluation and improvement, which characterizes the enlightened period which succeeded and profited from the Renaissance. As England's—and perhaps the world's— greatest satirist, he thus represents the triumph of these aims and techniques; by exploiting them to their fullest degree, he gives them a permanent and challenging significance.

Notes and Index

Notes

I

EXPOSURE BY RIDICULE

1. Letter to Swift (1720), *The Correspondence of Jonathan Swift, D.D.* (ed. F. Elrington Ball, 1910-14), III, 446.

2. Ricardo Quintana, *The Mind and Art of Jonathan Swift* (1936), p. 364 and *passim*.

3. *A Tale of a Tub To which is added The Battle of the Books and the Mechanical Operation of the Spirit* (eds. A. C. Guthkelch and D. Nichol Smith, 1920), pp. 171-174. Many years later, Swift referred to himself in a similar way while attacking Joshua, Lord Allen: ". . . and I am afraid lest such a practitioner, with a body so open, so foul, and so full of sores, *may fall under the resentment of an incensed political surgeon,* who is not in much renown for his mercy upon great provocation: who without waiting for his death, will flay, and dissect him alive, and to the view of mankind lay open all the disordered cells of his brain, the venom of his tongue, the corruption of his heart, and spots and flatuses of his spleen—And all this for threepence." *A Vindication of his Excellency the Lord Carteret* in *The Prose Works of Jonathan Swift, D.D.* (ed. Temple Scott, Bohn's Standard Library, 1897-1911), VII, 236; my italics. Hereafter, this edition will be cited as *Works.*

4. *A Tale of a Tub,* pp. 66, 123, 173-174.

5. *Observations upon Lord Orrery's Remarks* (1754), pp. 148-149.

6. *A Tale of a Tub,* p. 172.

7. Letter to Alexander Pope (September 29, 1725), *Correspondence,* III, 277.

8. Letter to John Arbuthnot (June 16, 1714), *Correspondence,* II, 153; my italics.

9. *The Publick Spirit of the Whigs* in *Works,* V, 321.

10. *Of Public Absurdities in England* in *Works,* XI, 179.

11. "The Comic," *Letters and Social Aims* (1883), p. 154; my italics.

12. Letter to Alexander Pope (April 20, 1731), *Correspondence,* IV, 217; my italics.

13. Letter to Knightley Chetwode (July 19, 1725), *Correspondence,* III, 254.

14. "The Intelligencer, Numb. 111," *Works,* IX, 318; my italics.

15. *Works,* II, 89.

16. Letter to Miss Esther Vanhomrigh (July 13, 1722), *Correspondence,* III, 134.

17. Letter to John Gay and the Duchess of Queensberry (July 10, 1732), *Correspondence,* IV, 316.

18. "An Epistle to a Lady," *The Poems of Jonathan Swift* (ed. Harold Williams, 1937), II, 635, ll. 167-170.

19. *A Treatise on Good Manners and Good Breeding* in *Works*, XI, 81.

20. *Perilous Balance* (1939), pp. 23-24.

21. *Journal to Stella* (Jan. 3, 1712/13) in *Works*, II, 410.

22. *Thoughts on Religion* in *Works*, III, 309.

23. Letter to the Duchess of Queensberry (March 23, 1732/33), *Correspondence*, IV, 404.

24. Letter to Miss Esther Vanhomrigh (July 8, 1713), *Correspondence*, II, 53.

25. Letter to Viscount Bolingbroke and Alexander Pope (April 5, 1729), *Correspondence*, IV, 76-77.

26. Letter to John Arbuthnot (June 16, 1714), *Correspondence*, II, 153.

27. Letter to the Reverend James Stopford (July 20, 1726), *Correspondence*, III, 322.

28. Letter to the Reverend Thomas Sheridan (Sept. 2, 1727), *Correspondence*, III, 417.

29. Letters to Alexander Pope (March 30, 1733; May 1, 1733), *Correspondence*, IV, 414, 429-430.

30. Letter to Mrs. Moore (Dec. 7, 1727), *Correspondence*, III, 436.

31. "The Restoration and Eighteenth Century (1660–1789)," *A Literary History of England* (ed. Albert C. Baugh, 1948), pp. 867-868.

32. Letter to Alexander Pope (June 1, 1728), *Correspondence*, IV, 34.

33. Letters to Alexander Pope (Sept. 29, 1725; Nov. 26, 1725), *Correspondence*, III, 276-277, 293.

34. We may compare, in this connection, Swift's remark to Pope—"I have often endeavoured to establish a friendship among all men of genius, and would fain have it done. They are seldom above three or four contemporaries, and if they could be united, would drive the world before them" (Letter to Alexander Pope [Sept. 20, 1723], *Correspondence*, III, 175)—with Pope's comment, almost ten years later—"I fancy, if we three were together but for three years, some good might be done even upon this age" (Letter to Swift from Viscount Bolingbroke and Alexander Pope [April 1732], *Correspondence*, IV, 290).

35. Letter to the Earl of Oxford (June 14, 1737), *Correspondence*, VI, 22.

36. *A Tale of a Tub*, pp. 53-54.

37. Letter to Mrs. Howard (Nov. 27, 1726), *Correspondence*, III, 366.

38. Robert B. Heilman in *Gulliver's Travels* (Modern Library College Edition, 1950), pp. xii ff.

39. Letter to the Reverend Thomas Sheridan (Sept. 11, 1725), *Correspondence*, III, 267.

40. *A Letter to a Young Gentleman, Lately enter'd Into Holy Orders* in *Works*, III, 206, 205, 215; my italics. Cf. "I imagine myself talking with you as I used to do, but on a sudden, I recollect where I am sitting, banished to a country of slaves and beggars,—my blood soured, my spirits sunk, fighting

with beasts like St. Paul, not at Ephesus, but in Ireland" (Letter to Lady Worsley [Nov. 4, 1732], *Correspondence*, IV, 357).

41. *Mr. C—ns's Discourse of Free-thinking, Put into plain English, by way of Abstract, for the Use of the Poor* in *Works*, III, 182.

42. Letter to the Reverend Thomas Sheridan (Sept. 25, 1725), *Correspondence*, III, 274-275.

43. *Remarks on the Life and Writings of Dr. Jonathan Swift* (Dublin, 1752), p. 97; my italics.

44. "Epilogue to the Satires," II, ll. 208-211.

45. "The Examiner, Numb. 39," *Works*, IX, 253. How little confidence Swift had in the effectiveness of preaching is suggested by one of his *Thoughts on Various Subjects* in *Works*, I, 280: "The preaching of divines helps to preserve well inclined men in the course of virtue, but seldom or never reclaims the vicious."

46. Letter from Viscount Bolingbroke and Alexander Pope (April 1732), *Correspondence*, IV, 290; my italics.

47. "An Epistle to a Lady," *Poems*, II, 637, ll. 225-226.

48. *Works*, VIII, 303-304; my italics.

49. Letter to Alexander Pope (Nov. 26, 1725), *Correspondence*, III, 293. For one of many repetitions of this belief, see *Thoughts on Various Subjects* in *Works*, I, 278: "The motives of the best actions will not bear too strict an inquiry. It is allowed, that the cause of most actions, good or bad, may be resolved into the love of ourselves; but the self-love of some men, inclines them to please others; and the self-love of others is wholly employed in pleasing themselves. This makes the great distinction between virtue and vice. Religion is the best motive of all actions, yet religion is allowed to be the highest instance of self-love."

50. George F. Meier, *The Merry Philosopher; or, Thoughts on Jesting,"* (translated from German, 1765), p. 40.

51. Thomas Nowell, *A Dissertation upon that Species of Writing Called Humour, when Applied to Sacred Subjects* (1760), p. 11.

52. *Philebus* (trans. Jowett), 47-50.

53. Z. Grey, *Notes Upon Hudibras* (1752), pp. 3, 4; my italics.

54. Francis Hutcheson, *Reflections upon Laughter and Remarks upon the Fable of the Bees* (1750), p. 19. Hutcheson is speaking here of the "spirit of burlesque." He offers no exception to the general confusion of terms in the period, but his meaning is clarified a few pages later (p. 33) when he says: "Nothing is so properly applied to the false grandeur, either of good or evil, as ridicule."

55. Corbyn Morris, *An Essay Towards Fixing the True Standards of Wit, Humour, Raillery, Satire, and Ridicule* (1744), p. 32.

56. Bk. III, ll. 275-277.

57. "Shade of Alexander Pope," *The School for Satire* (1802), pp. 215-216.

58. Lord Kames, *Elements of Criticism* (1795), II, 13-14.

59. Mark Akenside, *The Poems of Mark Akenside* (1772), pp. 114-115.

60. *Essays on the Characteristics* (1764), p. 104.

61. *The Works of Henry Fielding, Esq.* (ed. Leslie Stephen, 1882), IV, xiii-xiv, xi.

62. *Elements of Criticism,* II, 15.

63. Chap. IX, pt. 13; my italics.

64. *Reflections upon Laughter,* p. 13.

65. *Elements of Criticism,* I, 114, 345, 347.

66. John Brown, "An Essay on Satire," *A Collection of Poems* (ed. Dodsley, 1765), III, ll. 121-122.

67. G. A. Stevens, *A Lecture on Heads* (1806), p. 103.

68. William Combe, "The Justification: A Poem," (1777), p. v.

69. "Number 49; 31 August, 1754," *The Gray's Inn Journal* (1753-54), p. 293. Murphy followed Akenside in detail: "The Emotions here intended [in ridicule] are Laughter and Contempt, and these it is the Business of Comedy to excite, by making striking Exhibitions of inconsistent Circumstances, blended together in such a thwarting Assemblage, that a gay Contempt irresistibly shall take Possession of us" (p. 292).

70. Lord Kames considered contempt, alone, to be the proper punishment of serious "improprieties"; but this contempt was not to be confused with ridicule. For ridicule, consisting of a mixed emotion, was the proper method of treating minor foibles. "The emotion of contempt and of laughter occasioned by an impropriety of that kind, uniting intimately in the mind of the spectator, are expressed externally by a peculiar sort of laugh, termed a *laugh of derision* or *scorn.* An impropriety that thus moves not only contempt but laughter, is distinguished by the epithet *ridiculous;* and a laugh of derision or scorn is the punishment provided for it by nature" (*Elements of Criticism,* I, 344).

71. *Elements of Criticism,* II, 1.

72. *The History of Tom Jones* in *Works,* II, 219. Richard Cambridge, with a similar ideal in mind, defends his "Scribleriad" (1751) by the statement that "I have shewn throughout my Book that the Follies of Mankind provoke my Laughter and not my Spleen" (p. xvi).

73. Alexander Gerard, *An Essay on Taste* (1759), p. 68.

74. John Brown, "An Essay on Satire," ll. 269-270.

75. *Philosophical Works* (1854), II, 195.

76. *Poems,* pp. 115, 116; "The sensation of ridicule is not a bare perception of the agreement or disagreement of ideas; but a passion or emotion of the mind consequential to that perception. So that the mind may perceive the agreement or disagreement, and yet not feel the ridiculous, because it is engrossed by a more *violent emotion.* Thus it happens that some men think those objects ridiculous, to which others cannot endure to apply the name; because in them they excite a much intenser and more important feeling" (p. 115; my italics).

77. *Laughter, An Essay on the Meaning of the Comic* (trans. C. Brereton and F. Rothwell, 1921), p. 5.

78. John Brightland, *A Grammar of the English Tongue* (1746), p. 172.

79. "Epistle to a Lady," *Poems*, II, 634, 636-637, ll. 137-146, 197-216, 221-230.

80. *The Art of Satire* (Cambridge, Mass., 1940), p. 16.

81. *A Tale of a Tub*, p. 124.

II

SATIRIC DETACHMENT: INVECTIVE, DIMINUTION, AND IRONY

1. *The Poems of Jonathan Swift* (ed. Harold Williams, 1937), III, 1039.

2. *The Poetical Works of John Dryden* (ed. G. R. Noyes, Cambridge Edition, 1908), p. 313.

3. Romans 1:29-31.

4. *Arte of Rhetorique* (ed. G. H. Mair, 1909), p. 115.

5. *The Art of Satire* (1940), pp. 17-18.

6. *Gulliver's Travels* in *Works*, VIII, 196.

7. *A Letter of Advice to a Young Poet* in *Works*, XI, 111.

8. *Works*, VIII, 287-288.

9. *Attitudes Towards History* (1937), I, 53-54.

10. *Works*, VII, 288, 295, 290, 299.

11. Pp. 108 (I omit the bracket after "Physicians"), 79, 179.

12. Decorum in the Renaissance use of *meiosis* has been ably treated by Rosamunde Tuve in *Elizabethan and Metaphysical Imagery* (Chicago, 1947), pp. 196 ff.

13. *Remarks upon a Book, Intituled, "The Rights of the Christian Church, &c."* in *Works*, III, 83. Similarly, Swift speaks of Tindal's treatise as being ". . . wholly devoid of wit or learning, under the most violent and weak endeavours and pretences to both" (p. 87), and he denies Tindal the satisfaction of believing he has, through his attacks, done any "mischief to religion": for then Tindal "will reply in triumph, that this was his design; and I am loth to mortify him, by asserting he hath done none at all" (p. 88). A similar point of departure is taken by Swift against Wharton: "He seems to be but an ill dissembler and an ill liar, though they are the two talents he most practices, and most values himself upon. The ends he has gained by lying, appear to be more owing to the frequency than the art of them; his lies being sometimes detected in an hour, often in a day, and always in a week." *A Short Character of His Excellency, Thomas Earl of Wharton, Lord Lieutenant of Ireland* in *Works*, V, 9. In a different manner but with similar effect, Swift mentions the author of one political pamphlet as a man who ". . . Takes upon him the three characters of a despiser, a threatener and a railer; and succeeds so well in the two last, that it has made him miscarry in the first." *Some Remarks upon a Pamphlet, Entitl'd A letter to the Seven Lords of the Committee Appointed to Examine Gregg* in *Works*, V, 34. Thus Swift reduces the author to impotency in the one quality which could be

dangerous to Swift's own self-esteem. The same pattern is followed in *A Tale of a Tub* when Swift describes Wotton's *Reflections* as "made up of half Invective, and half Annotation. In the latter of which he has generally succeeded well enough" (p. 11).

14. *Works*, VI, 39. See Swift's observation: ". . . the church appeareth to me like the sick old lion in the fable, who, after having his person outraged by the bull, the elephant, the horse, and the bear, took nothing so much to heart as to find himself at last insulted by the spurn of an ass." *Remarks upon a Book* in *Works*, III, 87.

15. *Of Irony, Especially in Drama* (Toronto, 1948), p. 7.

16. "The Intelligencer, Numb. 111," *Works*, IX, 318; my italics.

17. As the Examiner, Swift's notebook filled somewhat more quickly, but his subject matter had changed: "I have likewise in my cabinet certain quires of paper filled with facts of corruption, mismanagement, cowardice, treachery, avarice, ambition, and the like, with an alphabetical table, to save trouble." "The Examiner, Numb. 29," *Works*, IX, 182.

18. *Swift's Remarks on Dr. Gibbs's Paraphrase of the Psalms* in *Works*, IV, 235, 237, 240.

19. *Works*, V, 265, 266.

20. *Ibid.*, pp. 267, 268, 264.

21. *Works*, VII, 232-233.

22. *Works*, V, 268.

23. *The Augustans* (ed. Maynard Mack, 1950; Vol. V of *English Masterpieces: An Anthology of Imaginative Literature from Chaucer to T. S. Eliot*, ed. Maynard Mack), p. 11.

24. *Works*, III, 207.

25. *Works*, III, 29.

26. *Works*, XI, 63-64; my italics. Other characteristic illustrations of Swift's elaborate computation of statistics may be found in: *The Swearer's-Bank* in *Works*, VII, 41-46, *A Vindication of His Excellency, the Lord C———t* in *ibid.*, pp. 246-249, *A Proposal for an Act of Parliament, to Pay off the Debt of the Nation, without Taxing the Subject* in *ibid.*, pp. 253-258, *A Serious and Useful Scheme, to Make an Hospital for Incurables* in *ibid.*, pp. 296-298. Much of the verisimilitude in *Gulliver's Travels* depends upon statistical detail: see, for example, *Works*, VIII, 20, 22, 25, 26, 31, 32, 40, 88, 94, 97, 114-117.

27. *Works*, VIII, 307.

28. "Situational Satire: A Commentary on the Method of Swift," *University of Toronto Quarterly*, XVII (January 1948), 135.

29. *The Augustans*, p. 12.

30. *Works*, VII, 207, 212, 208, 214, 209, 216. Cf. Swift's *Answer to the Craftsman* for an almost equally powerful use of dehumanizing statistics; Swift ironically supports the license granted to the king of France to export from Ireland "some thousand bodies of healthy, young, living men, to supply his Irish regiments," and Swift demonstrates "by computing the maintenance of a tall, hungry Irishman, in food and clothes, to be only at five pounds a head,

here will be thirty thousand pounds per annum saved clear to the nation."
Works, VII, 220, 221.

31. *Works,* VIII, 195.

32. Letter to Mrs. Howard (Nov. 27, 1726), *The Correspondence of Jonathan Swift, D.D.* (ed. F. Elrington Ball, 1910-14), III, 366.

33. *Works,* VIII, 109.

34. *Gulliver's Travels* (ed. Robert B. Heilman, Modern Library College Edition, 1950), p. xiv.

35. See Kathleen M. Williams, "Gulliver's Voyage to the Houyhnhnms," *ELH, XVIII* (December 1951), 275-286.

36. *The Augustans,* pp. 15-16.

III

THE RHETORIC OF SATIRE

1. *Remarks on the Life and Writings of Dr. Jonathan Swift* (Dublin, 1752), pp. 10-11.

2. Quoted by C. Kerby-Miller, ed. *Memoirs of the Extraordinary Life, Works, and Discoveries of Martinus Scriblerus* (New Haven, 1950), p. 244, n. 6.

3. A. C. Fraser, ed. (1894), II, 402, 391; Bk. IV, chap. xvii, sect. 6, 4. ". . . God has not been so sparing to men to make them barely two-legged creatures, and left it to Aristotle to make them rational . . . God has been more bountiful to mankind than so. He has given them a mind that can reason, without being instructed in methods of syllogizing: the understanding is not taught to reason by these rules; it has a native faculty to perceive the coherence or incoherence of its ideas, and can range them right, without any such perplexing repetitions" (p. 391; sect. 4).

4. *A Treatise on Good Manners and Good Breeding* in *Works,* XI, 84.

5. A. C. Guthkelch and D. N. Smith (eds., 1920), *A Tale of a Tub,* p. 85.

6. *Treatise on Good Manners* in *Works,* XI, 81.

7. *An Argument to Prove that the Abolishing of Christianity in England May, as Things now Stand, be Attended with Some Inconveniences, and Perhaps not Produce Those Many Good Effects Proposed Thereby* in *Works,* III, 16.

8. *Mr. C—ns's Discourse of Free-Thinking Put into plain English by way of Abstract, for the Use of the Poor* in *Works,* III, 186.

9. *Remarks upon a Book, Intituled, "The Rights of the Christian Church, &c."* in *Works,* III, 87.

10. *A Letter to a Young Gentleman, Lately enter'd Into Holy Orders* in *Works,* III, 202.

11. *An Argument Against Abolishing Christianity* in *Works,* III, 7.

12. *Remarks upon a Book* in *Works,* III, 83. Cf. Swift's observation in the same essay that "it requireth more knowledge, than his, to form general rules,

which people strain (when ignorant) to false deductions to make them out"
(p. 114).

13. *Rhetorica* (trans. W. Rhys Roberts) in *The Basic Works of Aristotle*
(ed. R. McKeon, 1941), pp. 1317-1451.

14. *Works*, IV, 226.

15. *Thoughts on Various Subjects* in *Works*, I, 285; my italics.

16. *A Sketch of the Character of Aristotle* in *Works*, XI, 185.

17. *Remarks upon a Book* in *Works*, III, 114.

18. *Gulliver's Travels* in *Works*, VIII, 206.

19. *A Letter to the Bishop of St. Asaph* in *Works*, V, 267.

20. *Letter to a Young Gentleman* in *Works*, III, 205.

21. *The Public Spirit of the Whigs* in *Works*, V, 329.

22. *A Proposal that All the Ladies and Women of Ireland Should Appear
Constantly in Irish Manufactures* in *Works*, VII, 195.

23. *Works*, III, 19.

24. *Works*, III, 215, 205.

25. *Works*, VI, 103.

26. Quoted by Herbert Davis (ed., 1935), *The Drapier's Letters to the
People of Ireland Against Receiving Wood's Halfpence*, p. 332.

27. *A Letter of Advice to a Young Poet* in *Works*, XI, 105.

28. "The Poet's Complaint of his Muse" (1680), pp. 9, 18.

29. Walter Savage Landor, *A Satire on Satirists*, (1836), p. 15. Typical of
the antagonism to satire in the period is Edward Fowler's rather weak denunciation of Hobbes, Shaftesbury, and the author of *A Tale of a Tub:* "Wit,
Liberty, and Ridicule reign; and yet we lie in all our Vices and Maladies, as
if they reigned not. So far as I see, they only produce greater Degrees of
Liberty and Licentiousness, of Fantastry and Impiety; and the Plague is but
still propagated by the Plague" (*Reflections upon a Letter Concerning Enthusiasm* [1709], p. 28). The moral purpose of satire was ridiculed by other writers
as being a mere pretense to conceal malice; one popular writer said he
"abhors"

> The name of Satirist, who to his share
> Needs but an ear to rhime and front to dare,
> To hide his splendid bile in moral mask,
> And set himself at once about his task ("Patriotism, a Mock
>   Heroic Poem" [1765], Canto VI, ll. 155-158, reprinted in
>   *The School for Satire* [1802], p. 336).

30. "Sensus Communis: An Essay on the Freedom of Wit and Humour,"
Characteristics of Men, Manners, Opinions, Times, etc. (ed. J. M. Robertson,
1900), I, 85.

31. "A Letter Concerning Enthusiasm," *Characteristics*, I, 10.

32. John Brown objected strenuously to this confusion of terms; see "Essay
on Ridicule," *Essays on the Characteristics* (1764), p. 71.

33. Charles Bulkley, among others, attempted to allay the controversy begun
by Shaftesbury. He insisted that "the *Test of Ridicule* is no other than the test

of free and chearful inquiry," and that Shaftesbury meant ridicule to be "synonimous to *freedom, familiarity, good humour,* and the like." (*A Vindication of My Lord Shaftesbury, on the Subject of Ridicule* [1751], pp. 19-20, 33.)

34. Typical is Anthony Collins's *Discourse Concerning Ridicule and Irony in Writing* (1729). Collins urges the use of ridicule as "the most effectual Method to drive Imposture, the sole foundation of their [grave men's] credit, out of the world." Any "true proposition," Collins said, will "withstand the test of Ridicule," and the "gravity" with which religious men corrupt mankind from common sense into a belief in miracles cannot excuse them from the tests (pp. 7, 9, 10).

35. *Essays*, p. 97.

36. *The History of Tom Jones, a Foundling* in *The Works of Henry Fielding* (ed. Leslie Stephen, 1882), I, 31.

37. *The Poems of Mark Akenside* (1772), pp. 114-118.

38. *Reflections upon Laughter and Remarks upon the Fable of the Bees* (1750), p. 32.

39. *An Essay on Taste* (1759), pp. 1, 2, 66.

40. *The Elements of Criticism* (1795), II, 13-14. "For this subject comes not," Kames continues in the same paragraph, "more than beauty or grandeur, under the province of reason. If any subject, by the influence of fashion or custom has acquired a degree of veneration to which naturally it is not entitled, what are the proper means for wiping off the artificial colouring, and displaying the subject in its true light? A man of true taste sees the subject without disguise: but if he hesitates, let him apply the test of ridicule, which separates it from its artificial connections, and exposes it naked with all its native improprieties."

41. "To apply the test of ridicule *here*, what is it but to scoff at religion, and deride its author? Though the sacred oracles will stand the test of any kind of examination, and however tortured by the severity or levity of its enemies will like silver tried in the fire come forth pure and unsullied; yet will this method of treating it prejudice weak minds, who are more taken with appearance than reality" (p. 11).

42. *Essays*, pp. 12, 16.

43. *Essays*, pp. 31, 19, 95, 68, 73-74, 97.

44. *Arte of Rhetorique* (ed. G. H. Mair, 1909), pp. 1, 2.

45. Dudley Fenner, *The Arte of Rhetorike* (1588), p. 1.

46. *Arte of Rhetorique*, p. 6.

47. Edmund Arwaken, *Truth in Fiction: or, Morality in Masquerade* (1708), p. iii.

48. *A Grammar of the English Tongue* (1746), p. 172.

49. Corbyn Morris, *An Essay Towards Fixing the True Standards of Wit, Humour, Raillery, Satire, and Ridicule* (1744), p. xv.

50. *The Gray's Inn Journal*, No. 49 (August 31, 1754), p. 291; my italics.

51. *Essays*, pp. 100 ff. A similar view is taken by, for example, Charles Abbott, *An Essay on the Use and Abuse of Satire* (1786), pp. 8 ff.

52. *Works*, I, 270.

53. *Works*, VI, 91.

54. *Works*, V, 267; my italics.

55. *Works*, VII, 21; my italics.

56. *Works*, IX, 145.

57. *Works*, IX, 203.

58. *Works*, IX, 198.

59. *Works*, VI, 128.

60. *Drapier's Letters* (ed. Davis), pp. 328-331.

61. *A Preface to the B—p of S—m's Introduction &c.* in *Works*, III, 161.

62. *A Letter from a Member of the House of Commons in Ireland to a Member of the House of Commons in England Concerning the Sacramental Test* in *Works*, IV, 17.

63. *Drapier's Letters* in *Works*, VI, 210.

64. *Works*, VI, 35-36.

65. *Works*, IV, 18. In the same *Letter*, Swift concludes an ironic defense of the good intentions of the English by presenting a vigorous double example which expresses his idea of the true relationship between Ireland and England more effectively than would an entire chapter of consecutive explanation: "In short, whatever advantage you propose to yourselves by repealing the Sacramental Test, speak it out plainly, 'tis the best argument you can use, for we value your interest much more than our own: If your little finger be sore, and you think a poultice made of our vitals will give it any ease, speak the word and it shall be done; the interest of our whole kingdom is at any time ready to strike to that of your poorest fishing towns; it is hard you will not accept our services, unless we believe at the same time that you are only consulting our profit, and giving us marks of your love. If there be a fire at some distance, and I immediately blow up my house before there be occasion, because you are a man of quality, and apprehend some danger to a corner of your stable; yet why should you require me to attend next morning at your levee with my humble thanks for the favour you have done me?" (pp. 10-11).

66. *Works*, III, 81-82; my italics.

67. See, for example, W. A. Eddy, ed. *Satires and Personal Writings by Jonathan Swift* (1937), pp. vii, xxx, 1-18, 497.

68. *Works*, III, 18-19; my italics.

69. *Memoirs of Martinus Scriblerus*, pp. 121-122.

70. *Elements of Rhetoric* (1865), Pt. I, chap. iii, sect. 7, p. 115; my italics.

71. *Works*, III, 170.

72. *Ibid.*, pp. 171-172.

73. *Ibid.*, p. 178.

74. Book I, chap. ii, sect. 3.

75. *Works*, III, pp. 182-184.

76. *Ibid.*, p. 183; my italics.

77. *Ibid.*, pp. 172-173.

78. *Works*, IX, 140.

79. "The Comic," *Letters and Social Aims* (1883), pp. 151-152.

80. *Works*, I, 322-323; my italics.

81. *Works*, I, 293.

82. *Mr. Collins's Discourse of Freethinking* in *Works*, III, 177.

83. *Works*, IX, 123-127.

84. *Works*, III, 62.

85. *A Proposal for the Universal Use of Irish Manufacture* in *Works*, VII, 21-22.

86. *Works*, III, 83, 115, 118, 119.

87. *Remarks*, p. 149.

88. *The Truth of Some Maxims in State and Government, Examined with Reference to Ireland* in *Works*, VII, 65.

89. *A Letter of Advice to a Young Poet* in *Works*, XI, 101, 104.

90. *Remarks upon a Book* in *Works*, III, 91.

91. *The Right of Precedence Between Physicians and Civilians Enquir'd Into* in *Works*, XI, 40.

92. *A Letter of Advice to a Young Poet* in Works, XI, 100.

93. *The Right of Precedence* in *Works*, XI, 35-37, 40, 41; my italics.

94. Quoted by Walter A. Kaufman, *Nietzsche: Philosopher, Psychologist, Antichrist* (Princeton, New Jersey, 1950), p. 112.

95. *A Tale of a Tub*, p. 4.

96. *Ibid.*, pp. 151, 152. How closely this logical fallacy is related to the superstitions of primitive magic is suggested by reading James G. Frazer, "Sympathetic Magic," *The Golden Bough* (abridged ed., 1947), chapter III, in which he discusses the relationship between magic and the false association of ideas. The fallacy of ambiguous terms, for example, is represented by the Malagasy soldier who would not eat kidneys because the word for kidney and "shot" is the same, hence to eat kidneys was to live in danger of being shot—and probably in the stomach.

97. *Works*, XI, 100.

98. *A Tale of a Tub*, p. 286.

IV

THE MECHANICAL OPERATION OF THE SPIRIT

1. A. Weber, *History of Philosophy* (1925), p. 316.

2. See, for example, Swift's scorn for Tindal's use of the phrase "the idea of government," which Swift calls a "canting pedantic way, learned from Locke" (*Remarks upon a Book, Intituled, "The Rights of the Christian Church, &c."* in *Works*, III, 100); see, also, the comment: ". . . this refined way of speaking was introduced by Mr. Locke . . . since our modern improvement of human understanding, instead of desiring a philosopher to describe or define a mouse-trap, or tell one what it is; I must gravely ask, what is contained in the idea of a mouse-trap?" (p. 95).

3. *Ibid.*, pp. 113-114.

4. *A Tale of a Tub To which is added The Battle of the Books and the Mechanical Operation of the Spirit* (eds. A. C. Guthkelch and D. Nichol Smith, 1920), p. 171.

5. *Ibid.*, p. 172.

6. *Ibid.*, p. 173.

7. *Gulliver's Travels* in *Works*, VIII, 278; my italics.

8. W. B. C. Watkins, *Perilous Balance* (1939), p. 18.

9. "The Dean's Reasons For not Building at Drapier's Hill," *The Poems of Jonathan Swift* (ed. Harold Williams, 1937), III, 900.

10. Walter J. Bate, *From Classic to Romantic* (Cambridge, Mass., 1946), pp. 72-73.

11. *A Tale of a Tub*, pp. 231-232; my italics.

12. *Works*, XI, 99.

13. *Poems*, I, 228.

14. *Laughter, An Essay on the Meaning of the Comic* (trans. C. Brereton and F. Rothwell, 1921), p. 14 and *passim*.

15. *A Tale of a Tub*, pp. 271-272, 268-269.

16. *Ibid.*, p. 62.

17. *Ibid.*, p. 289.

18. *Ibid.*, p. 291.

19. "The Tatler, Numb. 32," *Works*, IX, 5-10.

20. *Works*, III, 308.

21. *Works*, VIII, 35.

22. *Works*, VII, 269-270.

23. *Works*, VIII, 200-201.

24. *Remarks upon a Book* in *Works*, III, 90-91. A contemporary example of the converting imagination is relevant. *The New York Times* published, on August 30, 1951, this story of an Indian governmental decree: "A big wild animal of the antelope family and known as the 'Nehil Gae' was causing extensive damage to crops in the field. But the farmers would not harm it because 'Nehil Gae' means 'Blue Cow,' and the cow is sacred to the Hindu. So the Indian Government has changed the name to 'Nehil Goa'—which means 'Blue Horse.' Horses are not sacred, and so now the beast can be killed to protect the crops of food-short India." See, also, Swift's observation: "But will any man say, that if the words *whoring, drinking, cheating, lying, stealing,* were by act of parliament ejected out of the English tongue and dictionaries, we should all awake next morning chaste and temperate, honest and just, and lovers of truth? Is this a fair consequence? Or, if the physicians would forbid us to pronounce the words *pox, gout, rheumatism* and *stone,* would that expedient serve like so many talismans to destroy the diseases themselves?" *An Argument Against Abolishing Christianity* in *Works*, III, 12.

25. *Gulliver's Travels* in *Works*, VIII, 259, 261.

26. *A Serious and Useful Scheme, To make an Hospital for Incurables, of Universal Benefit to all His Majesty's Subjects* in *Works*, VII, 292.

27. *A Tale of a Tub*, p. 42.

28. *The Right of Precedence Between Physicians and Civilians Enquir'd into* in *Works*, XI, 34, 35.

29. *Remarks upon a Book*, in *Works*, III, 91-92. The play on words in the phrase "the poor man's head was full of nothing but worms," is worth noting. Swift depicts the man as thinking solely *about* worms, but he also interprets the brain as being, in the physical and literal sense, *filled* with worms. This latter meaning, of course, reduces the virtuoso's own thinking process to a purely physical (and, by the diminution of the comparison with worms, contemptible) reflex.

30. *Gulliver's Travels* in *Works*, VIII, 139.

31. *A Treatise on Good Manners and Good Breeding* in *Works*, XI, 81.

32. *Laughter*, pp. 37, 45, 46. A recent example of legal automatism is provided by the following account in *Time* magazine (March 21, 1949): "Nevada Assemblyman C. C. Boak, 79, introduced a bill to grant divorces by slot machine. The divorce seeker would punch the machine once a day for 42 days, to establish residence, then insert 200 silver dollars. As the divorce popped out of a slot, colored lights would flash, wheels spin and a jukebox would play *America*." The satire (if the ridicule is, indeed, conscious) in this "scheme" has a distinctive Swiftian flavor.

33. *The History of Tom Jones, A Foundling* in *The Works of Henry Fielding, Esq.* (ed. Leslie Stephen, 1882), Book V, chap. 1, pp. 184 ff.

34. *Thoughts on Various Subjects* in *Works*, I, 276.

35. *Gulliver's Travels* in *Works*, VIII, 260-261.

36. *Ibid.*, pp. 56, 69-70.

37. *Works*, III, 5-19, *passim*.

38. *Mr. C——ns's Discourse of Free-Thinking, Put into plain English, by way of Abstract, For the Use of the Poor* in *Works*, III, 171, 176.

39. *Works*, XI, 96.

40. *A Tale of a Tub*, pp. 190-192.

41. *Works*, III, 212.

42. *Ibid.*, p. 213.

43. *A Tale of a Tub*, p. 97. Cf. "When I went thro' That necessary and noble Course of Study [Reading prefaces, *etc.*] . . ." (p. 43) and ". . . the yawning Readers in our Age, do now a-days twirl over forty or fifty Pages of *Preface* and *Dedication* . . . as if it were so much Latin" (p. 131).

44. *Ibid.*, p. 131.

45. *Ibid.*, pp. 54, 64, 206-207.

46. Swift's judgments on mankind were not produced in an ivory tower but found their source and confirmation in his concrete experience with the human animal. We may note, in this connection, Swift's comment to Pope: "A great library always makes me melancholy, where the best author is as much squeezed, and as obscure, as a porter at a coronation. In my own little library, I value the compilements of Graevius and Gronovius, which make thirty-one volumes in folio, and were given me by my Lord Bolingbroke, more than all my books besides, because whoever comes into my closet, casts

his eyes immediately upon them, and will not vouchsafe to look upon Plato or Xenophon" (Letter to Alexander Pope [April 5, 1729], *The Correpondence of Jonathan Swift, D.D.* [ed. F. Elrington Ball, 1910-14], IV, 78).

47. *Memoirs of the Extraordinary Life, Works, and Discoveries of Martinus Scriblerus* (ed. C. Kirby-Miller, 1950), p. 100. Cf. Pope's lines on the same theme in the *Epistle to Dr. Arbuthnot*, ll. 115-122.

V

THE TRIUMPH OF ARTIFICE

1. Henri Bergson, *Laughter, An Essay on the Meaning of the Comic* (trans. A. Brereton and F. Rothwell, 1921), p. 48.

2. *A Tale of a Tub, To which is added The Battle of the Books and The Mechanical Operation of the Spirit* (eds. A. C. Guthkelch and D. Nichol Smith, 1920), p. 271.

3. *Works*, XI, pp. 79-84.

4. *Works*, XI, 100, 102. Cf. Pope's pun on "feet," *Dunciad*, I, 61-62.

5. *A Tale of a Tub*, p. 278.

6. *Works*, XI, 203, 205, 206, 228.

7. *Works*, VIII, 190; my italics.

8. *Ibid.*, pp. 193, 194.

9. *Memoirs of the Extraordinary Life, Works, and Discoveries of Martinus Scriblerus* (ed. C. Kerby-Miller, 1950), p. 108.

10. *In Praise of Comedy* (1939), p. 77.

11. *The Poems of Jonathan Swift* (ed. Harold Williams, 1937), I, 29-30.

12. *Memoirs of Martinus Scriblerus*, p. 136.

13. Acts 9:15; Romans 9:22.

14. *Poems*, II, 415.

15. *Works*, XI, 100.

16. *Laughter*, pp. 29, 30.

17. *Poems*, III, 1103, 1104.

18. *Works*, III, 133.

19. *Poems*, II, 592.

20. *An Essay on the Fates of Clergymen* in *Works*, III, 295.

21. *Works*, XI, 217, 215, 205.

22. *Works*, VIII, 61.

23. *Ibid.*, p. 30.

24. *Ibid.*, p. 22. Cf. p. 43: "After they were read, I was demanded to swear . . . ; first, in the *manner* of my own country, and afterwards in the *method* prescribed by their laws; which was to hold my right foot in my left hand . . ."; my italics.

25. *Poems*, I, 25.

26. Shane Leslie, *The Skull of Swift* (Indianapolis, 1928), p. 200.

27. *A Tale of a Tub*, pp. 157-158.

28. *Works*, III, 292, 291, 293, 297, 292, 298, 294.

29. *The Right of Precedence Between Physicians and Civilians Enquir'd into* in *Works*, XI, 30.

30. *An Essay on English Bubbles* in *Works*, VII, 34.

31. *Works*, IV, 255.

32. *Ibid.*, pp. 253, 254, 255. From the internal evidence of the use of "zeal," some doubt may be cast on Swift's authorship. For Swift's usual denigration of the word, see, for example, *A Tale of a Tub*, p. 137.

33. *Remarks upon a Book* in *Works*, III, 89.

34. *A Tale of a Tub*, p. 225.

35. *A Letter of Thanks from my Lord W****n to the Lord Bp of S. Asaph* in *Works*, V, 268.

36. *The Right of Precedence* in *Works*, XI, 33.

37. *A Tale of a Tub*, pp. 215-216.

38. *Ibid.*, pp. 183, 184, 113, 111-112, 189, 124.

39. *Ibid.*, pp. 75, 151, 153, 5, 6; cf. also "UPON all which, and many other Reasons of equal Weight . . ." (p. 175); "He had many wholesome maxims ready to excuse all miscarriages of state; Men are but Men; *Erunt vitia donec homines* . . .; with several others of equal weight" (*Essay on the Fates of Clergymen* in *Works*, III, 297).

Index

Note: Writings of Swift are entered by short title and appear in italic type.

Abbott, Charles, 203
Addison, Joseph, 185
Aeolists, 118, 119, 168, 174, 182, 190
Affectation, 24-29
Agesilaus, 157
Akenside, Mark, 27-28, 31, 32, 33, 34, 35, 77, 197, 198
Alexander, 157
Allen, Joshua, Lord, 195
Anne, Queen of England, 36, 52, 151
Answer to the Craftsman, 200
Antony, 55
Appearance and reality, 2-5, 70, 72, 126, 130-131, 141
Arachne, 86
Arbuthnot, John, 4, 11, 13, 47, 195, 196
Argument against Abolishing Christianity, An, 22, 73, 92, 98, 152, 201, 206
Aristophanes, 131
Aristotle, 33, 49, 50, 69, 70, 71-74, 76, 82, 83, 86, 87, 88, 93-94, 108, 109, 110-111, 113, 125, 201
Art (artifice), 129-131, 158-192
Arwaken, Edmund, 203
Ashburnham, Lady, 9
Atterbury, Francis, 137

Bacon, Francis, 69, 74, 107, 111
Bacon, Montagu, 26
Bailey, N., 50
Ball, F. Elrington, 195, 201, 208
Bate, W. J., viii, 128-129, 206
Battle of the Books, The, 117, 129, 138, 174, 175, 176, 178, 186, 188
Baudrier, Sieur de, 56
Baugh, Albert C., 196
Bentley, Richard, 160, 187
Bergson, Henri, 34, 132-134, 149, 151, 158, 171, 208
Bickerstaff, Isaac, 6, 56, 105-107
Bolingbroke, Viscount, *see* St. John
Brightland, John, 34, 35, 81, 199
Brobdingnag, 62, 63-64, 180
Brown, John, 17, 25, 28, 31, 77, 78, 79-80, 81, 82, 198, 202

Brutus, 55
Bulkley, Charles, 202
Burgess, Daniel, 85
Burke, Kenneth, 44
Burnet, Gilbert, 88, 172
Butler, Samuel, 26, 131-132

Caesar, Julius, 109
Cambridge, Richard, 198
Campbell, George, 99, 100
Carteret, John, 54-55
Cartesian, *see* Descartes
Charles I, King of England, 109
Chesterton, G. K., 68
Chetwode, Knightley, 195
Cicero, 63, 74, 115, 157
Coleridge, Samuel Taylor, vii, 67
Collier, Jeremy, 17
Collins, Anthony, 97-102, 120, 153, 203
Collins's Discourse of Freethinking put into plain English, Mr., 97-102, 120, 197, 205, 207
Combe, William, 198
Comedy, 5, 6-8, 29-37, 39-43, 81, 104; of mechanism, 132-134
Common sense, *see* Reason
Compleat Collection of Genteel and Ingenious Conversation, A, 161-162, 176
Conrad, Joseph, 45
Contempt, 29-37; *see also* Irony, Praise-blame inversion
Correspondence, 2, 6, 10, 11, 12-13, 14, 15, 21, 23, 195, 196, 197, 201, 208
Corusodes, 176, 184
Craik, Henry, 74
Crambe, Conradus, 94

David, 51, 83, 84
Davis, Herbert, viii, 87, 202
"Dean's Reasons for not Building at Drapier's Hill, The," 128, 206
Defoe, Daniel, 17
Delany, Patrick, 3-4
Delusion, 2-3, 8-9, 25, 61-66, 125-126
Demosthenes, 62, 74, 87, 157

Descartes, 58, 125, 145, 147
Detachment, 34, 38-67, 68
Diminution, 44-49, 53
Diotima, 19
Discourse Concerning the Mechanical Operation of the Spirit, A, 119-120, 134, 135, 138, 159, 161, 167-168, 174-175, 176, 183, 185
Discourse of the Contests and Dissensions . . . in Athens and Rome, A, 82-83
Dodsley, Robert, 198
Don Quixote, 134, 144
Donne, John, 36
Drapier, M. B., 48, 56, 57, 74, 75, 83, 87, 89
Drapier's Letters, The, 83, 85, 87-88, 89-90, 204
Dryden, 15, 17, 18, 24, 39, 156

Eddy, W. A., 204
Elliston, Ebenezer, 56
Eloquence, *see* Rhetoric; Ridicule
Emerson, Ralph Waldo, 5, 104
Epicurus, 117-118, 125, 147
"Epistle to a Lady, An," 8, 34-35, 196, 197, 199
Erasmus, Desiderius, 53
Essay on English Bubbles, An, 209
Essay on the Fates of Clergymen, An, 184, 208, 209
Examination of Certain Abuses in the City of Dublin, An, 137
Examiner, The, 22-23, 87, 102-103, 109, 197, 200

Faulkner, George, 171
Feibleman, James, 164
Fenner, Dudley, 81, 203
Fielding, Henry, 28-29, 32, 77, 149
Fleetwood, William, 52-54, 56, 85, 187
Fowler, Edward, 202
Fraser, A. C., 201
Frazer, James G., 205
Freud, Sigmund, 43
"Furniture of a Woman's Mind, The," 169

"Gay contempt," *see* Contempt
Gay, John, 195

Gerard, Alexander, 32, 78, 198
Gibbs, James, 51-52, 56
Glubbdubdrib, 73
Goliath, 83, 84
Grey, Z., 197
Grub Street, 56, 76, 116
Gulliver, Lemuel, 8, 9, 14, 15, 23, 43, 56, 60, 62-66, 73, 87, 136, 138, 146, 151, 163, 177-181
Gulliver's Travels, 7, 8-15, *passim,* 23, 42, 43, 60, 62-66, 82, 92, 134, 137-138, 142-143, 151-152, 177-181, 192, 199, 206, 207
Gutchkelch, A. C., 195, 201, 206

Harley, Robert, 14, 52, 196
Heilman, Robert, 196, 201
Henry IV, King of France, 165
Hervey, Lord, 47, 170
Hobbes, Thomas, 30, 77, 202
Home, Henry, Lord Kames, 26, 30, 32, 78, 197, 198, 203
Homer, 73
Hope, Thomas, 56
Horace, 7, 18, 35, 190
Houyhnhnm, 15, 20, 64, 65, 91, 127-128, 142, 146, 147, 150
Howard, Henrietta, 196, 201
Hume, David, 33
Hutcheson, Francis, 26, 30, 77, 78, 197
Huxley, Aldous, 130

Imagination, 2; "converting," 134-148, 154-155
Intelligencer, The, 195, 200
Irony, *see* Satire; Swift
Invective, 32-35, 38-44

Job, 9
Johnson, Esther, 11
Johnson, Maurice, 130
Johnson, Samuel, 80, 82, 85, 128-129
Jonson, Ben, 32
Journal to Stella, The, 7, 196
Juvenal, 7, 15, 18

Kames, Lord, *see* Home, Henry
Kant, Immanuel, 104, 133
Kaufman, Walter, 205
Keats, John, 10

Kerby-Miller, Charles, 201, 208
Ketch, Jack, 39
Kipling, Rudyard, 14

Lagado, 62, 163
Landor, Walter Savage, 75, 202
Laputa, 164
Laughter, *see* Comedy
Leslie, Shane, 208
Letter Concerning the Sacramental Test, A, 89, 90, 204
Letter of Advice to a Young Poet, A, 119, 129-130, 153-154, 160-161, 169, 199, 202, 205
Letter to a Young Gentleman, Lately enter'd into Holy Orders, A, 19-20, 57, 74, 155, 196, 201, 202
Letter to the Bishop of St. Asaph, A, 52-53, 56, 85, 209
Letter to the Whole People of Ireland, A, 57
Levin, Harry, viii
Lilliput, 136, 142, 151, 152, 177, 178, 179, 180
Lipsius, 148
Locke, John, 69, 70, 79, 124-125, 144, 205
Logic, 68-122, *passim; see also* Rhetoric
"Love Song, A," 38

Mack, Maynard, viii, 56, 61, 65, 200
Mair, G. H., 199, 203
Mandeville, Bernard de, 77
Marius, 157
Marlborough, John Churchill, Duke of, 109, 110
Maxims Controlled in Ireland, 111
McKeon, R., 202
Mechanism, 123-192; subjectivity in, 123-132; comedy of, 132-134; misdirection in, 148-157
Meier, George, 197
Method, *see* Art
Milton, John, 45, 91
Misorarum, Gregory, 56
Modest Defence of the Proceedings of the Rabble in all Ages, A, 14, 51
Modest Proposal, A, 5, 61-62, 64
Morris, Corbyn, 27, 197, 203

Moore, Mrs. John, 196
Murphy, Arthur, 31-32, 81-82, 198

Nature, 70, 128-130, 158-170
Newman, John Henry, 21-23
Nietzsche, Friedrich, 116-117
Nowell, Thomas, 78, 197
Noyes, G. R., 199

"Ode to the Athenian Society," 181
"Ode to the Honourable Sir William Temple," 164-165
Oedipus, 9
Of Public Absurdities in England, 195
Of the Education of Ladies, 57, 58-59
Orrery, John Boyle, Earl of, 22, 69, 111
Otway, Thomas, 75
Ovid, 86
Oxford, *see* Harley

Pallas, 86
Panegyric, *see* Praise-blame inversion
Panegyrical Essay upon the Number Three, A, 51
Panegyrick upon the World, A, 14, 51, 62
Parmenides, 131
Partridge, John, 105-107
Peacham, Henry, 81
Persius, 18
Plato, (Platonic, etc.), 25, 27, 30, 32, 72, 110, 125, 135, 136, 164, 178, 208
Pope, Alexander, 4, 6, 11, 12, 18, 22, 23, 24, 27, 35, 36, 47, 56, 109, 130, 170-171, 195, 196, 197, 207, 208
Praise-blame inversion, 50-56, 62-66
Predictions for the Year 1708, 105
Preface to the Bishop of Sarum's Introduction, A, 88, 172, 204
Pride, 15, 22, 65-66
"Progress of Beauty, The," 130
Project for the Advancement of Religion, A, 24, 58
Proposal for an Act of Parliament, A, 200
Proposal that all the Ladies and Women of Ireland should appear constantly in Irish Manufactures, A, 73

Public Spirit of the Whigs, The, 57, 195, 202
Puppet, *see* Symbol
"Puppet-Show, The," 171
Puttenham, Richard, 45, 46, 50

Queensberry, Lady Catherine Hyde, Duchess of, 195, 196
Quintana, Ricardo, viii, 2, 61, 195
Quintilian, 51

Rabelais, 41, 42, 48
Reason, 2-3, 20, 91, 126-128, 132-133
Remarks on Dr. Gibbs's Paraphrase of the Psalms, 51-52, 200
Remarks upon a Book Entituled The Rights of the Christian Church Asserted, 46, 73, 91, 111, 141, 186, 199, 200, 201, 205, 206, 207, 209
Remarks upon a Pamphlet, Entitl'd A Letter to the Seven Lords, Some, 199
Rhetoric, 55, 68-122; Aristotle on, 50, 71-72, 93-94, 108, 113; ambiguous terms in, 112-122; enthymeme in, 71, 92-122; example in, 82-92; maxims in, 108-112; ridicule as branch of, 75-82; spurious enthymemes in, 113-122; *see also* Logic
Ribbeck, Otto, 49
Ridicule, 1-37; as "eloquence," 75-82; Akenside on, 26-28, 31; Brown on, 78-81; Dryden on, 17; Fielding on, 28-29; Shaftesbury on, 21-22, 25-26, 76-78; Socrates on, 25-26
Right of Precedence between Physicians and Civilians enquired into, The, 114-116, 119, 145, 205, 207, 209
Robertson, J. N., 202
Rochefoucauld, François, Duc de la, 23
Rochester, John Wilmot, second earl of, 53

St. John, Henry, 10, 196, 197, 207
St. Paul, 40, 41, 42, 103, 136, 197
Sancho Panza, 144
Santayana, George, 66
Satan, 45

Satire, general characteristics of, 1-2, 16-18, 21-22, 39-41, 75-82; utility of, 7-8, 50, *see also* Shame; Swift's theory of, 7, 34-37; detachment in, 34, 38-67; irony in, 49-67, 92-108; ironic masks *(personae)* in, 56-67; dramatic irony in, 60-66; computation in, 58-59; rhetoric of, 68-122; mechanism in, 123-192
Saul, 84
Scaliger, Joseph, 148
Scott, Temple, 185, 195
Scriblerus, Cornelius, 69, 94, 157, 163
Scriblerus, Martin, 94, 157, 163, 164, 167
Sedgewick, G. G., 49, 60
Sentiments of a Church of England Man, The, 110
Serious and Useful Scheme to make an Hospital for Incurables, A, 44, 200, 206
Sermon upon Sleeping in Church, A, 72
Shaftesbury, Anthony, Earl of, 17, 18, 21, 22, 25, 26, 28, 76-77, 78, 80, 81, 202, 203
Shakespeare, William, 55
Short Character of the Earl of Wharton, A, 199
Shame, 16-24; *see also* Contempt
Sharp, John, 190
Sherburn, George, viii, 12, 191
Sheridan, Thomas, 6, 11, 15, 20, 87, 196, 197
Sherry, Richard, 81
Singer, Irving, viii
Sketch of the Character of Aristotle, A, 72-73
Smith, D. Nichol, 195, 201, 206
Socrates, 19, 25, 49, 88, 110, 131
Sophocles, 164
Starkman, Miriam, viii, 116
Stella, *see* Johnson, Esther
Stephen, Leslie, 198, 203, 207
Stevens, G. A., 198
Stopford, James, 11, 196
"Strephon and Chloe," 131, 172
Sturdy, Charles, 135
Subjectivity, 119, 123-132
Swearer's Bank, The, 200

Swift, comedy in, 6, 38-39, 42-43; contempt in, 3-5, 29-37; detachment in, 5, 7, 38-67; idealism in, 1-4, 20; indignation in, 3-5, 9-14, 38-39, 67; realism in, 1-4, 20; distrust of rhetoric, 71-72, knowledge of rhetoric and praise of its proper use, 72-75, *see also* Rhetoric; satiric theory of, 7, 34-37; satiric techniques of, *see* Irony, Mechanism, Rhetoric; his view of life as ridiculous tragedy, 1-16

Symbol, puppet, 171-181; height and depth, 181-192

Tale of a Tub, A, 2-8, *passim*, 14, 42, 44, 46-48, 51, 62, 70, 73, 76, 82, 92, 116-122, 126-127, 130, 134-135, 138-141, 144, 146-147, 151, 152, 154, 156, 160, 161, 165-169, 170, 173-175, 176, 182, 183, 185-186, 188, 189-191, 195, 196, 200, 205, 206, 207, 208, 209

Taylor, Jeremy, 108
Temple, William, 164
Thoughts on Religion, 10, 136, 196
Thoughts on Various Subjects, 197, 207
Tighe, Richard, 55
Timon, 13, 67
Tindal, 46, 47, 70, 73, 91, 103, 111, 112, 114, 141, 186, 199, 205
To the Gentlemen Freeholders, and Freemen of the City, 87
Tragedy, 5, 6, 8-9, 14-15
Treatise on Good Manners and Good Breeding, A, 159, 196, 201, 207
Tritical Essay upon the Faculties of the Mind, A, 107-108
Tully, *see* Cicero
Tuve, Rosamunde, 199

Vannessa, *see* Vanhomrigh, Esther
Vanhomrigh, Esther, 2, 8, 10, 182, 195, 196
"Verses on the Death of Dr. Swift," 50
Vindication of Carteret, A, 55, 195, 200
Vindication of Isaac Bickerstaff, 105

Wagstaff, Simon, 56
Walpole, Horace, 5
Walpole, Robert, 13, 36, 123, 137
Watkins, W. B. C., 9, 127, 206
Weber, A., 205
Webster, John, 69
Wharton, Thomas, 56, 85, 123, 199
Whately, Richard, 97, 101
Whiston, William, 108, 123
Whitehead, A. N., 21, 128
Williams, Harold, 171, 196, 199, 206, 208
Williams, Kathleen M., 201
Wilson, Thomas, 40, 80, 81
Wood, William, 57, 83-84, 85, 89, 90
Worcester, David, 37, 40
Worde, Wynken de, 50
Wordsworth, William, 56
Worsley, Frances, 197
Wotton, William, 123, 170, 175, 176, 200
Wylie, Philip, 75

Xenophon, 208